Second Edition

D1219848

Study Skills for
Learning Power

Regina Hellyer

Carol Robinson

Phyllis Sherwood

English Department
Raymond Walters College
of the University of Cincinnati

HOUGHTON MIFFLIN COMPANY   Boston   New York

Director of Student Success Programs and College Survival: Barbara A. Heinssen
Assistant Editor: Shani Fisher
Senior Project Editor: Cathy Labresh Brooks
Senior Production/Design Coordinator: Carol Merrigan
Senior Manufacturing Coordinator: Marie Barnes
Editorial Assistant: Ryan Vine
Editorial Assistant: Jonathan Wolf

COVER IMAGE: Kimura/Photonica; © Beverly Brown/ Photonica; © Minori Kawana/Photonica.
COVER DESIGN: Rebecca Fagan

TEXT CREDITS: Page 41, *The Little Engine That Could* retold by Watty Piper, from *The Pony Engine* by Mabel Bragg. NY: Platt and Munk, 1976. *The Little Engine That Could* and *I think I can, I think I can* are trademarks of Platt & Munk, Publishers and are used by permission; page 52, from *Memory: surprising new insights into how we remember and why we forget* by Elizabeth Loftus; page 53, from *Take Control of Your Life* by Sharon Faelten and David Diamond. Copyright © 1988 by Rodale Press. Reprinted by permission; page 102–104, from Levine and Miller, *Biology: Discovering Life,* Second Edition. Copyright © 1994 by D.C. Heath and Company. Used by permission of Houghton Mifflin Company; page 116, excerpt from *Concentration: Strategies for Attaining Focus* by Becky Patterson. Dubuque, IA: Kendall/Hunt, 1993. Reprinted by permission of the author; pages 125–126, untitled poem #1263 by Emily Dickinson, from *The Complete Poems of Emily Dickinson,* ed. Thomas H. Johnson. Reprinted by permission of Little, Brown and Company; page 132 (diagram), 133 (paragraph), from Sylvia S. Mader, *Inquiry Into Life,* 7th edition. Copyright © 1994 Times Mirror Higher Education Group, Inc., Dubuque, Iowa. All rights reserved. Reprinted by permission of The McGraw-Hill Companies; pages 169–170, excerpts: "First things first," from *Efficient Study Strategies: Skills for Successful Learning* by George M. Usova. Pacific Grove, CA: Brooks/Cole Publishing Company, 1989; pages 216–217, from *Introduction to Child Development,* 4th edition by John P. Dworetzky. Copyright © 1990 by West Publishing. Reprinted by permission.

Printed in U.S.A.

Library of Congress Catalog Card Number: 00-133826

Student Text ISBN: 0-618-04657-7

123456789-FFG-04 03 02 01 00

As part of Houghton Mifflin's ongoing commitment to the environment, this text has been printed on recycled paper.

Table of Contents

Preface

The title of our book, *Study Skills for Learning Power*, comes from our conviction that students have the power within themselves to take control of their learning and their lives. Our ultimate goal is to have students put critical thinking into action as they learn academic and life skills. In response to this conviction and goal, we have created a concise, practical, readable, down-to-earth, student-oriented, hands-on, reader-friendly textbook. We have made a concerted effort to set an appropriate tone, using vocabulary suitable for college students. This text expects students to use the study skills as they learn them, rather than complacently reading about theories and study techniques. Students using the first edition have commented enthusiastically that the book "talks to them," is very easy to understand, and provides solid, practical strategies that have brought about positive changes in their academic and personal lives.

SPECIAL FEATURES OF THE SECOND EDITION

- An emphasis on critical thinking in every chapter.
- A whole new dynamic chapter entitled "The Power of Critical Thinking" includes information about critical reading and evaluation of various print and online sources.
- An "Introduction for Students" includes summaries of each chapter, highlighting special features and information about working in groups and writing journal entries.
- "Myths and Facts about College" that promote classroom interaction.
- A chapter on self-knowledge and discovery with an emphasis on the Myers-Briggs Type Indicator (MBTI) instrument, now available shrink-wrapped with the text.
- Two comprehensive study methods: GREAT for taking notes and STUDY-READ for reading and marking textbooks.
- A proactive method for solving problems called SOLVE.
- An extended section on understanding and managing stress.
- A new, enlarged section on motivation.
- An extensive list of web sites on academic and personal topics related to the chapters available on the Houghton Mifflin Student Success Programs web site http://college.hmco.com (select "student success").
- Extra wide left-hand margins that allow students to mark the text, turning it into a study guide.
- "Critically Thinking Together" **group activities** for the classroom.
- "Critically Thinking in Writing" **journal entries.**

- A summary question or statement box at the end of each chapter.
- A list of terms at the end of each chapter.

STUDENT INTERACTIVENESS

Study Skills for Learning Power is an interactive textbook that encourages students' participation in their own learning on several different levels. Each chapter encourages student interaction with the textbook information through its format—wide left-hand margins for the application of STUDY-READing as well as summary question boxes and lists of terms. On a second level, students interact with new concepts by trying out each new skill as it is presented to them through the chapter "Exercises." On another level, students interact with other students as they solve problems and critically assess situations through "Critically Thinking Together." On a fourth and very personal level, students are given the opportunity for introspection as they consider their own experiences and opinions through personal journal entries in "Critically Thinking in Writing." Finally, the many "Web Site Information" references were selected because they extend rather than duplicate textbook information, allowing students the opportunity to explore certain concepts of special interest to themselves. In the final analysis, the true test of interactiveness requires having students apply their new skills and knowledge in all their other courses and in everyday life.

JUST FOR TEACHERS

Not only is *Study Skills for Learning Power* student-friendly, it is also teacher-friendly. Instructors who have used the previous edition will notice that the organization of chapters has changed. These changes are in response to instructors' preferences that personal knowledge of self, goals, and motivation come before actual study skills. All chapters, however, are autonomous, so that they can be taught according to teachers' preferences or studied according to students' needs. We realize that every chapter is necessary to students' success and could be considered the one chapter students should read and understand first. Because each chapter does stand alone, teachers may make their own decisions about the chapter order they will use.

Because of its fundamental emphasis on critical thinking as well as its practicality, comprehensiveness, and conciseness, *Study Skills for*

Learning Power is an excellent textbook choice for a variety of courses, namely, the freshman-year experience, freshman orientation, study skills, effective reading and study skills, the college seminar, pre-college workshops, and summer study programs. The textbook can be adapted readily to a quarter or semester system or a year-long seminar with students typically earning one, two, or three credit hours.

VALUABLE CLASSROOM SUPPORT

- Houghton Mifflin now offers in its Student Success Programs the Myers-Briggs Type Indicator® (MBTI®) instrument*—the most widely used personality inventory in history—shrink-wrapped with this text for a discounted price at qualified schools. The standard Form M self-scorable instrument contains 93 items that determine preferences on four scales: Extraversion-Introversion, Sensing-Intuition, Thinking-Feeling, and Judging-Perceiving.
- Houghton Mifflin's Student Success Roundtable Discussion Videotapes can be used to supplement the text. These two videos, "Study Strategies" and "Life Skills," are ideal for promoting student discussion and for providing quick reinforcement of strategies and skills to students.
- Additional activities and web sites to visit are available on the *Study Skills for Learning Power* web site located at http://college. hmco.com (select "Student Success" and then "*Study Skills for Learning Power*").
- For information on offering a shrink-wrapped package to your students or purchasing a video, contact your local sales representative or Faculty Services at 1-800-733-1717.
- Instructors will be delighted to use the *Instructor's Resource Manual* that is available with this textbook. It contains **sample syllabi** for various length courses and **chapter by chapter information,** including suggestions for teaching and classroom activities, answers to exercises, as well as factual quiz questions and critical thinking application questions. In addition, we have included **transparency masters** for each chapter and an extensive **test bank,** organized by chapter content and by types of questions (definition, true-false, multiple choice, essay, etc.) from which instructors can design their own tests. Finally, instructors will also find a list of **web sites** for each chapter that contains additional information on teaching particular topics and skills.

---

*MBTI and Myers-Briggs Type Indicator are registered trademarks of Consulting Psychologists Press, Inc.

Acknowledgments

Our thanks go first to the many students we have taught over the years. We certainly have learned as much from them as we have taught them. Their questions, comments, concerns, and needs guided us to formulate the contents of this textbook. A special thanks to those students who allowed us to use their work in the book as examples.

Next, we wish to thank the reading and study skills monitors, tutors, and lab staff at Raymond Walters College of the University of Cincinnati for their emotional support, information, and analytical skills. Specifically we thank: Pam Bauer, Beverly Claunch, Della Colmar, Sharon Disher, Sue Gross, Mary McClellan, Maureen Nestor, Paula Spievack, Sylvia Thompson, and Judy Whitton. We realize it took courage to walk the fine line between critiquing our writing and hurting our feelings.

We are especially grateful to Mary McClellan for her precise critiquing of our text and her many excellent suggestions, to Ann Chisko for her assistance in writing the section on reading math, and to Beverly Claunch for assistance in the section on reading in the sciences.

We also offer a round of applause and special gratitude to John Sherwood who allowed us to transform first his living room and then most of the rest of the house into our office and who gave us food for thought—gourmet style.

We owe a special thanks to Barbara Heinssen, the Director of the Student Success Programs at Houghton Mifflin, for her continual encouragement, support, and helpful comments and suggestions. We would also like to thank other members of the editorial staff, namely Shani Fisher, Jonathan Wolf, Cathy Brooks, and Ryan Vine, for their assistance in helping to create the 2nd edition of *Study Skills for Learning Power*.

We would also like to thank the following reviewers who offered us helpful suggestions for revising this textbook:

Dr. Julia Beyeler	The University of Akron-Wayne, Ohio
Mary Hackler	Northwestern College, Ohio
Barbara Howard	Northwest Nazarene College, Indiana
Michael Johnson	Western Kentucky University, Kentucky
Peg Mauzy	Frederick Community College, Maryland
Mary Lee Mikkola	Suomi College, Michigan
Lorna Lou Moir	Indiana University, Indiana
Mary Jane Mullins	University of Louisville, Kentucky
Fiona Pearson	DeVry Institute of Technology, Georgia
Terrel L. Rhodes	University of North Carolina, North Carolina
Jim Stepp	University of Maine at Presque Isle, Maine
Leesa Young	Asheville-Buncombe Technical Community College, North Carolina

Introduction
for Students

Study Skills for Learning Power is your guide to learning and self-discovery; as such, it is designed to enable you to achieve your maximum learning power—power for success in college as well as in life. The power that already exists within you can blossom into academic and personal success as you learn and use critical thinking, critical reading, and effective study strategies. Each chapter focuses on either a basic study skill or individual growth through personal knowledge, or a combination of the two. In addition, you will find interactive exercises that examine your own experiences, reflective journal questions, stimulating group activities, related exercises, and web sites for further information. The chapters can be read and studied in any order, so if your instructor chooses to teach in an order different from the one listed in the Table of Contents, you should feel comfortable beginning at any point in the book.

The information that follows will give you an overview of this textbook, and you will benefit from reading it. This information summarizes the contents of each chapter, describes special features in the chapters, and explores some myths and facts about college.

SUMMARY OF TEXT

Chapter 1, "The Power of Self-Knowledge," allows you to discover which sense you use the most to learn—sight, hearing, or touch. You will identify your own personality type and learn how to use this knowledge to your best advantage. The chapter presents different teaching styles so that you can learn to cope with teaching styles that don't match your learning style. You will also learn that your attitudes toward responsibility can have a great impact on your success, both academically and personally.

Chapter 2, "The Power of Managing Goals, Problems, and Stress," helps you to examine your short- and long-term goals, and to adjust them if necessary, so that they are personally fulfilling, realistic, and flexible enough to be achievable. You will also learn how to motivate yourself to reach your goals. The chapter presents a step-by-step, critical-thinking method to solve problems, including the causes of stress and how to identify and manage your own stress.

Chapter 3, "The Power of Note Taking," instructs you in one of the most important skills for your college success, the skill of listening and taking good notes in class and placing the information into your long-term memory. The GREAT Note Taking System provides you with five steps to help you prepare for class, take good notes, and master the material. In addition to good note-taking skills, you will discover three ways to record, organize, and learn technical terms that relate to the courses you are taking.

Chapter 4, "The Power of Reading for Meaning," helps you to increase your overall reading comprehension and to adjust your reading speed to a variety of materials. Your comprehension can be increased by understanding main ideas and major and minor supporting details; by recognizing transitions and patterns of organization; and by correctly interpreting visual aids. Because a faster reading speed is not always desirable in reading, you will learn how your purpose for reading and the difficulty of the material influence your reading speed.

Chapter 5, "The Power of STUDY-READING," helps you to turn your textbook chapters into personal study guides. By using the systematic STUDY-READ method, you will be able to turn passive reading into dynamic, active reading and learning. You will also learn how to adjust the basic STUDY-READ method to accommodate specific courses and class handouts.

Chapter 6, "The Power of Critical Thinking," explains why critical thinking is essential to understanding, interpreting, and evaluating the world around you. You will learn how to recognize common errors in thinking and reasoning. The discussion on critical reading provides information about how to evaluate printed material and on-line sources. In addition, you will research questions about television and movies to determine the value and effectiveness of these two media.

Chapter 7, "The Power of Time Management," encourages you to become aware of how you spend your 168 hours per week. It guides you to become more time "wise," organized, and efficient.

Chapter 8, "The Power of Memory," presents ways to improve your long-term memory and to increase your powers of concentration. The memory discussion focuses on ways to strengthen your memory process and explains the five classic memory techniques. The chapter also explains how distractions can interfere with concentration and memory; then it provides ways to manage common distractions.

Chapter 9, "The Power of Making Your Own Visual Organizers," offers several methods to analyze and condense large amounts of information into one page or so for study. This application of critical thinking is especially useful when you are preparing for exams and writing papers.

Chapter 10, "The Power of Taking Tests," gives you techniques for reading and answering objective, short answer, and essay test questions, and ways to alleviate test anxiety. You will analyze your own test results using the detailed Test Analysis Chart and evaluate your own test-taking strategies.

SPECIAL FEATURES IN THE CHAPTERS

In addition to providing basic academic and everyday survival skills, each chapter contains special features to further enhance your learning: exercises, journal writing, group activities, and web site information.

Exercises

Each chapter features exercises that let you make new discoveries about yourself, practice new skills, or expand the new skills and information to new situations. In order to truly participate in your own learning, you must do all the exercises in the chapters as you read them. Because this textbook has a workbook format, your answers to exercises should be written in the book, unless the directions or your instructor indicate otherwise.

Journal Writing

Journal writing, called "Critically Thinking Alone," helps you to reflect on your own personal experiences, to express your thoughts and opinions, to logically analyze your ideas, and then to evaluate your thinking process, or even to solve problems that may have surfaced. Journal writing encourages deeper thought about situations and ideas so that you can grow academically and personally. Your journal entries may be handwritten on regular notebook paper, printed out from a word processor, or e-mailed to your instructor, depending upon your instructor's directions.

Group Activities

Group activities, called "Critically Thinking Together," allow you to express your own ideas, listen to others' input, brainstorm together, learn from each other, and find solutions, insights, and creative ideas. Group work can be a very rewarding experience because several people are contributing to reach a goal, whether it is to understand yourself and others better, generate new ideas, rewrite goals, find solutions to problems, evaluate printed information, or accomplish a learning task. Cooperative group work is an essential life skill that helps you to achieve academic goals while in college and career goals as a member of a work team or group. Following are some guidelines that will help you to understand what it takes to be a good group member.

How to Be Successful as a Group Member

- Always be prepared by completing any assigned pre-meeting work.
- If the group is meeting outside class, arrive on time.
- Carefully read or listen to directions to clarify what the group's task is.
- Participate in, but do not monopolize, the discussion.
- Give everyone else a chance to contribute.
- Be positive and encouraging.
- Try to involve everyone in the discussion.
- Be certain that you understand what other group members are saying; ask for clarification if necessary.
- Be open to others' ideas and opinions.
- Respect differences in cultures, backgrounds, and experiences.
- Stay on track; keep the task in mind. Gently guide others back on track if they begin to talk about an unrelated subject.
- If no one is designated as group leader, take a leadership role yourself when necessary, but let others do the same.
- Reach a group conclusion; this should be a collaborative effort.
- If individual tasks are assigned at the end of the meeting, make certain that each person understands how each assignment contributes to the whole picture, knows exactly what assignments belong to which members, and has a firm deadline for completion.

- If necessary, the group should agree on the time and place for the next meeting.

Web Sites

In several places, a "Web Site Information" box appears so that you will have the opportunity to delve deeper into exciting and informative aspects related to the concepts in the chapters. Ample educational information is available today on the Internet, and the sites listed for you have been selected because they are highly interactive, visually appealing, or enhance and expand the textbook information without undue repetition of textbook concepts. Following is an example of how this information appears in the text:

WEB SITE INFORMATION

To complete a self-assessment study skills checklist and to learn tips on how to be a successful student, visit our web site:

<http://college.hmco.com/success/>

MYTHS AND FACTS ABOUT COLLEGE

1. **Myth:** Since many professors in college do not take attendance, I can skip classes when I want to or need to. It's not a big deal if I am there or not.

   Fact: Get real! Would you say that about seeing your favorite rock star live and in concert versus hearing a CD? Would you say that about experiencing the Fourth of July fireworks display vs. watching it on TV? When it comes to attendance, the old saying holds true: "You have to be there."

2. **Myth:** If I am a full-time college student, I only need to attend classes approximately twelve hours a week; therefore, I can easily hold a full-time job, go to classes, and fulfill all family obligations.

   Fact: What you see is not always what you get! "Full-time" as a student is a 36-hour commitment disguised as a 12-hour pastime. Colleges expect that you spend approximately two hours studying outside of class per week for every credit hour you take. College is a balancing act.

3. Myth: Reading is reading. The way I read a textbook is really no different from the way I read a magazine, a newspaper, or a novel.

Fact: Who are you kidding? A textbook is heavy-duty reading! It's a matter of purpose, approach, and accountability. Would you want your doctor to read medical journals the same way he/she would read *Sports Illustrated*?

4. Myth: If a professor does not collect my homework or check up on my reading assignments through quizzes, then I don't need to worry about doing any of those assignments.

Fact: You can lead a horse to water but you can't make him drink. Homework means just that: learning at home or on your own. Sitting in a classroom gives you limited information and practice and should make you "thirsty" to learn more. If you don't worry about homework, maybe you won't need to worry about graduation either.

5. Myth: If I don't like a particular required class or if I get too far behind in a class, it is best to stop attending. The teacher really won't notice if I disappear, and I can take the course some other time.

Fact: Think again! A computer never forgets. When your body disappears from class, your name and GPA don't disappear from your academic records.

6. Myth: In college, my success in a given course depends mostly upon the professor's teaching abilities. If he or she cannot hold my interest, it's not my problem.

Fact: Oops! If this were true, your former high-school driving instructor would be arrested if *you* were arrested for drunk driving.

7. Myth: If I attend classes and do all my homework in a course, then I am guaranteed a passing grade.

Fact: Sorry, Charlie! Life has no guarantees. The only sure things in life are death and taxes. Seriously, no doubt attending classes and doing homework are extremely important. However, you must still demonstrate mastery of the course by passing tests.

8. Myth: If I go to an instructor for help outside of class, he/she might think that I'm not smart enough to be in the course.

Fact: Whoa! Silence may be golden, but not when dealing with doctors or teachers. You're paying for school, so get your money's worth.

9. **Myth:** Tutoring and learning centers in college are not for regular students like me.

  Fact: Don't kid yourself! Presidents and kings use cabinet members and advisors. Shouldn't you take advantage of experts, too?

10. **Myth:** If I arrive late for class or leave early, it's no big deal.

  Fact: Come on! Try telling that to Delta Airlines. Whether you miss a plane or miss a class, you have missed the boat.

1 The Power of Self-Knowledge

Who knows you better than yourself? After all, you have been inside your skin for *x* number of years. Until you actually begin to explore what makes you tick, however, you may not know yourself as well as you think you do; you may not be making the most of yourself and your talents.

The focus of this chapter is you yourself and your personal preferences. Would you rather get up early or stay up late? Do you learn better by listening to a teacher or by reading a textbook? Are you more comfortable working alone or with others? Your answers to these questions and others may indicate your preferences.

To get the most out of this chapter, it is important that you understand the differences between preferences and nonpreferences. *Preferences* refer to those actions and attitudes that feel natural, comfortable, easy, and stress-free, requiring little energy. *Nonpreferences* imply the opposite. These actions and attitudes may feel uncomfortable, awkward, and stressful, requiring extra effort.

This chapter will examine certain key factors concerning you and your preferences and will demonstrate how an awareness of these factors can add to your self-power because, taken all together, they form your learning style. Your *learning style* is your unique way of gaining knowledge and making sense of the world by using your preferences. In particular, you need to be in tune with and capitalize on the strengths of your sensory preferences and your personality type. Your knowledge of teaching style preferences and your own attitude toward responsibility will add to your self-knowledge database. This deeper sense of self-knowledge will empower you in college, career, and interpersonal relationships.

SENSORY PREFERENCES

From birth, people use their senses to learn about themselves and the world around them. The five senses are our keys to learning and exploring. For example, small babies spend hours looking at their hands and feet: sense of sight. Those same babies are soothed to sleep by lullabies: sense of sound. From first-hand experience, they learn that stoves are hot and ice cubes are cold: sense of touch. As they grow older, they put everything from rocks to cat food in their mouths: sense of taste. Finally, they are suddenly drawn to the kitchen when chocolate chip cookies are baking: sense of smell. A child, like all learners, uses all five senses to become acquainted with the world.

As an adult, you still rely on your senses to acquire information, even though your learning at this point is more sophisticated than that of a small child. Granted, you seldom learn in college by tasting your textbooks or smelling them for that matter, but your other three senses are still hard at work.

Most academic learning occurs when you take in information by sight, sound, or touch. A *sensory preference* refers to your use of either sight, sound, or touch as the most reliable means of taking in information. Thus, you may be primarily a visual learner, an auditory learner, or a tactile (also called kinesthetic) learner. *Visual* learners prefer to *see* information, *auditory* learners prefer to *listen* to information, and *tactile* learners prefer *hands-on* experience. Although you can learn by using any one, two, or all of these senses, you probably have a sensory preference. An awareness of your preference is another way to help you get the most out of your study sessions and classes.

Exercise 1-A

Directions: In order to determine your preferred learning style, read each descriptive sentence. If you say, "Yes, that is usually true of me," put a check next to that sentence. Leave the line blank next to those sentences that do not apply to your learning style. Check as many or as few sentences in each category as apply to you.

(continued on the next page)

Exercise 1-A (continued)

Gaining meaning from seeing

_____ I prefer having written directions.

_____ Don't tell me; show me.

_____ I have to see a word written out to tell if it is spelled correctly.

_____ I like to use maps, pictures, and charts.

_____ I usually remember where I saw an item in printed material.

_____ I prefer to read things for or by myself.

_____ I take lots of notes in class and write "to-do" lists.

_____ I read labels on cans, signs, notices—anything that's available.

_____ I notice differences in colors, shapes, and forms.

_____ I need to write out math problems, see them written, or use flash cards.

Gaining meaning from listening

_____ I prefer to have oral directions.

_____ Don't show me; tell me.

_____ I need to sound out words (using phonetics) in order to pronounce them.

_____ I like to work in study groups.

_____ I would rather listen to oral reports than read written ones.

_____ I like to interview people or get information from talking to them.

_____ I enjoy the sounds of words and like to play word games.

_____ I'm good at remembering jokes or the words to songs, jingles, rhymes, and limericks.

_____ I think it is fairly easy to learn foreign languages.

_____ I learn math best by having someone explain it orally.

Gaining meaning from hands-on activities

_____ I prefer doing or experimenting with things like computers, rather than reading directions or manuals.

_____ I like to manipulate objects physically.

(continued on the next page)

Exercise 1-A (continued)

Gaining meaning from hands-on activities

_____ I learn to spell words by writing them out.

_____ I enjoy handicrafts—cross-stitching, sculpting, building models, etc.

_____ I am mechanically inclined.

_____ I find texture to be important in decorating or selecting clothing.

_____ I like to "talk with my hands."

_____ I enjoy being physically active (I don't like to sit still!).

_____ If I am learning something, I need to "walk through" the steps.

_____ I like to learn by using contour maps, scientific models, or other touchable materials.

Count how many check marks you have in each of the three sections. The section in which you have the highest number of checks indicates your sensory preference. You may have the same number (or almost the same) in two categories. That simply means that you are equally comfortable processing information with either of those senses. If you have an equal number of answers in every section, you are quite adaptable. Most people, however, tend to have one or two sensory preferences.

The number of sentences each person checks will also vary. Remember, no single sensory preference is better than any other. Once you know your sensory preference(s), you can assess the best ways to enhance your studying and to perform better in both the classroom and your daily life.

Visual Learners

Visual learners find reading assignments more to their liking than auditory or tactile learners do. In fact, almost all educational material is geared to visual learners. Thus, in class, as a visual learner, you will benefit most from viewing films, slides, transparencies, and information written on the board. Your learning is enhanced by reading handouts, charts, graphs, maps, and sample assignments or papers and by viewing molecular models or skeletons. Doing computer exercises or writing with a word processor will provide you with additional visual reinforcement.

Because notes provide you with visual reinforcement, you need to take plenty of notes in class so that you will have a good visual record of each lecture. This is especially true if your instructor is teaching using primarily auditory methods, such as lecture, class discussion, or group work. If you are in a lab situation, where a lot of tactile learning takes place, again you need to reinforce your visual learning by taking notes on your procedures and outcomes. If you create your own drawings, graphs, maps, and charts, you will benefit by seeing this organized information on paper.

You may reinforce your visual learning preference in any subject by adding auditory and tactile approaches. For instance, for auditory reinforcement, you might form a study group, have a question-answer session with a study buddy, or use a tape recorder. To add tactile learning to your visual preference, you might make a model, a diagram, or drawing.

Auditory Learners

Auditory learners process information primarily by listening; therefore, auditory learners have an advantage because many college classes are taught through the lecture method. As an auditory learner, you will benefit considerably by hearing yourself as you recite your notes after class. Reciting aloud should be easy and natural to you because you will be stimulated to increase your learning by hearing your own voice.

As an auditory learner, when you read a textbook assignment, you might also consider reading it aloud. The use of a tape recorder—not necessarily in the classroom, but as a study aid—will also enhance an auditory learning style. For example, you could record questions on the tape recorder, then pause, leaving blank space to recite the answers. When you are ready for your own recitation, you simply play the taped questions and fill in the blank segments with your verbal answers. If you are taking a foreign language, you could tape conversations or vocabulary, again with blank time for responses. You could play these tapes in the car while you are driving to and from school or work. With a little bit of thought, you might devise some other ways to use a tape recorder. As an auditory learner, you may want to become a member of a study group because you will be stimulated to learn by the verbal interactions of the study group members.

One of the best methods of adding visual and tactile aspects to your auditory preference is to take notes. Note taking gives you the opportunity to use tactile learning as you write, and it also provides you with a visual record of the lecture or discussion.

Tactile Learners

Tactile learners, who learn best through the sense of touch, generally prefer courses that have lab components or courses that provide hands-on learning. However, most learning situations in college cater to visual or auditory learners, so tactile learners must devise ways to use their hands-on talent for learning. As a tactile learner, you want to enhance your learning by adding a physical component whenever possible. For example, using the computer gives you a hands-on approach to learning. You can use the word processor to write papers and keep your lists of vocabulary words or terms for courses. You can make charts and graphs and other visual organizers (see Chapter 9). You can also explore the Internet for information. You might also consider working with models or prototypes or make your own models whenever possible. When some tactile learners read a textbook chapter, they not only enjoy highlighting or underlining their text, but they also like to write questions and key word answers on notebook paper. Writing is actually a tactile learning experience. Many tactile learners frequently use 3 x 5 flash cards for studying vocabulary, terms, math and science formulas, and other concepts. In addition, since tactile learners seem to absorb more information if they move about, you might want to walk around as you recite your notes or textbook information.

Tactile learners should take as many notes as possible in class and resist the urge to doodle. For classes that seem to have no hands-on component, you might consider forming a study group with auditory and visual learners in it so that you can benefit from their sensory perspectives.

Complementing Your Sensory Preferences

Knowledge of your sensory preferences provides a powerful way for you to get the most out of your learning. However, you should also develop more strength in your less preferred senses. Most knowledge is gained through the senses, so the more senses you engage in learning, the more likely you are to remember the information. Also, practice in nonpreferred senses gives you versatility in learning. Always keep an open mind and be willing to try new approaches.

PERSONALITY PREFERENCES

Your learning is not only affected by the use of your sensory preferences, but also by your personality type. Personality type influences such areas of learning as (1) the source of energy, (2) the methods used to gather information, (3) the way decisions are made, and (4) approaches to work and play. These four categories may be discussed in terms of four pairs of opposites.

1. Extraverts or Introverts (sources of energy)
2. Sensors or iNtuitives (methods of taking in information)
3. Thinkers or Feelers (means of making decisions)
4. Judgers or Perceivers (approaches to work and play)

Each of these terms refers to personality preferences and is based upon the research of Carl Jung and the later work of Katharine Briggs and Isabel Briggs Myers. (*Note:* The word *Extravert* is purposely spelled with an *a* to conform to the official spelling on the Myers-Briggs Type Indicator or MBTI.)

In 1923, some of the writings of Carl Jung, a Swiss psychologist, were published in English. He proposed the Theory of Motivation and Personality, which describes people as being predominately Extraverts or Introverts, Sensors or iNtuitives, and Feelers or Thinkers. The meanings and implications of these paired, opposite terms will be explained throughout the rest of this chapter.

Katharine Briggs, who had long been interested in differences among people's personalities, had previously and independently made similar observations about her friends and acquaintances in terms of their lifestyles and personality preferences. When Jung's findings were published in the United States, she read his works and recognized the similarities to her own studies, and then she and her daughter, Isabel Briggs Myers, continued their research. Subsequently, they began developing a systematic and reliable way to understand differences in people. Their inventory, which was first published for public use in the 1970s, is called the Myers-Briggs Type Indicator (MBTI). This mother-daughter research team added an additional paired category to the personality preferences recognized by Jung, namely, Judgers and Perceivers.

If you want to take the official MBTI survey, a trained, qualified individual who can interpret the data and explain the results accurately must administer it. Taking the official MBTI survey and having it interpreted and discussed by a qualified person is really the only reliable way of discovering your true preferences. Many colleges and universities have a qualified MBTI person on the staff who will administer the inventory free or at a minimal cost. However, if such a resource is unavailable to you, you can get a sense of your personality preferences by reading the following explanations of the four pairs of contrasting preferences mentioned above.

As you read about the categories of the MBTI, it is essential to remember that all preferences are *good*. When you are able to operate according to your preferences, you feel comfortable and normal. However, since this is not a perfect world, sometimes you will need to work outside your preferences, using your nonpreferences. This may make you feel awkward and uncomfortable, but you still have the ability to function well in these situations.

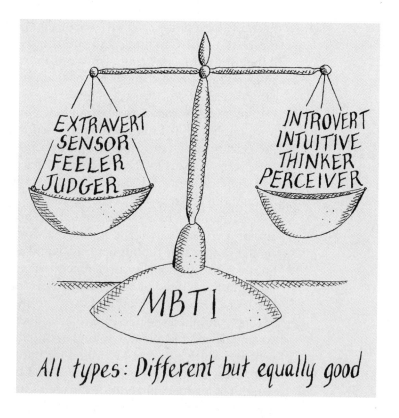

All types: Different but equally good

Once you use your preferences for a period of time, they tend to become habits. A simple comparison might be found in such an everyday occurrence as putting on your shoes and socks. Do you start with the left foot or the right? It really doesn't make any difference which foot you start with, but you probably always begin with the *same* foot. The way you perform this action demonstrates a preference. Now try putting your socks and shoes on in the opposite way. How did that feel? You may not have been as comfortable because you were using a nonpreference.

Like the right and left foot illustration, the preferences in the four categories of the MBTI are set up as opposites. As you consider these categories, you will likely identify more with one preference than the other. Your *honest* responses are important here. You will recognize yourself in parts of both opposites; however, you will usually feel more identification with one than with the other because that one is your preference.

No matter what your preferences are, view them as an empowerment or strength for you, not as an excuse for dodging responsibilities.

Extraverts and Introverts

The first pair of opposites deals with where you get your energy and how you interact with others. *Extraverts* (E) get energy from people and the outside world, whereas *Introverts* (I) find their energy from within themselves. Read the following descriptions to see which of the two opposites applies to your personality.

You are an Extravert (E), as the name implies, if you are energized by being with people and talking to them. An Extravert tends to

- talk instead of listen.
- speak before thinking carefully.
- say, "I wish I'd kept my mouth shut!"
- respond quickly in class.
- talk about writing assignments with others before actually writing.
- enjoy studying and working in groups and sharing ideas.
- talk to strangers as well as friends.
- be easily distracted while studying.
- have many friends.
- enjoy parties.
- like talking on the phone.
- be outgoing and talkative socially.
- be energized by social activities.

If you are an Introvert (I), you are energized by being alone or with a small group of close friends. An Introvert tends to

- listen instead of talk.
- think before speaking.
- say, "I wish I'd speak up more."
- hesitate to answer in class.
- think alone about a writing assignment before actually writing.
- prefer studying or working alone.
- dislike talking to strangers.
- concentrate so well that the outside world is sometimes forgotten.
- prefer having a few good friends.
- hesitate to attend large social events.
- resent telephone interruptions.
- seem quiet and shy socially.
- need peace and quiet to recuperate after social activities.

After reading the descriptions of an Extravert and an Introvert, you may now be able to determine which one best describes you. Of course, you may very well have characteristics of both an E and an I, but one most likely is your preference. Check *one* of the following:

I am primarily an E _____, or I am primarily an I _____.

Sensors and iNtuitives

The next two categories, Sensors (S) or iNtuitives (N), indicate the way you prefer to learn information. The abbreviation for iNtuitives is the letter N because the letter I has already been used as an abbreviation for Introverts.

If you are primarily a *Sensor,* you depend heavily on your five senses to learn. A Sensor tends to

- speak using specific facts and details.
- be comfortable with repetition.
- be practical and down-to-earth.
- prefer information given in a clear, logical, step-by-step order.
- want specific directions.
- write with great detail but may have trouble developing the main idea.
- be comfortable with facts.
- be tuned into the present and not worry about the past or future.

- prefer reality over fantasy.
- focus on the task itself at work or college rather than how it relates to the company or career.
- say, "If it ain't broke, don't fix it!"
- resist change.

If you are an *iNtuitive* person, your preferred way of learning is just the opposite of a Sensor. Rather than relying mostly on your five senses, your approach to learning is driven by your "sixth" sense, your intuition. An iNtuitive tends to

- speak in generalities.
- dislike repetition.
- be impractical at times or even seem absentminded.
- understand information even if it is not in order.
- disregard directions or change them.
- write with many generalizations, assuming the reader can fill in the details.
- like theories and ideas.
- be driven by thoughts and concerns about the future and unconcerned about the past and present.
- prefer fantasy over reality.
- focus on how a task at work or college contributes to the big picture.
- say, "There must be a better way to do this!"—preferring creativity and originality.
- welcome changes and love challenges.

Once again, you probably see characteristics of both the Sensor and the iNtuitve in yourself. One preference, however, is more predominate than the other. Check *one* of the following:

I am primarily an S _____, or I am primarily an N _____.

Thinkers and Feelers

The categories of Thinking (T) and Feeling (F) relate to how people are most apt to arrive at their decisions. The names of these categories should not be taken too literally. People who are predominately Feeling *do* think, and people who are predominately Thinking have feelings for others. However, when it comes to making a decision, one or the other preference, T or F, influences our choices.

A *Thinking* person makes decisions based upon what he or she considers to be right, fair, and truthful. A Thinker tends to

- evaluate with head, not heart.
- love to analyze situations.
- appear to be cool, calm, collected, perhaps even calculating.
- be logical, precise, and to the point.
- be surprised if anyone disagrees with him or her.
- be strong-minded and is sometimes seen as overbearing.
- present ideas in a logical organization and expect the same from others.
- expect ideas to be proven by reason or by scientific fact.
- be capable of making tough decisions.
- hurt people's feelings, knowingly or unknowingly.

A *Feeling* person is usually very conscious of the emotional reactions of others and bases his or her decisions on what will make people happy. A Feeling person tends to

- decide with heart, not head.
- analyze people's feelings and needs and respond to them.
- appear to be emotional and sensitive.
- ensure peace and harmony even if he or she must bend logic or soften the truth.
- take comments very personally when others disagree with him or her.
- be kindhearted, caring, and nurturing.
- develop ideas by referring to his or her own feelings and those of others (logic is secondary).
- view ideas and facts selectively based on how they affect people's well-being.
- procrastinate on tough decisions or let others make them.
- get feelings hurt easily.

From reading about the decision-making processes of Thinkers and Feelers, you may now identify your major method for making decisions. If you are more concerned about right and wrong and logical conclusions, you are primarily a T. If you are more concerned with how your decisions will affect those involved, you are primarily an F. Check *one* of the following:

I am primarily a T _____, or I am primarily an F _____.

Judgers and Perceivers

The last two opposites, Judging (J) and Perceiving (P), relate to your approaches to work and play. If you prefer to live in a relatively organized and structured way, you are a J, but if you tend to be more spontaneous and flexible, you are probably a P.

A *Judger* appreciates and needs organization in his or her life. A Judger tends to

- be on time and meet deadlines.
- want closure and dislike leaving anything unfinished.
- like to be in control.
- make everyone in a group stay on track.
- keep lists.
- know what he or she is going to do in advance.
- get a lot done early and on time.
- feel frustrated by interruptions.
- dislike last-minute changes.
- manage time well.
- work before playing.

A *Perceiver* likes to be spontaneous and flexible. A Perceiver tends to

- run late for appointments and sometimes miss deadlines.
- stay open to incoming information and not worry about closure.
- be free and easy; control is not essential.
- get off the topic frequently because each topic is interesting and should be explored.
- keep lists in his or her head; if writing a list, it may be trashed, lost, or ignored.
- act on the spur of the moment and enjoy surprises.
- produce work at the last minute.
- be easily distracted.
- welcome change and variety.
- appear disorganized.
- prefer play to work and often turn work into play.

These opposites, Judging and Perceiving, indicate how much structure you prefer in your life. Often both Js and Ps are forced to compromise because of people or situations at home, at work, or at school. Thus, you may want to consider the following situation to determine if you tend to be a J or a P: Suppose you were independently wealthy, retired, or in some other way responsible only for yourself. Which description best fits the way you would live? A J prefers living an organized, scheduled, predictable life, whereas a P prefers living a spontaneous, flexible life, where time and structure are of little importance. Check *one* of the following:

I am primarily a J _____, or I am primarily a P _____.

Your Personality Type

Your *personality type* is a combination of your four preferences from the descriptions above. Look back at the letters you checked, and write those four letters in the blanks below to identify your preferred personality type.

E or I	S or N	T or F	J or P
_____	_____	_____	_____

These four letters indicate one of the sixteen MBTI personality types.

Understanding MBTI Types

According to the MBTI, when the four pairs of opposite characteristics are arranged in all possible combinations, sixteen different types exist. No one type is better, or for that matter worse, than any other type. They are all merely different. Similar types, however, will share similar characteristics. However, people who are the same type may be very different because the degree of preference in each of the four categories could fluctuate greatly from one individual to another. The following illustration will help you to understand the concept: Just because a number of people enjoy rock concerts doesn't mean they all go to the same concerts or like the same singers, the same songs, or the same instruments. In a similar sense, you *do* have a personality type that you share with others of the same type, but you are still unique as an individual.

WEB SITE INFORMATION

If you want more information about learning preferences and personality types, visit our web site:

<http://college.hmco.com/success/>

Web sites about majors and careers are also listed.

Appendix: To learn more about your own and others' MBTI profiles, go to the Appendix.

MBTI in the Classroom

Extraverts & Introverts   In the classroom, Extraverted and Introverted students often behave differently. Extraverts may respond quickly and vocally and enjoy working in groups. Introverts, on the other hand, take time to rehearse their answers silently and may seldom or never respond aloud, and they usually prefer working alone.

The way you use your natural E or I preference may influence your rapport with your instructor and your fellow students; it may even affect your grade. For example, all students need to participate actively in class regardless of their comfort level. Extraverts are good at asking questions and giving quick answers in class; however, they should make a special effort to listen and not to monopolize class discussions. As group leaders, Extraverts are comfortable with their role, but they need to make a deliberate effort to include all group members in the discussion, particularly the quiet ones. Introverts, on the other hand, need to answer and ask questions in class more often. When Introverts act as group leaders, they must tolerate their feelings of discomfort and make the effort to interact with everyone.

Sensors & iNtuitives   Differences also exist in the classroom for the second category, Sensors and iNtuitives. Sensors like to have step-by-step directions, with everything spelled out for them in detail. Students who are iNtuitive do not need sequential directions and prefer more open-ended assignments. Whether you are an S or an N, you may have to adapt to a classroom where the instructor is teaching in a preference opposite to your own. Your ability to adapt to the other preference can help you stay open-minded and ensure your learning.

For a Sensing student, an iNtuitive instructor may seem to jump from one idea to another, start with the big picture, and assume that everyone will pick up the details. Even if a Sensing student comes to class well prepared, he or she may sometimes feel lost. An S in an N's classroom must gain structure by being thoroughly prepared before class and by meticulously editing notes and perhaps even outlining notes and the text after class to make the material completely understandable. These students should also not hesitate to ask for clarification, more details, or examples.

For an iNtuitive student, the Sensing teacher may seem to dwell on specific details and endless facts. The N student may feel frustrated, and even bored, with too many details because the N student wants the class to move on to larger issues and future implications. The N in an S's class needs to respect the knowledge of the instructor, be tolerant of the lecture style, and understand that the majority of students are S's and need to have all the details outlined. Ns can use this time to make mental connections and think about the topic as a whole. In terms of assignments, an N student could try to negotiate for some flexibility, or be realistic and say, "Okay, if that's the assignment, that's what I have to do."

Knowing how you prefer to learn or to process information is not going to change the way assignments are given or the way individual instructors teach. However, this awareness of MBTI types will allow you to understand your preferences, cope with your frustrations, and adapt to your classroom situation in a positive way.

Thinkers & Feelers   The third set of opposites, Thinkers and Feelers, arrive at decisions differently. These differences, too, have an impact on learning. Thinking types base their decisions on logic and what they perceive as right and wrong. Feeling types base their decisions on personal values and their perception of how others will be affected. Sometimes miscommunication occurs between instructors and students when Thinking and Feeling types are interacting. In class, T instructors tend to be more direct and to the point, wanting students to respond in a logical, matter-of-fact way. Their feedback is also likely to be direct and factual. F instructors tend to be open to many varied responses to a question; they encourage students to give personal answers and may lavish praise and encouragement on the student. Student-instructor conferences may also be affected by the instructor's T or F preference. For example, when a student is trying to resolve an issue, problem, or discussion with a T instructor, the student would be wise to use objective and logical reasons rather than subjective and emotional language. When having a conference with an F instructor, the opposite would be true. The F instructor would want to hear factual reasons as well as the personal implications of the problem or discussion.

Judgers & Perceivers   The fourth area of differences in the classroom involves the Judging and the Perceiving types. Judgers are well-organized, time-conscious people who like to keep schedules and lists. Therefore, their preference for structured environments allows them to fit comfortably into most academic situations. Perceivers, however, are more spontaneous and flexible and not as concerned with time. They may often prefer leaving completion of tasks until the last minute.

Both Perceivers and Judgers must appreciate that time is valuable and that poor time management can defeat students in achieving their goals. Judgers are generally good time managers, but they should be cautious not to finish tasks too quickly just to be finished, thus compromising quality. They also should avoid being so controlling that they create undue negative stress for themselves. Perceivers may have more difficulty meeting the structured deadlines in college. If you are a Perceiver and wait for that last-minute adrenaline rush, you might consider leaving enough lead-time to stay on top of your tasks, breaking large tasks into smaller ones to help you get started on a project, or using a loosely constructed time management list or schedule.

In conclusion, knowing your MBTI personality type and preferences will allow you to understand yourself and others better, to use your preferences as strengths in learning situations and everyday life, and to realize that sometimes you may choose—or be required—to work outside your preferences.

Learning to Use Your Nonpreferences

Although using your personality preferences makes you feel comfortable, normal, and stress-free, you also need to be able to adapt to situations where you want to—or need to—use your nonpreferences. Nonpreferences are those actions and attitudes that feel uncomfortable, awkward, and stressful. The purpose of adapting to a nonpreference is not to attempt to change your personality type (you couldn't if you wanted to), but to practice using nonpreferences enough to enable you to feel more comfortable in situations that require using them. If you have taken the official MBTI, you will know by the numbers how clear your preferences are in each area. If you have not taken the MBTI, then rely on your instincts and self-knowledge to know how clear your preferences are in each area. The clearer the preference, the more challenging it may be to use your nonpreferences comfortably.

The following tips provide some ways to practice using your nonpreferences. You will probably think of many more ways. To keep from overloading yourself, take small steps, perhaps even working in only one area at a time.

Extraverts could learn from an Introvert by

- letting others speak before impulsively giving their opinions.
- working alone on a project.
- taking time to think carefully before speaking or acting.
- listening carefully before reacting to others.

Introverts could learn from an Extravert by

- speaking up in class and in small group discussions.
- joining and participating in a college or community group or organization.
- sharing ideas without being asked.
- going out of their way to say "hello" to people and generally being more sociable.

Sensors could learn from an iNtuitive by

- trusting intuition when making a judgment.
- imagining where they will be in five years, then ten years.
- reading articles in a magazine in a random order.
- driving home on a different route from school or work.

Intuitives could learn from a Sensor by

- noticing specific details as they drive to work or school.
- paying attention to details about people: their dress, hairstyles, etc.
- patiently explaining a process to a child or another adult.
- investigating as many details as possible before reaching a conclusion.

Thinkers could learn from a Feeler by

- writing a short note to someone who is important to them, telling the person why he or she is important.
- making a conscious effort to compliment people.
- persuading someone to do something by asking instead of commanding.
- listening to others' reasons and considering their views and feelings instead of saying, "You're wrong."

Feelers could learn from a Thinker by

- saying "no" without giving reasons or feeling guilty.
- hanging up on phone solicitors without apologizing for not listening.
- accepting criticism without "crying" inside or outside.
- making a decision they know is right even if it has to hurt someone's feelings.

Judgers could learn from a Perceiver by

- doing something on the spur of the moment.
- forgiving people who are not on time.
- thinking of three more ways to improve a task instead of saying, "I've finished this task."
- going outside and playing for ten minutes.

Perceivers could learn from a Judger by

- making a to-do list for the day and using it.
- finishing one task before starting another.
- saying "No!" if someone tries to distract them from an important task.
- getting to appointments on time for a whole week.

Critically Thinking Together

Form small groups. One person should act as a recorder for each group. Keeping in mind that all preferences are good, make a list of advantages of being a Judger and an equally long list of being a Perceiver. Be prepared to discuss your lists with the whole class.

Teaching Style Preferences

Instructors teach in different ways because they are influenced in part by their own preferred learning styles and their personality types. Think about all the teachers that you have had in the past and that you have this term. They all have unique teaching styles and techniques. Whether you consider their teaching styles "good" or "bad" depends to some degree on your preferences. If your preferences match those of the teacher, then that match may facilitate your success in that class. For example, if you are an auditory learner, you will have an advantage over visual or tactile learners in a class where an instructor teaches only through lectures. If you and your teacher are both Judgers, you may understand each other's desires for logic and reason. If, however, your style is a mismatch with that of your teacher, then you need to recognize the difference and work a bit harder in the class to adjust to that teacher's style. Mismatches cannot be used as an excuse for not learning. Such differences can be opportunities to adapt to a nonpreferred style.

Teaching styles can be divided into several categories, and, of course, any given teacher might demonstrate a variety of styles depending on the class size, course content, amount of material to be covered, or time restraints. The basic elements in teaching styles include the format, the organization of information, and delivery.

Format

Lecture Format   In the lecture format, the instructor is the central figure at all times, and students are expected to listen and take notes. There is little time for questions or interaction between the instructor and the students; in fact, some lecturers may resent being interrupted. The classroom is arranged in the traditional fashion—the teacher stands at a lectern, and the students sit at desks in neat, orderly rows. At times, some of these classes are so large that they meet in an auditorium. Some lecturers arrive early so that they can write information on the board before they start their lectures. Note taking is the primary way to gain information in this type of class. Because this is true, you will want to arrive early and sit near the front of the room. If the lecturer is a rapid-fire speaker, take notes as quickly as you can, but if you miss something, leave white spaces to fill in later. Basically, the instructor is providing all the information, which the student is expected to record and know. One advantage of the lecture format is that it provides a great deal of information in a relatively short period of time; some disadvantages to you, as a student, are that you might feel overwhelmed and unimportant because you are not verbally contributing to the class.

Interactive or Shared-Learning Format   In the interactive format, the instructor uses a variety of ways to present materials—mini-lectures, class discussions, group work, peer readings, student presentations or debates, and hands-on projects. The classroom structure is flexible with desks arranged in rows, a circle, or small groupings, depending upon the activity. Whatever the arrangement, the instructor moves around the classroom in response to those activities. These instructors encourage students to discover answers and ideas themselves by interacting in class discussions and small groups. Even though the setting seems to be informal, students need to take their learning seriously by participating actively in discussions and taking notes on ideas contributed by other students. One advantage is that learning seems easier and more enjoyable because you are actively involved. A disadvantage is that some students do not take notes and falsely believe that "nothing happened" in class because most of the learning occurred through a discovery method.

Organization

Structured Organization   Teachers who use structured organization in the classroom provide information in an orderly, exact, detailed, often sequential way. These instructors tend to use words like "the definition is," "first . . . , second . . . , third . . . ," "I have provided you with an outline of . . . ," and "Finally, the most important ideas to remember are . . ." Directions from structured teachers tend to be very specific. Because these teachers are highly organized themselves, they have little tolerance for disorganized work from students. On tests, these teachers will probably focus on factual information rather than abstract ideas. Some advantages to students in a structured classroom are that students find it easy to follow the instructor's train of thought and to take notes because major points and supporting details are clearly outlined. In addition, test items from a structured class are usually predictable. A disadvantage might be that some students would feel hemmed in by the exactness and daily routine of a highly structured class. Because the syllabus is so carefully constructed and the teacher doesn't want to get behind, some of these classes may lack time and opportunity for student input.

Spontaneous Organization   Instructors who use spontaneous organization in the classroom are often creative people who focus on possibilities, ideas, and applications that connect textbook information to real life experiences. They often introduce a topic with a broad concept or theory and explore it in many directions. They pepper their comments with words such as "concept, theory, discuss, interpret, and justify." Their exams will probably be composed of some factual questions but may be heavily weighted toward analytical and theoretical questions. Sometimes they omit the concrete details because they assume that everyone can see the big picture and is following the discussion. An advantage to a spontaneously organized class is that it stimulates critical thinking and creativity in students. Also, these classes will seldom be predictable or boring because of the wealth of ideas presented. A disadvantage is that the lectures or discussions can be so abstract that some students have a hard time following the logic behind these discussions. Taking notes in a spontaneous class can also be a challenge because the information is so randomly organized. You probably will need to reorganize your notes after class and perhaps outline the major points and details by referring to your textbook.

Delivery Styles

Besides format and organization, every teacher has his or her own style of delivery. These styles range from the extremely dynamic, entertaining, and enthusiastic presenter to the more matter-of-fact, less animated presenter, who might speak in a monotone. All of these qualities must be viewed on a progressive scale. That is, most instructors are not at either extreme, but have delivery styles that are somewhere in the range between dynamic and matter-of-fact. Delivery styles do influence your feelings about a course and your interest in the class. No one can deny that interesting, creative delivery can make information seem more fun to learn. However, the real purpose of instruction is to gain information, and you cannot expect all your instructors to be entertainers or comedians. Whatever the person's delivery style, you are the one who is responsible for learning the information.

The discussion of teaching styles has included format, organization, and delivery methods—three components that can be combined in many different ways and to many different degrees. Individual instructors may vary or adjust their styles of format, organization, and delivery according to the class size, subject, or particular needs of students. For example, particularly in a class period lasting several hours, a teacher might give a lecture, then divide the class into groups for discussion, and then have students go to a lab to complete a hands-on project.

Your knowledge of your sensory preferences and your personality preferences act as a means of helping you to cope with any situation. The more you know about yourself, the more you are able to be in control of your life.

Exercise 1-B

Directions: Now that you have read about your sensory preferences, personality type, and teaching style preferences, summarize your preferences below:

Preferences Summary

My major sensory preference: _____

My secondary sensory preference: _____

My personality type: _____

My teaching style preference:

Format _____

Organization _____

Delivery _____

> ## Critically Thinking in Writing
>
> In a journal entry, choose one of the following topics:
>
> 1. Describe the ideal class for you, keeping in mind all your learning preferences (sensory preferences, personality preferences, and teaching style preferences) and your major.
>
> 2. Write about your most challenging class, describing your instructor's teaching style and your learning style. Create a plan that will help you to achieve success in that class.

ATTITUDES TOWARD RESPONSIBILITY

Another aspect of self-knowledge is having an understanding of attitudes that influence your behavior. When you were a child or teenager, your life was probably less complicated than it is today. You did what you wanted to do, or very often you did what you were told to do by a parent or another adult in charge. Do any of the following statements sound familiar, or, if you are now a parent, do you hear yourself saying words like these:

"It's time to put away your toys."
"I will read just one more story, and then you have to go to bed."
"You have to do your homework before you go out."
"Clean your room first; then you can go to a movie."

When you were a child and even a teenager, your choices and actions were often dictated by others who were responsible for you. In one sense, that is good because children do need guidance. However, now that you are a college student, you need to become responsible for yourself and your own decisions. In other words, you should strive to be a self-motivated person. Examining what motivates you can help you understand your actions better, which allows you to gain more control.

Exercise 1-C will give you an opportunity to begin thinking about your motivation.

Exercise 1-C

Directions: Answer each question by checking the appropriate line.

	Yes	Partly	No
1. I am going to college to get a degree.	____	____	____
2. I am in college because my friends are.	____	____	____
3. I study because I know I should.	____	____	____
4. I regularly procrastinate when I should be studying.	____	____	____
5. I don't think instructors grade me fairly.	____	____	____
6. I am responsible for the grades I receive.	____	____	____
7. It is not my fault if I don't attend class.	____	____	____
8. I don't finish my assignments on time because I'm a busy person.	____	____	____
9. I tend to be an unlucky person.	____	____	____
10. My grades directly relate to how thoroughly I study.	____	____	____

If you answered "yes" to 1, 3, 6, and 10 and "no" or "partly" to the rest of the questions, you are likely to be a self-motivated person. If most of your responses to 2, 4, 5, 7, 8, and 9 were "yes," then you may be letting the outside world control you too much.

Locus of Control

A psychologist named Julian B. Rotter introduced the term *locus of control* in 1966. Locus means "place." If you place responsibility for your life within *yourself*, then you are said to have *internal locus of control*. On the other hand, if you place primary responsibility for your life on others and on circumstances outside yourself, then you are considered to have *external locus of control*.

People who are self-motivated have developed internal locus of control and are generally positive thinkers who are responsible for their actions. For example, if they cannot get to school, they do not blame their cars for breaking down or children for being sick. They have alternative plans already in place—a ride from someone else, a baby sitter, or a classmate who takes good notes and agrees to share them in an emergency. If they do not do well on a test, they say, "What did *I* do wrong?" and then analyze how they can improve their study habits in order to do better.

People who need to be pushed by other people or circumstances have external locus of control and are often very negative, blaming the world around them or "fate" when things don't go their way. They can be heard making comments like these:

"It's not *my* fault the car wouldn't start!"
"I wasn't able to do the work because my baby kept me up all night."
"I don't think the teacher went over half the stuff on that test. No wonder I didn't do well."
"How can I be expected to study when I have to work all night?"

In addition to blaming cars, jobs, or others, people who have external locus of control may turn to drugs or alcohol to "solve" their problems instead of attacking the problem itself. This so-called solution could lead to their being even less in control of their lives.

Obviously, dealing with serious situations that are not under your control is difficult. However, you do have the power to determine your actions and reactions. For example, even though you cannot control a health problem or a family crisis, you can determine how to accept the situation, face the reality of it, adjust your plans and goals, and move on with as positive an attitude as possible.

The chart on page 27 indicates some of the major differences between the attitudes of people with internal locus of control and people with external locus of control:

Locus of Control

=

where you place responsibility for control over your life

− External	+ Internal
Other people or things seem to control me.	I'm responsible for myself.
Others must push me.	I make my own choices.
My outlook on life is often negative.	My outlook on life is usually positive.
Professor Smith *gave* me a D!	I worked *hard* for this C!
I don't like change. I have my *own* ways of doing things.	Changing wasn't easy, but now I'm glad I did.
I'm unlucky. I never get any breaks!	Sure, I've had some bad breaks, but they're not an excuse to quit.
It's not my fault! I couldn't help it.	I take full responsibility for what happened.
I give up! I can't do anything about it.	I made a mistake. Now I'll figure out how to correct it.

External locus of control actually takes away your own self-power when you point the finger of blame at other people or at your surroundings or circumstances.

In order to achieve internal locus of control, you must be willing to give up the security of making excuses and to take responsibility for *all* your decisions and actions. A person with internal locus of control has successfully made the transition from childhood to adulthood. With an awareness of locus of control, you can replace the tired, external cliché of "It's just not fair!" with an action statement: "So, life is not fair; now how can I solve the problem?" The decision to take responsibility for your life is up to you.

WEB SITE INFORMATION

To assess your own locus of control, visit our web site:

<http://college.hmco.com/success/>

Exercise 1-D

Directions: Here are statements that a person with external locus of control might make. Explain what a person with internal locus of control might do to motivate himself or herself. Be prepared to share your answers in class.

1. "I signed up for a class; that teacher can't expect me to go to labs, too!" _____

_____

_____

2. "I don't know why I have to take this class." _____

_____

_____

3. "This instructor is so boring I can hardly stay awake." _____

_____

_____

4. "Why do I get all the tough teachers, and you get all the easy ones?" _____

_____

_____

Summary

In this chapter, you discovered your own learning styles and preferences and how to use them to help you become a more powerful learner.

First, you discovered your preferred sensory style(s): visual, auditory, or tactile. To get the most out of your learning, you need to capitalize on your sensory preference, but also learn to incorporate other sensory perceptions to get the most out of your classroom and study time.

Next, you learned about personality preferences through the Myers-Briggs Type Indicator (MBTI), which isolates four pairs of contrasting preferences: Extravert or Introvert, which is an indication of where you get your energy; Sensing or iNtuition, which is the way you prefer to gather information; Thinking or Feeling, which indicates your preferred way to make decisions; and Judging or Perceiving, which is how you prefer to live your life. The composite of these variables creates sixteen different personality types, all of which are equally good. Knowing your type, and that fifteen others exist, can help you better understand yourself and others. You should not try to change your own type, but sometimes you will benefit by using your nonpreferences.

Then, you learned about teaching style preferences. These include the instructor's format, organization, and delivery. Awareness of these preferences can help you understand your comfort level in a given class.

Finally, you learned about two different attitudes toward responsibility. Students who have internal locus of control accept responsibility for their actions as opposed to those who have external locus of control and blame others.

List of Terms

preferences	tactile learners	Feelers
nonpreferences	Extraverts	Judgers
learning style	Introverts	Perceivers
sensory preference	Sensors	personality type
visual learners	iNtuitives	internal locus of control
auditory learners	Thinkers	external locus of control

> **In this box, write your summary question or statement for this chapter.**

2 The Power of Managing Goals, Problems, and Stress

Knowing where you want to go and how to get there is an important aspect of life. In a simple physical sense, knowing how to get where you want to go is rather easy. All you need is a map and some kind of transportation. In a more complex psychological and mental sense, however, knowing where you want to go in life and how to get there generally requires planning, effort, and critical thinking. The path to your future is not always clear cut; you have many choices and decisions to make and may encounter many unforeseen road blocks along the way.

In this chapter, you will learn how to reach long-term goals by setting short-term goals and how to use motivation to make the process happen. You will also learn a powerful critical-thinking technique, SOLVE, for overcoming both large and small problems. Finally, you will learn to understand and manage stress better, especially as it relates to college. The techniques you will learn in this chapter will help you find direction and gain the power to manage your life better.

GOAL SETTING

A *goal* is the objective or purpose toward which an effort is directed. *Long-term goals* are large achievements that often take a significant amount of time, such as graduating from college, being accepted in your profession, buying a house, or making your first million. *Short-term goals* provide the smaller steps that you need to take in order to reach your long-term goals, such as STUDY-READING an assignment (see Chapter 5), creating an effective résumé, saving a certain amount of money every week, and making wise financial investments.

For a goal to be meaningful to you, it must have three components:

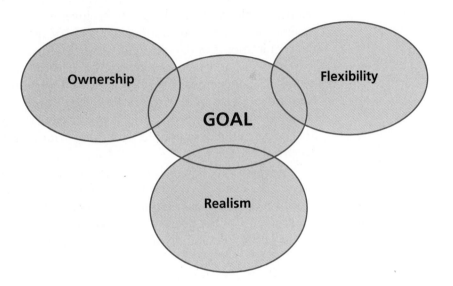

Ownership

The first criterion for a meaningful goal is that it must be something that *you* really want. This is especially true for all of your long-term goals. Even if a relative or friend says, "This is something I think would be good for you," unless you yourself truly want to do it, it will not be your goal, but rather something you are doing to please someone else. In other words, a goal must be something that you choose for yourself and must be something that you personally value.

An effective way of determining if you really *own* a goal is to ask yourself the following questions:

- Am I personally and genuinely interested in this goal?
- Am I willing to change old attitudes, behavior, or habits if necessary?
- Am I willing to devote the necessary time to accomplish it?
- Am I willing to sacrifice some comforts and some interests to achieve it?

If your answers to these questions are yes, then the goal is yours, *you own it,* and you will probably be motivated enough to pursue it.

Realism

When you set your long-term goals, ownership is not the only consideration. You also must consider what you can realistically achieve. Setting realistic goals must involve taking an inventory of your personal talents, qualifications (physical and mental), and background to see if they meet the requirements of that particular goal. If, for example, you are twenty-five years old and have never played a musical instrument, deciding to become a concert pianist probably would be unrealistic. On the other hand, if you have studied the violin since the age of seven and have been accepted into a college of music, it would be realistic to have a long-term goal of playing in a symphony orchestra. Your goals must realistically reflect your capabilities.

You must also be realistic about the requirements of the goal itself. You must decide if you are willing to master the necessary knowledge and skills. This means you must seek out sufficient information about the requirements of the goal. For example, if you think you would like to be a nurse, is the picture in your head realistic? Do you see a nurse as a person who has a pleasant job, going from patient to patient, offering them pills and encouraging words? Are you aware of the course requirements in a nursing program? Some of the courses are very challenging. Have you realistically learned about the day-to-day duties of a nurse? Nurses do much more than take blood pressure and have a good bedside manner. They also give shots, empty bedpans, change bloody bandages, and bathe patients. Sufficient information about a long-term goal is necessary to make a realistic choice.

The length of time it will take to reach the goal must also be realistic. Whatever your goal, you need to establish a beginning point and an ending point when you can say, "Yes, I've accomplished that goal." Whether you are seeking a two-year or a four-year degree or are in a program of some other length of time, you should plan the time you will need to fulfill the requirements. For example, some two-year programs leading to an associate's degree cram in as many as nineteen hours a quarter (when twelve hours is a full-time load) and require attendance during the summer. Although completing such a program in two years could be a realistic goal, you also need to weigh all the other factors that might make a two-year time frame unrealistic for you. For instance, do you have to work part time? Do you have family obligations that would make going to school full time difficult? Are there prerequisites that you need to take before you start your program? These and other factors might mean that your goal would be more realistic if you allowed three, four, or even five years or more to complete your associate's degree.

When considering your career goals, you might want to visit the career planning and placement center at your college. It can offer you resources such as books, audiovisual materials, computer software, career testing, and career counseling. These services are usually offered to you free or with a minimal fee to cover the cost of testing materials. You might want to begin your search on the Internet by going to your college's home page.

WEB SITE INFORMATION

For additional information on majors and careers, visit our web site:

   <http://college.hmco.com/success/>

As you evaluate how realistic your career goal is—or any other goal, for that matter—you would do well to ask yourself several questions:

- Do I have the mental ability to accomplish this goal?
- Do I have the physical ability?
- Do I have the talent?
- Do I fully understand what is involved in achieving this goal?
- Do I have the resources—including opportunity, time, and means (financial and other)—to accomplish it?
- Do I have a support system (cooperation from family, advisors, boss, friends) that I can rely on for help?
- Are there any other factors that might keep me from reaching this goal? If so, what can I do to overcome these obstacles?

Being realistic does not necessarily mean that you should give up a goal if you don't have the skills, because skills can be acquired. If you have the ability and the desire, you need to focus your energy on practical and creative ways to accomplish your goal.

Flexibility

A third criterion for a meaningful goal is flexibility; that is, you must be willing to evaluate your goal continually and to revise it if necessary. Because situations change and unforeseen obstacles arise, you must be prepared to face these possibilities realistically and then make whatever adjustments are needed in order to reach your goal. Although you may have some setbacks due to your own poor choices, other setbacks are really out of your control. For example, you often have no control over schedule changes at work, illness, injury, unforeseen expenses, or other circumstantial difficulties.

However, a setback should not be viewed as a failed goal; it simply means you need to adjust your plans and your timetable. For example, suppose your old, reliable car finally gives out on you. It cannot be repaired, and if you buy another car, even a used car, you won't have enough money for tuition the following term. This might mean that you would have to drop out of school for a while to earn enough money to buy the car. This setback, however discouraging, does not mean you have to quit college completely, but it does mean you must be flexible enough to adjust your time frame.

SHORT-TERM GOALS TO LONG-TERM GOALS

Long-term goals by their very nature often seem far away and beyond reach. The means of reaching a long-term goal, therefore, may seem like a monumental task. For example, if you are just beginning college and are planning to become a doctor, having to complete four years of undergraduate school, four years of medical school, and another three or more years of internship and residency may seem impossibly demanding. However, by setting short-term goals, you can gradually work your way up to achieving your long-term goal, even one as far away as ten years from now. Completing an assignment, completing a course, and completing a term of classes may be considered short-term goals because they can be accomplished in the foreseeable future.

Short-term goals by definition are smaller, more immediate, and more readily attainable than long-term goals. Therefore, in order to stay motivated and to encourage yourself along the way, you need to focus on short-term goals that you can meet within a month, a week, a day, or even a class period. Each short-term goal that is completed builds confi-

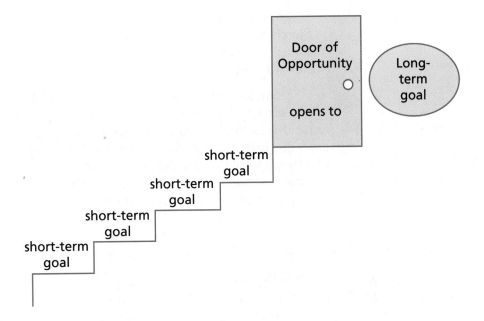

dence and, like climbing the steps of a staircase, brings you closer to reaching your long-term goal.

In order for short-term goals to be effective, they must be very specific and action-oriented. As you write out your short-term goals, you should keep the following guidelines in mind:

- Make positive statements, not negative ones. Instead of stating, "I will not be late to class," write, "I will arrive on time to class."
- Make statements based on personal behaviors that are in your control. If you state, "I'm going to get an A in my chemistry course," you are focusing on the outcome, which is not completely in your control because it involves more than just your behavior. Instead, write, "I will attend and prepare for each lecture and lab, take thorough notes, study notes and text for at least an hour and a half daily, and consult a chemistry tutor, as needed." This kind of statement will make your goal more reachable because these specific behaviors are in your control.
- Make your goals specific by using exact times and amounts. Instead of stating, "I will study harder," write, "I will work 10 math problems every day even if they are not assigned," and "I will go to the math lab to work with a tutor every Monday and Wednesday at 11:00."

- Make your short-term goals easy enough that you can achieve them, but challenging enough to make you feel that you have accomplished something worthwhile.
- Reward yourself when you have completed a short-term goal.

Setting and achieving goals for yourself is a learned art and can be a very rewarding experience. You don't want to set your goals too low because that is an insult to your intelligence. You don't want to set your goals too high either because you probably won't achieve them and the experience would be frustrating. Strive to set goals that are challenging, but also achievable. Stretch yourself through hard work and perseverance to surpass even your own expectations.

Exercise 2-A

Directions: Using the guidelines above, choose one course you are taking. In pencil, write one long-term goal for that course, and then write five short-term goals that you can use to reach the long-term goal. Be prepared to discuss your list of goals in class and adjust the wording of your goals as needed.

Course: _____

Long-Term Goal: _____

_____

_____

Short-Term Goals:

1. _____

_____

2. _____

_____

Exercise 2-A (continued)

3. _____

_____

4. _____

_____

5. _____

Critically Thinking Together

In a group of three or four, share your long-term and short-term goals from Exercise 2-A. Evaluate these goals according to the guidelines, and help each other rewrite any goals that fall short of the guidelines.

MOTIVATING YOURSELF TO ACHIEVE GOALS

An important factor in achieving goals is your motivation. *Motivation* is an internal driving force that stimulates you to take action to achieve a goal. As a human being, you are very complex and generally have a variety of motivations. For example, although you may eat because you are hungry, a primary motivator, sometimes you may eat to relieve stress, anger, or boredom, to enjoy companionship, or just to please your taste buds. Motivation is extremely complex. In terms of its importance, however, self-motivation is just as necessary to your performance as are your goals.

Goals and abilities will be wasted unless you have enough motivation and desire to take action. You may have top-notch goals and above-average skills and intelligence, but without self-motivation, your high goals and great abilities will probably not show in your performance level.

Motivation is impossible to acquire from others because true motivation comes from within yourself. Others might encourage your motivation, but they cannot give it to you. If you want to be successful in life, then you must find the means to become self-motivated. The following suggestions may help you become more self-motivated.

Goals as a Motivator

Although motivation is needed to achieve goals, the goals themselves can also provide motivation. That statement may sound like circular logic or the old adage, "Which came first, the chicken or the egg?" However, it really is true. If you have written down specific short-term goals with definite time frames, these written statements can help motivate you to actually do them. As each goal is completed, you will probably feel a sense of accomplishment and a desire to continue to meet your remaining goals. As you complete your short-term goals, you might want to cross them out in order to help motivate yourself to do more. Crossing out completed goals gives you a sense of satisfaction and accomplishment. Eventually, by completing your short-term goals, you will achieve your larger long-term goals.

Believing in Yourself as a Motivator

Some self-confidence is basic to all motivation. Few people perform at a genius level, but many people achieve success in college and in life because they believe that they are capable. When you have this basic belief in yourself, then you will understand that for most average people achievement comes from hard work and perseverance. Belief in yourself does not mean fooling yourself about abilities you do not have, but it means that with enough time and effort you know that you, too, can learn most skills well enough to reach your goals. It also means that when you make excuses you will recognize them for what they are—a cop-out. Belief in yourself also implies that you will take risks and make changes in yourself. Risk-taking is not always comfortable because, when you challenge yourself this way, your efforts might result in failure. If you expect to make changes, then failure must be viewed in a positive way.

Failure should be seen not as defeat, but as an opportunity to adjust and make changes. To a self-motivated person, "If at first you don't succeed, try, try again" means that a so-called defeat becomes a reason for trying a new and better approach.

Positive Self-Talk as a Motivator

Have you ever said to yourself, "I *know* I'm going to fail (this quiz, this test, this final exam, this course)"? If you tell yourself often enough that you cannot do something, your *self* will believe it, and you will likely become incapable of achieving your goals. Psychologists call this phenomenon a *self-fulfilling prophecy*—you predict what you are going to do, and then you psychologically work for or against yourself to make it happen. If your prediction about yourself is negative, full of doom and gloom, then you are likely to have a negative outcome.

Fortunately, however, a self-fulfilling prophecy can go in the opposite direction as well. Henry Ford once said, "Think you can, think you can't; either way you'll be right." By using *positive self-talk* as a motivator, you tell yourself that you can achieve your goals. This repetition of positive statements to yourself should greatly increase your chances of success. In other words, your mind is willing to accept the "truth" as you see it; your mind knows only what you tell it. By using positive self-talk, you fill your mind with good, positive, successful words and images that can motivate you to achieve your goals.

The opposite of positive self-talk is *negative self-talk*, and it is guaranteed to drag you down. Have you ever met anyone who is constantly negative? That person makes a habit of belittling ideas and opportunities, often even before they have been explored or discussed. Such people make all kinds of negative statements, such as "That won't work." "You shouldn't even try to do it that way." "Boy, that will be disastrous." "I couldn't do that if I tried, so I won't." This kind of talk and attitude is self-defeating and can result in inaction and hopelessness. Sure, at times, you will feel "down"; that is only normal. Everyone has bad days. However, you should try to replace negative self-talk with positive self-talk, and, if you can, remove yourself from others who have made negativity a habit or even a way of life.

Exercise 2-B

Directions: Turn these negative self-talk statements into positive self-talk. Be prepared to share your statements in class.

1. "I'll never get this assignment finished!" _____

   _____

2. "I hate math!" _____

   _____

3. "I can't learn this material!" _____

   _____

WEB SITE INFORMATION

To take a quick survey to discover how positive or negative you are, visit our web site:

   <http://college.hmco.com/success/>

Visualization as a Motivator

Another way to motivate yourself is called mental visualization. *Mental visualization* involves actually picturing yourself as successful. People in all walks of life use this technique to build their confidence. Both amateur and professional sports figures use this technique very frequently to improve their performances. Golfers, for example, visualize what they must include for the perfect stance, grip, swing, and follow-through to make the perfect tee shot or the perfect putt. Public speakers envision their ideal audience, eager and receptive, hanging on their every word, applauding wildly at the conclusion of the speech. If you see yourself as successful and reinforce this vision with positive words, then you'll have a better-than-average chance of successfully achieving your goals.

In the same way, when faced with a difficult task at work, home, school, or play, you can envision yourself performing at your best. For example, you might visualize yourself taking a test in your hardest subject. You see yourself entering the classroom, sitting in your usual seat, getting the test, beginning to calmly answer the questions, completing the test successfully, and handing it in to the instructor. You may even want to extend this vision to when you get the test back with a very good grade on it. Having visualized success, you will feel more confident when the actual experience happens. Using visualization as a motivator is a learned skill. For visualization to be truly effective, you need to repeat your visual images of success many times.

Using positive self-talk and visualization, when accompanied by good preparation, will definitely increase your chances for success in all areas of your life. Like the little engine struggling up the mountain in the children's story who said, "I think I can; I think I can; I *think* I can®,"— and he could—you, too, can use mind over matter in the successful achievement of your goals.

Outcomes as a Motivator

Another form of motivation directly involves using critical thinking to make choices. When you consider the results of your actions, your awareness of possible outcomes (positive or negative) can motivate you to perform. If you prepare for each class beforehand, for example, you will probably feel comfortable in class and get more out of the lecture. This is a positive outcome. If you go to class unprepared, the result might be that you will feel less familiar with the information and even confused in class. This is a negative outcome that could eventually lead to other negative effects, such as poor grades. By carefully considering the outcomes of your choices, you are less likely to procrastinate and are more likely to be motivated to take positive actions.

Rewards as a Motivator

Rewarding yourself after you have completed a goal or task is another means of motivation. We all have tasks that we do not look forward to doing, whether it is reading an assignment that seems boring, cleaning the kitchen, or doing some other unappealing job. You have probably experienced the snowball effect when you keep ignoring an unpleasant task—the longer you wait, the harder it gets. Looking at a task undone can actually make you uncomfortable enough to motivate you to do it today rather than tomorrow. Once you get the task out of the way, you can sigh and say, "Aha, that's done!" Your reward is that you feel a sense of relief and control.

Sometimes actual physical rewards can also act as motivators. After you have reached a goal or completed a task, you might want to create a reward by being nice to yourself. The reward could be small or large, short or long—eating a candy bar, calling a friend, reading a magazine, watching a TV show, going out with friends. The reward should be something *you* want, something that will spur you on to finish your task.

Less materialistic, but just as rewarding, are psychological rewards. Sometimes you will find motivation through a good grade on a test or paper or praise from another person for doing something well.

WEB SITE INFORMATION

For more information about increasing your own motivation, visit our web site:

<http://college.hmco.com/success/>

Critically Thinking in Writing

In a journal entry, describe what motivates you in college, at home, at work, and in your social life. Your personal motivators may include some or all of those listed above, as well as any other factors that motivate you.

PROBLEM SOLVING

If you are like most people, when you set short-term and long-term goals for yourself, you probably hope that everything will go according to plan. However, as you read in the section on flexibility, the best-made plans may sometimes go astray when problems interfere. An integral part of setting and achieving goals is being able to overcome problems.

Everyone has problems. Some are simple, like what to wear or where to go for lunch. Others are more complex, like how to finance a college education, what to choose as a major, or, in your personal life, whether or not to get married or divorced. Instinctively, almost everyone uses some method for solving problems. However, some methods may be more effective than others.

When facing a difficult problem, some people just sit back and take a wait-and-see attitude, hoping that the problem will go away or that somebody will rescue them. On occasion, such inaction may work; however, if you use this technique, you run the risk of being mowed down while waiting to see what develops. Your lack of action might even make the problem worse.

A more powerful means of solving difficult problems involves using a critical-thinking approach. Critical thinkers recognize when situations are getting out of hand. Instead of avoiding the situation, they act in a timely way, approaching the problem directly and logically, and trying to alleviate possible negative, painful, or embarrassing consequences.

Once you develop a systematic way to solve your problems, you, too, can approach your problems as a critical thinker. A five-step way to *SOLVE* problems is illustrated below:

> **S** = *Search out* the *real* problem
> **O** = *Open* your mind to *all* options
> **L** = *Line up* your plan of action
> **V** = *Venture* upon your plan
> **E** = *Evaluate* the results

Search Out the Real Problem

What your true problem is may seem self-evident. But often you, like many other people, may deceive yourself. For example, if you are not doing well in a class, you might say, "I'm not getting good grades because the teacher doesn't like me." Chances are that this is just an excuse and not the real reason your grades are poor. More probable reasons may involve your own behavior.

By searching out the real problem through a series of questions, you are better able to assess the situation. Are you studying as much as you should? Do you dislike the teacher, and are you using that negative attitude as an excuse? Do you lack the educational background or experience to do well in the class? Whatever the problem, you need to be honest with yourself in order to identify the real problem.

If you have trouble identifying a real problem and separating it from excuses, you may want to focus on a questioning method that will lead you to the real problem. The following questions are good ones to use when trying to determine the real cause(s) of your problem:

- What or whom do I blame for this problem? Is this really a reason or an excuse?
- When do I feel the impact of the problem the most?
- Who is involved (directly and indirectly) in this problem?
- Where am I when the problem occurs?
- Why do I feel defeated in this endeavor?

Eventually, you will search out the major cause or causes of the problem, and then you can state it in words: "My real problem is . . ."

Exercise 2-C

Directions: **Search out the *real* problem.** On a piece of summary paper, write down a problem you are having at work, at school, or at home that you need to solve. Then ask and answer questions, including *who, when, where,* and *why,* in writing. Finally, state your real problem.

Open Your Mind to All Options

Once you have searched out the real problem, your second step is to open your mind to all options by brainstorming all the possibilities available for solving that problem. *Brainstorming* entails jotting down a list of possible solutions without being judgmental. Brainstorming is one of the creative aspects of critical thinking. While you are brainstorming, do not inhibit yourself by trying to decide whether an idea is silly, dumb, unworkable, okay, or even great. Simply write down everything and anything that comes to mind until you think you have exhausted all possibilities.

In the process of brainstorming, you might even find it especially useful to have a friend help you think of ideas because that is a good way to come up with as many options as possible. You may be too close to the problem to see all the options. The other person may offer additional ideas that you would never have thought of yourself. The more possible solutions you identify, the better chance you have of finding a workable one.

Exercise 2-D

Directions: **Open your mind to *all* options.** Using the problem you described in Exercise 2-C, on the same piece of paper, brainstorm at least ten possible solutions. Remember, do not be judgmental as you make your list.

Line Up Your Plan of Action

Once you have brainstormed your options, you are ready to evaluate each option critically. In this third step of the problem-solving process, *lining up a plan of action,* you begin by weeding out the options that seem silly or unlikely to work. Those that remain are your best possible solutions. At this point, assuming that you have more than one solution, you should prioritize what remains on your list and select one action or a combination of actions that will serve as an appropriate plan for solving your problem.

Finally, in order to make a firm commitment to yourself, write out your plan of action, including a realistic time to begin and to complete each step. Start with statements that say, "I will . . ." Then fill in the steps you plan to take and when you plan to take them. Writing out your plan will help you get motivated and be firmly committed to solving the problem. Keep this written plan handy so that you can check your progress daily and maintain your focus and motivation.

Exercise 2-E

Directions: **Line up your plan of action.** Select the best option(s) from your list in Exercise 2-D, and line up your plan of action by writing "I will _____" statements. Include a time to begin and end each step.

Venture Upon Your Plan

Now you are ready to take action—to venture upon your plan. Tackle the first step, no matter how small it is, today, for as you know, tomorrow never comes. Even if that step is just making a phone call or seeking information, taking action will begin to solve the problem.

Exercise 2-F

Directions: **Venture upon your plan**. Take the first step in your solution, and then continue to follow your plan of action. Keep a written record of what you do, including dates.

Evaluate the Results

Finally, once you have acted upon and completed your plan, you have to evaluate how successful it was. You may have done this along the way to adjust for setbacks or changes, but it is essential that you evaluate the whole process once it is finished. If your plan solved your problem, congratulations; the process is completed. If your plan didn't solve the problem to your satisfaction, you need to analyze why it did not work. Then you will have to back up a little, repeating Steps 2 (Open your mind to all options) and 3 (Line up your plan of action) to devise and enact a new plan.

Exercise 2-G

Directions: **Evaluate the results**. Once you have completed your plan of action, evaluate the results in a paragraph. If you were successful, wonderful! If not, reconsider your options and write another plan of action. Then, complete all the other steps.

The SOLVE method is an effective approach to problem solving because it employs basic critical-thinking skills. When the problem is crucial to your happiness or progress, then each step should be written out according to the previous guidelines. Using SOLVE will give you the power to overcome your problems in an objective, methodical, and logical way.

WEB SITE INFORMATION

For more information about problem solving, visit our web site:

<http://college.hmco.com/success/>

UNDERSTANDING STRESS

Even with clear goals, high motivation, and a critical-thinking approach to problem solving, you, as a college student, will sometimes feel the uncomfortable pressures of stress. Most people think of stress as a negative factor in their lives. However, believe it or not, stress is a natural and necessary part of everyone's life. Or, thinking about it another way, if no one ever felt any pressure or stress, little or nothing would ever get accomplished!

Stress is an emotional, psychological, or physical reaction to a disruptive situation. As such, it can be good and healthy, a driving force that helps you get things done and live up to your own or others' expectations. *Positive stress* is the adrenaline surge that great athletes experience—what might give them their "winning edge." Or it can be likened to the personal magnetism of great singers, speakers, and performers when they work their audiences—what their fans would call charisma. For you the student, positive stress can help you keep your college learning on course by helping you keep up with assignments and set personal study goals. Positive stress may also allow you to compete with yourself to do your best when you take a test or exam.

On the flip side, *negative stress* can affect you in a bad way, both physically and mentally. Stress that lasts too long or that causes you to feel so helpless that it hinders you from performing well can take its toll. Usually this kind of debilitating stress will express itself in physical ways.

Some symptoms that may indicate that you are under too much stress include:

- Tightness in neck, shoulders, or back
- Trouble falling asleep or staying asleep
- Irritability, anger, and short-tempered reactions
- Feeling scared
- Lowered self-esteem through negative self-talk
- Headaches
- Forgetfulness
- Excessive worry
- Frequent illnesses, such as colds or the flu
- Stomach and intestinal upsets
- Butterflies in the stomach
- Poor concentration
- Depression
- Overeating or undereating
- Nervous tics
- Accelerated heart rate
- Elevated blood pressure
- Crying for no apparent reason
- Smoking more than usual
- Escape through alcohol or other drugs

Some Causes of Stress

Many students who are entering college for the first time find that college itself creates its own kind of stress. If you are a recent high school graduate, college may represent the very first time you are fully and completely on your own. While initially that may sound wonderful, along with this new-found freedom come all the responsibilities of adulthood. Although your parents may back you emotionally and maybe even financially, you realize that now your decisions and success in college are in your hands, and this can be scary and stressful.

On the other hand, if you have been out of school for several years, you may feel a different kind of stress stemming from a lack of confidence. When you think of competing with recent high school graduates, you may feel that your education is outdated. You may even imagine that your ability to learn may have mysteriously evaporated over the years.

Whether you are just out of high school or a returning student, you may find yourself showing some of the symptoms of negative stress.

Although going to college is a major change in your life which can cause stress, other life changes that can be very stressful include moving, getting married, becoming a parent, changing jobs, losing your job, experiencing divorce, or losing a loved one to death. Other causes of stress might come from your internal thoughts and feelings, an unwholesome environment, other people, or even improper eating habits. Although major changes that cause stress are clearly recognizable, you also can be stressed by smaller everyday occurrences. What may seem like a little problem to someone else might be a big stressor for you. These daily stressors might include getting stuck in traffic, being interrupted, working with a negative person, losing your purse or billfold, unreturned phone calls, or a friend or family member who constantly disappoints you. The root of most stress-related problems seems to be a feeling of loss of control over one's life. If this is the case, and it usually is, the general cures for stress must be control-related.

WEB SITE INFORMATION

To take a 45-question stress test, visit our web site:

<http://college.hmco.com/success/>

Critically Thinking in Writing

In a journal, each day for three to five days, describe briefly the events of the day that caused you the most stress. After you write each one, rate it on a scale of 1 to 5 (1 = a little stressful; 5 = extremely stressful). At the end of the three to five days, look over your whole list and try to describe in writing some causes for your most stressful times. If you see a pattern (repeated stressors or causes) in your list, describe how you feel when you are in this situation. Write down possible ways you can relieve these stressors.

Tips on Managing Stress

Here are some general guidelines for better controlling your negative stress in college:

Time Management and Organization

- Get and stay organized in your studies.
- Faithfully use proven time-management techniques, especially scheduling (see Chapter 7).
- Start all projects early, allowing for a crisis or two; if there are none, you will certainly meet your deadlines.
- Realize that studying for a given course begins on day one and that reviews should be a regular daily activity.

- Understand that the desire to procrastinate is normal for most people, but it is childish to play such a risky game with your education.

Reaching Out to Others

- Ask for help and cooperation from other members of your family; explain that college is a commitment, not a hobby.
- Talk to your professors if you have concerns or need additional information or help.
- Don't try to do everything alone: Seek out the student support services available on campus (for example, tutoring, writing lab, math lab, test review services, career counselors, your academic advisor, the financial aid office, learning needs counselors, special interest support groups, and so on).
- Find somebody to talk to; a good listener can help relieve your stress.
- If your stress is so severe that it overwhelms you, seek professional help.

Assertiveness

- Understand that you may have to say "no" sometimes, but your family, loved ones, and friends should still be a significant part of your life.
- Delegate routine tasks to others.
- Remember, you can't please all of the people all of the time.

Goals and Motivation

- Remind yourself of your goals.
- Set priorities according to your goals.
- If something is interfering with your goals, use SOLVE to overcome the obstacle.
- Realize that if you are a parent, you will have to put your children's needs first and perhaps take college at a slower pace.
- Put test scores into perspective; they are not a measure of your self-worth.
- Remember that test anxiety is a learned response and can be un-learned (see Chapter 10).
- Make it a habit to use positive self-talk when your confidence is in a slump.
- Focus on your achievements, not your shortcomings.

Physical

- Make sure your schedule includes some free time for yourself every day to do whatever you want to do.
- Do something constructive to replace your negative stress with positive stress.
- Eat well-balanced meals; the healthy body/healthy mind connection is genuine.
- Make exercise a part of your daily routine, even if that means parking in the farthest parking spot in order to walk a regular distance each day.
- Find humor in your life (laugh!), and enjoy yourself.
- Learn and use deep breathing, meditation, and other relaxation techniques.

By using the preceding guidelines for relieving negative stress, you can make your college experience and your daily life more positive. The objective is not to get rid of all stress, but rather to control your stress well enough for you to perform at your best.

Exercise 2-H

This relaxation exercise, devised by Herbert Benson, M.D., author of *The Relaxation Response,* flicks "the switch that turns off tension and turns on physical and mental peace" (Faelten and Diamond, 253–254).

1. Once or twice a day, sit comfortably in a quiet place and close your eyes.
2. Deeply relax all your muscles, beginning at your feet and working up to your face. Keep your muscles relaxed.
3. Breathe naturally through your nose and become aware of your breathing. As you exhale, silently say to yourself the word "one" (or another word of your choosing).
4. Maintain a passive attitude. Don't worry about whether you're achieving a state of deep relaxation. Let relaxation come to you. When distracting thoughts enter your mind, try not to dwell on them. Instead, return to your word. Dr. Benson emphasizes that this passive attitude is perhaps the most important element in bringing on the Relaxation Response.
5. Continue for ten to twenty minutes. You may open your eyes to check the time, but don't use an alarm clock. After you finish, sit quietly with your eyes closed for a few moments. Then open your eyes and sit still for a few more minutes before you stand up.

Summary

In this chapter, "The Power of Managing Goals, Problems, and Stress," you examined three valuable means for keeping your life on course. After separating short-term goals from long-term goals and understanding how they relate to each other, you learned how to identify meaningful goals. Meaningful goals have three basic criteria: ownership, realism, and flexibility. You also learned motivational techniques to help you achieve your goals.

A second major consideration is problem solving. By applying the steps in SOLVE, you can logically tackle problems, however large or small. The five steps of SOLVE are:

- Search out the real problem.
- Open your mind to all options.
- Line up your plan of action.
- Venture upon your plan.
- Evaluate the results.

The third related factor is learning to manage your stress level. This includes recognizing the signs and causes of negative stress and, more importantly, taking steps to manage stress.

By setting clear goals, staying motivated, dealing with your problems in an objective and logical way, and managing your personal stress, you will be better able to take powerful control of your life.

List of Terms

goal
long-term goal
short-term goal
mental visualization
brainstorming

motivation
self-fulfilling prophecy
positive and negative self-talk
SOLVE
positive and negative stress

In this box, write your summary question or statement for this chapter:

3 The Power of Note Taking

One of the most important skills needed in college is the ability to take good notes. In this chapter, you will learn why you should take notes and the importance of listening. Not only will you learn how to take good notes, you will learn how to take GREAT notes. You will also learn three effective strategies for organizing and learning new vocabulary words and technical terms.

THE EBBINGHAUS FORGETTING CURVE

Have you ever started to tell a joke and then realized that you could not remember the punch line? Has an appointment ever slipped your mind? Have you ever sat in a classroom and listened to an interesting lecture only to forget the details the next day? Have you ever taken a test and forgotten an important bit of information? Most of you will answer yes to all those questions because you do forget on occasion; that is only human.

In the late 1800s, Hermann Ebbinghaus, a psychologist, studied forgetfulness by researching the human mind and its ability to remember new information. Because of his thoroughness and precision in studying the human memory, his findings are still considered valid today and are often cited in basic psychology and study skills textbooks, as well as in books about memory. Although some numbers vary slightly in different texts, the results, called the *Ebbinghaus Forgetting Curve* (Loftus 67), look like this:

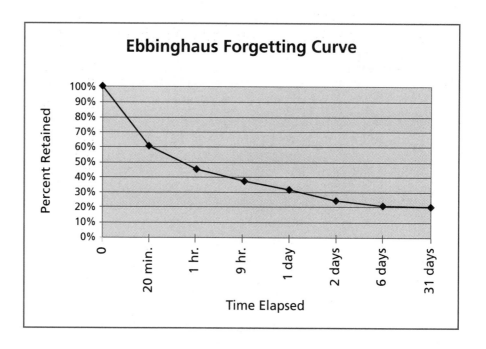

From the Ebbinghaus Forgetting graph, you can see that within twenty minutes you are likely to forget approximately 40 percent of what you hear or read, but by the time twenty-four hours have elapsed, you may have forgotten almost 70 percent. It is rather frightening to think that you can forget more than half of what you have heard or read in one day.

Knowing this information, you will not be surprised by the following conversation between Derrick and Katrina:

"Hey, Derrick. How did you do on the psych test?"

"Oh, man, I really bombed that one! I don't know what happened. I went to class and read the book, but I couldn't remember a thing!" Derrick moaned.

"Well, maybe your notes were lousy. After all, the test was mostly on the lectures," Katrina said. "Let me see your notes."

"Notes? What notes?" Derrick said indignantly. "I don't take notes! I go to class and listen."

"I listen, too, but I can't remember unless I write it down," Katrina responded.

Derrick is not unique in his forgetfulness. The Ebbinghaus Forgetting Curve indicates that everyone has a tendency to forget a great deal. In fact, the Ebbinghaus Curve shows that a month after hearing a lecture or reading an assignment you may have forgotten up to 80 percent of what you have heard or read—not good news in terms of taking exams.

However, by using good study skills, you can reverse this forgetting trend and remember as much as 80 percent or more of what you hear or read. Cultivating this ability to remember requires listening carefully and taking effective notes during class, skills that will be discussed in this chapter. In Chapters 4, 5, and 6, you will learn how to improve your ability to remember what you read.

POWER LISTENERS AND PASSIVE LISTENERS

Power listeners are quite different from passive listeners. *Power listeners* are people who actively listen to what is being said. They realize that the classroom is a learning environment where information is exchanged. Power listeners, like power walkers, are easily recognizable in class. They are intense, focused, and critical thinkers (see Chapter 6). They have the right equipment, the right attitude, and the right mental focus, not letting anything distract them from listening to a lecture. Just as power walkers appear to have everything working together to build a better body, so do power listeners have everything working together to build a better mind.

Passive listeners, on the other hand, physically hear the words being said, but they make little attempt to engage their minds to understand the message. Unlike power listeners, passive listeners are like window shoppers strolling through the mall. These listeners are occupying space in the classroom, relaxed and unfocused. They are filling in time and often seem to have this attitude: "OK, I'm here. Entertain me." To them, it is not themselves but the teacher who is responsible for their learning.

From the descriptions above, you can see that listening involves more than *just* hearing. Students' actions and attitudes are also important. Obviously, the power listener is going to get a great deal more out of class than the passive listener.

Take the following survey to determine what your actions and attitudes indicate about you in the classroom.

Exercise 3-A

Directions: Check the answers that best describe your behaviors and attitudes in your *least* interesting class.

	Always	Usually	Sometimes	Never
1. I arrive at class on time.	____	____	____	____
2. I have my homework completed.	____	____	____	____
3. I take lots of notes.	____	____	____	____
4. I look out the window.	____	____	____	____
5. I am distracted by other students.	____	____	____	____
6. My mind wanders in class.	____	____	____	____
7. I expect the teacher to be entertaining.	____	____	____	____
8. I work on homework for other classes in this class.	____	____	____	____
9. I think using a tape recorder is just as good as taking notes.	____	____	____	____
10. I sit in the front row.	____	____	____	____

If you answered questions 1, 2, 3, and 10 "always" or "usually" and questions 4, 5, 6, 7, 8, and 9 "sometimes" or "never," you are a power listener. If you did not, then you may need to reexamine your attitudes and behaviors so that you can get the most from your classes.

The examples that follow will provide you with models of power listeners and passive listeners.

Power Listeners

Concetta and Jerome are power listeners who begin preparing for class before they ever enter the classroom. They have done their homework and arrive on time, sometimes even a little early. If the class is the first of the day and they are commuters, they realize the need to leave home early enough to allow for delays in driving time, particularly in bad weather. By the time the instructor begins, they already have their notebooks open and their pens out, ready to take notes. They sit in the front of the room so they will not be distracted by other students.

Both Concetta's and Jerome's behaviors in class increase their listening skills. Their body language, especially their postures, indicates positive attitudes. They make eye contact with the instructor when they are not taking notes. Because they are really listening to what the instructor has to say, their body language indicates they are doing their best to comprehend the information. Concetta sometimes nods when she clearly understands a point and frowns as she tries to grasp a difficult idea. Jerome participates in class discussions and sometimes raises his hand to ask for further clarification during a lecture. They appreciate an interesting instructor, but still pay attention even if the lecturer is dull. They are power listeners who take extensive notes.

Concetta and Jerome do not close their notebooks until after the instructor has finished speaking, even if it is a minute or so after class is supposed to end. They also know the simple rules of etiquette: the classroom is like a conversation—one person does not walk away (or pack up) while the other is speaking. They know the importance of getting as much out of the class as possible.

If for some valid reason, Concetta or Jerome is unable to attend a class, each calls the other to ask for his or her notes, knowing that the notes will be comprehensive. As power listeners, they know the value of having a *study buddy,* someone they can rely on as a back-up person, in every class.

Passive Listeners

Ruth and BJ are passive students. They don't always attend class, and when they do, they may not be prepared. They barely arrive on time or are even a few minutes late, so they don't have their notebooks out when the instructor begins speaking. To avoid being noticed by the instructor, they choose the most inconspicuous seats, such as in the back row or on the fringe.

Both Ruth and BJ believe that since they have appeared in class, learning will magically happen. They slouch or lounge in their seats, gaze out the window, or check out their classmates. Ruth frequently looks at her watch, and BJ yawns and sometimes dozes off when the lecture is not "entertaining." They physically *hear* what is being said, but they do not mentally *listen.* Sometimes they do homework for another class. The few notes they take are buried under elaborate doodling.

About five minutes before class ends, Ruth and BJ begin getting ready to leave. They close their notebooks, unzip their backpacks to stuff everything in, and zip them up again. They are oblivious to the fact that all the noise they are making is disturbing those around them. One or two minutes before class is over, BJ stands up and puts on his jacket. Ruth struggles into her coat while sitting in her chair. They are the first ones out the door.

One day BJ overslept and missed class. When he saw Ruth later in the day he said, "Did I miss anything in class today?"

"No," Ruth replied, "we just did the same old stuff."

As passive listeners, neither BJ nor Ruth seems to realize the need for active participation and responsibility in the college classroom.

Exercise 3-B

Directions: List the characteristics of power listeners.

Column 1: Attitudes   **Column 2: Actions**

_____   _____

_____   _____

_____   _____

_____   _____

_____   _____

_____   _____

TAKING GREAT NOTES

Now that you know how easy it is to forget and what it takes to be a power listener, you need to learn how to take not just good notes but GREAT notes. Sure, you've been taking notes before this, but your system may not be as efficient and effective as it could be.

Note taking, the focus of this chapter, is a process that involves a great deal more than simply the physical act of writing. Not only does it help you remember information from your lectures, but it also helps you concentrate, condense information, and discover important points. It is a process that begins before class and lasts until you have mastered the information. Taking effective notes and reading textbooks are the two major means of receiving information in college.

To begin an effective note-taking system, you must have the basic tools: summary paper and a three-ring binder with tabs to separate your notes for each class. Using a three-ring binder gives you great flexibility. One of the advantages of using a binder is that you can insert handouts, syllabi, homework, or other pages of information in the appropriate places for each class. Other advantages are that you can add to or change your notes easily and take out the pages you need to study instead of always carrying around the whole binder. Next, you need loose-leaf summary paper, that is, paper with a three-inch left margin. If you do not have summary paper, you can draw a line three inches from the left edge of your paper.

To organize your three-ring binder, you should think of it as a mini filing cabinet. Each tab is like a file that names each course. In some cases, if you are taking a course that has a lab and a lecture segment, you may want to put your notes for each in different sections if that seems more appropriate. Use your knowledge of the course and common sense to determine whether you need to subdivide a particular course in your binder. Assuming each course is a tabbed section, you will likely put your syllabus first, followed by your dated class notes in chronological order. Then, when you receive handouts, insert them as close as possible to related information in your notes. Homework to be turned in should be in a place where you can find it easily. You might want to put it in front of your syllabus or right behind it. Wherever you put it, be consistent. Returned homework and quizzes or tests might be placed at the end of the tabbed section or inserted into your notes that pertain to that information. Again, be consistent because you will use this information for studying.

All study skills books describe at least one system for taking notes. The GREAT note-taking system combines the best features of them all. GREAT is an acronym, a word formed by the first letter (in the case of wRite, the first audible letter) of each important word in a phrase. The letters G-R-E-A-T stand for the five steps in the note-taking process. Each letter in GREAT represents one step in the system. The five steps are:

Get ready

wRite

Edit

Ask questions

Test yourself

Step One: Get Ready

Preparing for note taking *before* you enter the classroom to hear a lecture is as important as the actual note taking itself. This preparation will directly affect the quality of your listening and note taking.

The Get-ready stage can be compared to preparing for a vacation or trip. To go on a trip, you usually do some mental work, such as selecting your destination, deciding where to go, choosing a place to stay, deciding on transportation, reading about what sights are considered special enough to visit, and deciding what to pack. You usually make physical preparations as well if you want the trip to be successful, such as getting your car in good running order if you are driving, packing your suitcases, loading the car, or getting to the airport if you are flying.

Similar to making your vacation plan, you must prepare before you enter the classroom. Getting ready to take notes involves three tasks that are performed before attending each class.

First, in order to Get ready, you must read your textbook assignment and do any other homework. (In Chapter 5 you will learn the most productive way to read your textbook assignments.)

Second, you need to review the notes from the previous lecture. When you have reviewed, you have the material in mind, which makes learning additional material easier because the human brain functions best when new information is attached to already learned ideas.

This ability to learn new information by relating it to something you already know can be demonstrated in several ways. Math courses, for example, are taught sequentially, each new component building on the one before. In drawing classes, you also start with simple figures and techniques and progress to more complex ones. In all learning situations, whether your previous knowledge is something you learned just minutes ago or years ago, your grasp of the new knowledge is enhanced by your previous knowledge, which creates a background of information. Thus, your mental preparation of reviewing your previous notes is an essential element of note taking. In fact, knowing that you are prepared will not only aid in your learning but also give you added confidence when class begins.

The third task in the Get-ready stage is a physical one: Make sure you have all the materials you will need for all of your classes. In addition to your binder and summary paper, you should bring to class your pens, textbooks, and other supplies, such as a calculator, a ruler, pencils, and any homework. Your backpack should literally serve as a portable desk, allowing you to get to work as soon as you enter the classroom.

Step Two: wRite

The second step, wRite, means to take notes during class. When the instructor arrives, have your notebook open and pen in hand. Put the date and page number in the top right-hand corner of your summary paper, and continue to do this on all subsequent pages. The illustration below shows the format of the summary paper you will be using to take notes in all your classes:

Three-inch column	Five-inch column Date Page #
	You will be taking your
	notes in this five-inch column
	of summary
	paper.

To begin taking lecture notes, you need to focus all your attention on the speaker. Write down all pertinent information: main ideas, facts, details, examples, definitions, and even "common sense" information—that is, information you think everyone should already know. Remember the Ebbinghaus Forgetting Curve: Even if you think you will remember something, chances are it will be "gone" before the day is over because you have only been exposed to the information, but you haven't had a chance to absorb it.

Generally, any information written on the board or shown on overheads contains major points that you should include in your notes. However, do not stop there. You should also include as much of what the lecturer says as possible. Listen carefully to what the instructor says, paying close attention to "cues," sometimes called signal words, that the speaker uses. *Cues* are transitional words that indicate what is coming next and often how important it will be. They are used by a speaker to connect one idea to another. Learn to tune in to cue words to guide you in your note taking. The following chart lists some of these words.

Samples of Cues or Transitional Words and Phrases

There are four parts to . . . first, second, third, fourth, or last . . .

This is important, a major factor, the primary reason, most, often . . .

Next, then, before, after, when . . .

Because, since, consequently, as a result . . .

On the other hand, however, but, nevertheless, meanwhile, yet . . .

For instance, for example . . .

Rarely, sometimes, occasionally, this is an exception, seldom . . .

In addition to listening for cues or signal words, you should be aware of other clues to help you discover major points. Generally, major points will be written in the main column next to the margin of your note paper, and supporting details will be indented under each major point. You may want to number the details or use dashes or dots to represent major details that come under each main point. (See the "Critical Thinking" example in this chapter.) Sometimes, you will find it helpful to add symbols, such as ex. for examples or stars (*) for important points.

Note when your instructor repeats information. Unless you have an absent-minded professor, *repeated* information should be considered *important* information. Also, pay attention to the speaker's body language. Often the speaker's hand gestures, facial expressions, tone and volume of voice, or other physical movements can signal to you the relative importance of the verbal information.

A legitimate question at this point might be, "Should I write down every word the speaker says?" The answer is, "No, you really can't do that; it's basically impossible." In the first place, unless the speaker talks as slowly as a turtle walks, it would be physically impossible to write down every word. Second, it is not important to take down every word; what is important is recording the major points and main ideas, with as *many* details as you are able to include. If you fall behind, realize you have missed a point, or cannot write as much as you want, leave space so that you can fill in information after class (see the Edit step).

One way to streamline your note taking is to use abbreviations. You should create your own personal system of abbreviations for every course. Below are listed some common abbreviations:

Common Abbreviations

"	inches	b	born
#	number	chem	chemistry
$	dollar(s)	comp	compare
%	percent	d	died
&	and	Eng	English
'	feet	ex	example
¢	cent(s)	esp	especially
+	plus	p	page
−	minus	psych	psychology
=	equals	soc	sociology
?	question mark	std	student or standard
*	important!!	vs	versus
@	at	x	by, multiplied by
A&P	anatomy and physiology		

Often you can anticipate what could be abbreviated when you read your assignment for the day. For example, if you read a chapter on Sigmund Freud's theories for your psychology class, you could abbreviate that expression as SFs theories. Take care, however, that you do not get carried away with your abbreviations.

Observe what this student wrote from a lecture on elephants:

Student's notes: "Ls r frm As or Af nd hv ivry tks, lv 60-80 yrs, nd n cptvy et brs, alf, nd frt."

This student's over-abbreviated sentence stands for "Elephants are from Asia or Africa and have ivory tusks, live 60 to 80 years, and in captivity eat berries, alfalfa, and fruit." The abbreviation certainly saved the student a lot of writing time, but translating it back into words is time consuming and defeats the purpose of using abbreviations. Your goal is to understand your notes at a glance, both now and weeks later.

Some students mistakenly believe that a tape recorder can serve as a substitute for taking notes. However, this is completely false. In certain circumstances, using a tape recorder in class might be helpful, but only as a back-up system for your own notes. For instance, if your instructor speaks very quickly, uses vocabulary that is over your head, or seems to be disorganized, you could use a tape recorder in class to help you clean up or edit your notes after class. Also, if you are taking a foreign language, you might want to tape the lecture to listen to and imitate the pronunciations of words. Finally, in the very rare circumstance when you know ahead of time that you must miss a class, you could ask someone else to tape that lecture for you. Of course, if you do use a tape recorder, you should always get your instructor's permission beforehand.

One more point needs to be made about note taking. As you well know, not all college professors use the lecture method. Many instructors use informal lectures, class discussions, group work, or other methods. It is just as important to take notes at these times as it is when the instructor is speaking. In nonlecture class meetings, the instructor is letting the class discover the information necessary for an understanding of the subject. This is information you will also need to study for tests. So when a discussion begins or when you are working in a group, do not lay your pen down and close your notebook: *listen, participate, and take notes!*

Step Three: Edit

The third step of GREAT, Edit, is done as soon as possible after class and is simply a "clean-up" stage. At this time you need to read over your notes to make sure they are clear, legible, and understandable. You may need to fill in missing words, check the spelling of technical words, or clarify abbreviations you used. You might even want to check with your instructor or another student, or consult your textbook if you missed something in order to fill any "holes" or blank spaces in your notes. During the Edit stage, you should not try to rewrite or even type your notes; that would be much too time consuming. Nor do you need to erase any information. Your goal is to make your notes usable and readable so that you can study them efficiently. Be sure you have numbered and dated each page.

One of the purposes of the Edit stage is to clarify your notes. Some students, therefore, prefer to take notes in the five-inch column on only *one* side of the page, using the back side for clarification. What might seem like a waste of paper really provides you with a way to get the most out of your notes. By leaving the back side of your notes blank, you have room to supplement your notes.

That empty page has all kinds of possibilities:

- Put vocabulary words or terms in the three-inch column and their definitions in the five-inch column.
- Make up your own example(s) to parallel examples your instructor gave.
- Include charts, diagrams, formulas, or other information to round out your notes.
- Add your own comments and observations.
- Draw pictures to illustrate your notes.
- Write down questions to ask your instructor about information that you do not understand or that you need clarified.
- Make a glossary of your abbreviations.

As you use the back side of your notes to enhance them, you will probably come up with even more ways to make this "scratch pad" a useful study aid.

The sooner you Edit after class, the more likely you will remember information that you were unable to write down during the class. If possible, the *best* time to Edit is right after class. In any case, try to Edit within the first eight hours after the class, but no later than twenty-four hours.

Critically Thinking Together

In a group of three or four people, share the abbreviations you have used in your study skills notes. Include answers to the following questions in your discussion: What worked well? What didn't? Did any of the abbreviations confuse you? Why? Use this exchange of information to improve on your own use of abbreviations. Be ready to share your best ones with the whole class.

Step Four: Ask Questions

The fourth step of GREAT, Ask questions, usually follows editing your notes. At this point, you put yourself in the role of teacher and of active learner to become the questioner. As you read through your notes, you look for chunks of information, ideas that fit together because they are related concepts, such as a main idea with supporting details or examples. Then you view each chunk of information as the answer to an implied question, the question that your teacher is likely to ask you on the next quiz or test. Write that question in the three-inch column of your notebook paper. (See "Critical Thinking" example on page 70.)

If you want to make a game of the Ask questions step, think of yourself as a contestant on the popular quiz show *Jeopardy*. On that show, contestants are given the categories with answers, and it is up to the contestants to give the appropriate questions to match those answers. In your case, your notes for a day's class are the answers, and your job is to create complete questions to the answers in your notes.

Your questions should be complete sentences, not just phrases or key words. Once you have written the questions, you might want to highlight key words in your notes that answer the questions. By writing questions, *you* are controlling the information and are making your own study guide at the same time.

By using this method, you are a critical thinker rather than a passive learner. You are a learner who is in control of your learning as you analyze the information and write meaningful questions. You are both physically and mentally involved. You are working in a positive framework, anticipating questions that might be asked and the way you might answer them. On the other hand, a passive learner waits for something to happen. That student might take notes in a class, thinking that is sufficient.

Critical Thinking   5/15
                                                                       p.1

How does critic. thinking differ from just thinking?	Thinking = the way we make sense of world ↳ Critical thinking = thinking about how we think ← to clarify and to improve it
Explain the word "critical."	"Kritikos" Greek origin – to question, make sense of, analyze "criticize" = to question, to evaluate (not destructive but constructive)
What are the 5 major components of thinking critically?	Components (5) of critical thinking 1. Thinking actively 2. Exploring situations w. ?s 3. Thinking for ourselves 4. Viewing situations fr. diff. perspectives 5. Discuss ideas in an organized way
Explain 4 elements needed to think actively.	Four elmts to thinking actively: 1. get involved (not on the side-line!) 2. take the initiative (make decisions on yr own) 3. follow thru (when going gets tuff) 4. take respons. for self (re: internal locus of control)
Give examples of the two kinds of outside influences on thinking.	Active and Passive influences Parenting = dictator vs. guide Managers = top down vs. grassroots Jobs = repetitive vs. creative
How does J. Chaffee classify questions?	Exploring situations w ?'s (#2) J. Chaffee's categories are • factual (obj. info.) • interpretive (relate by inferences) • synthesized (put parts together) • analytical (take apart) • evaluative (judge truth. reliability) • appreciative (apply to other situations)

This type of learner reacts with surprise when quizzes or tests are given, as if the instructor had pulled those questions from out of the blue.

When you are writing questions, you need to keep this guideline in mind: The *quality* of questions can be important. The better the quality of a question, the more information your response will include. If you begin your questions with words like "do/does," "can/could," "will/ would," "is/are," the answers they will generate are "yes" or "no." You want to avoid these types of questions. At first, you will have a tendency to write many questions beginning with "what," "who," or "when" because these are the first questions that come to mind. There is certainly nothing wrong with writing these types of questions, but you will discover that they allow you to answer with only one or two words. Consider the following example:

> **Your question:** "When did the Boston Tea Party occur?"
> **Your answer:** "December 16, 1773."

These so-called *literal questions* will allow you to answer only very factually, with limited information. Certainly you will need to know facts, dates, and names, but you will also need to understand relationships and complex material. To prepare yourself for tests that will require this kind of knowledge, you must venture into the realm of *critical-thinking questions.*

A more inclusive question about the same topic could be this:

> **Your question:** "Explain some of the Acts which led to the Boston Tea Party before the Revolutionary War."
> **Your answer:** It should include:

- Naming various Acts passed by the British Parliament government
- Describing how these Acts affected the colonies

This example illustrates how much more useful the critical-thinking questions are for studying the material. Critical-thinking questions are higher-quality questions that allow you to give in-depth answers that show relationships, such as comparisons, differences, causes, and effects.

Think of the various qualities of questions as being building blocks in a pyramid (see the Quality Questions Pyramid in this chapter). The higher you go, the more sophisticated your questions are, and, therefore, the more meaty your answers will be. When you ask higher-order critical-thinking questions like "why" or "how," you will be able to connect facts and ideas into larger explanations. Some of your questions may begin with words like "describe," "explain," or "contrast." These also are called critical-thinking questions because they advance your thinking beyond the simplest and most basic, literal level. At first, generating even literal-level questions may take time and effort, but with practice you will develop the ability to reach an even more sophisticated level of asking questions. You will be able to write both literal and critical-thinking questions comfortably.

One final kind of question at the top of the pyramid deals with the highest order of thinking needed to be creative and inventive, the "what if" or "what would happen if" kinds of questions. This kind of question, which is also used frequently in business, industrial, and scientific research, can help you *apply* the information you have.

For example, "what if" is the process a scientist, a physician, or an inventor uses to explore unknowns and create solutions. The "what if" has helped researchers develop low-fat foods. The "what if" has allowed doctors to use DNA information. The "what if" has inspired Steven Spielberg to create realistic special effects. Finally, not too many years ago a computer took up the space of a large room, but now, thanks to someone's "what if," a computer can fit nicely in a person's lap. Each year new innovations and improvements occur because of people asking "what if."

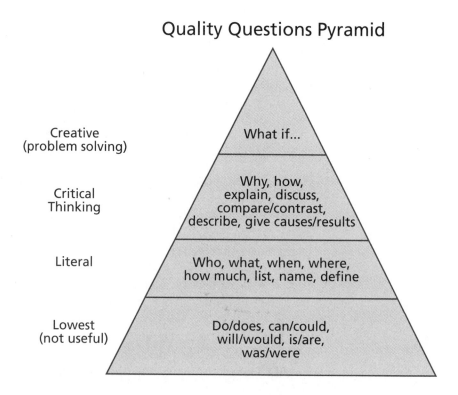

Quality Questions Pyramid

Creative (problem solving) — What if...

Critical Thinking — Why, how, explain, discuss, compare/contrast, describe, give causes/results

Literal — Who, what, when, where, how much, list, name, define

Lowest (not useful) — Do/does, can/could, will/would, is/are, was/were

These "what if" questions usually do not appear in students' notes, but they can be helpful to you as you creatively explore some topics for a more specialized purpose.

Although Asking questions is the fourth step of GREAT, when the instructor asks a question during class, note it in your three-inch column. The notes that you take during the discussion or lecture, which you will write in the five-inch section, should be the answer to that question. Also, instructors' questions are usually asked because that information will likely appear on tests or quizzes.

At the end of the day's lecture notes, you might want to write a *summary statement* or *question* capsulizing the lecture. In order to write a summary statement or question, you should skim your questions in the three-inch margins and write a *big* question that includes all the major points of that day's notes. Such a statement or question is likely to have multiple parts to it, depending on how much information was included in the lecture. You can make this summary stand out by writing all the way across the bottom of the page instead of writing it in the three-inch margin.

For example, in an economics course, after taking notes about where tax revenues come from, you will have written many questions in the three-inch column dealing with various aspects of tax revenue. When you have finished, glance back at your questions and determine how you could summarize the whole day's notes. Your summary question or statement at the bottom of your page might look like this:

Summary Statement: Describe the five sources of tax revenues (personal income taxes, payroll taxes, sales taxes, property taxes, and corporate income taxes), and explain how each is used.

This summary statement contains the major points from the lecture. Such statements or questions can provide guidelines for studying for comprehensive tests and essay exams.

Critically Thinking Together

Using the page of notes from the "Critical Thinking" example in this chapter, work in small groups and collaborate to write a summary question. When all groups are finished, ask one person from each group to write the group's completed summary question(s) or statement(s) on the board.

Step Five: Test Yourself

The "T" in GREAT stands for Test yourself, something that can be done *only* after you have written your questions. In this step, you begin to place information into your long-term memory.

The process is simple. Cover the five-inch column of your notes with a piece of paper or fold over the page, leaving the three-inch column with the questions uncovered. Then read the question and recite—out loud, in your own words—the answer to that question. If you cannot answer a question, study the notes in the main column, cover them once more, and read the question and recite the answer again. Strive to understand the material. In other words, do not try to memorize what your notes say, but rephrase the information in your own words. Repeat this procedure until you can recite the material without looking at your notes.

Repeated recitation, out loud and in your own words, is the most powerful tool known for placing new information into long-term memory. Think about information you already know. For instance, how did you learn the multiplication tables? By recitation. How did you learn your nine-digit social security number? By repetition.

Reciting *out loud* has a distinct advantage over silent study. You are using *sensory learning*—employing as many senses as possible. By reciting out loud, you are using your sense of hearing in addition to the senses of sight and touch. You use the sense of touch when you write and edit your notes, and you use the sense of sight when you read them. In addition to reciting out loud, you should recite by using your own words. If you do this, you cannot fool yourself into thinking you know the information when you really do not. If you can actually answer your questions meaningfully, that is a good indication that you *understand* the concepts and ideas, and understanding is the basis for all new learning.

The five steps of GREAT—Get ready, wRite, Edit, Ask questions, and Test yourself—will enable you to get the most out of your notes. The primary benefit of note taking is to help you remember information from lectures, but it also promotes learning in several other ways: Note taking stimulates your senses of touch (writing the information), sight (seeing the notes on paper), and hearing (reciting out loud). It also helps you stay focused and attain a higher level of concentration. Taking notes allows you to be selective as you listen actively, think critically about the information, and select the most important information to write down. Furthermore, note taking lets you organize the lecturer's ideas. Finally, good notes allow you to create a study guide from class information.

WEB SITE INFORMATION

For additional tips on note taking, visit our web site:

<http://college.hmco.com/success/>

Exercise 3-C

Directions: Turn on a 30-minute national news broadcast and take notes on summary paper for 15 to 20 minutes. At the top of your paper, write the name of the broadcast, the channel, the date, and the time. Try to include logical abbreviations as you take notes. Be sure to indent the supporting details under each main point. After taking the notes, go back and write appropriate questions in the three-inch margin.

Critically Thinking in Writing

In a journal entry, describe what you like about GREAT and explain why. Tell which actions or steps in GREAT are the most difficult for you, and explain why.

LEARNING TERMS AND VOCABULARY

New terms and vocabulary will repeatedly occur in your notes and textbooks. Often, finding the definition of words is easy, but learning them can be a challenge. Most textbooks include the definitions of terms either within the text itself, in a glossary, or at the beginning or end of each chapter. In addition, you can identify many new terms in your textbook because they will be printed in italics, bold-faced type, or within quotation marks. In lectures, teachers usually introduce new terms by giving definitions verbally, by writing them on the chalkboard, or by including them in class handouts. Learning new terms may seem like a simple task at the beginning of a course, but the amount and complexity of the terms can soon multiply. Within a few weeks, you may begin to feel overwhelmed. Thus, early on, you will want to find an organized way to master the terms and vocabulary in each discipline.

As you discover new terms in your textbooks and notes, you should circle them, underline them, or highlight them (with a different color highlighter than used for notes) so that they clearly stand out. Then, to organize and study new terms in every discipline, you will want to adopt one or more of these three methods: use 3 x 5 flash cards, list terms on the back side of notes, or make your own personal glossary.

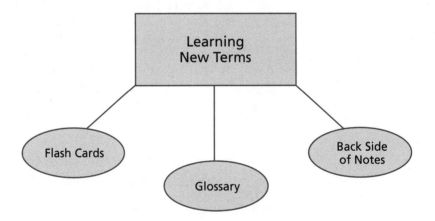

You may choose the method that best suits your learning style or needs. Or you may even choose different methods for different courses or use a combination of methods, depending upon the subject matter and the number of technical terms. Regardless of which method you choose, if you put the definitions in your own words, they need to be complete, accurate, and meaningful to you. Avoid circular definitions, that is, defining the word with the word itself. For example, to define "summary question," instead of saying, "A summary question summarizes the information in a day's notes," say, "A summary question is a brief overview of the major points in a day's lecture."

In addition to learning the definitions of words, you also need to be able to spell them. The ability to spell terms accurately can be a very important aspect of a course. For example, in biology or anatomy and physiology, *ileum* means the third and lowest division of the small intestine, and *ilium* means the broad upper portion of the pelvis. Knowing when to use an *e* or an *i* could make the difference between passing and failing a test, or later, in a medical procedure, the difference between curing or killing a patient.

Learning New Terms Using Flash Cards

Creating 3 x 5 flash cards for vocabulary development is probably the best method in terms of flexibility because the cards are portable. You can sort out what you know from what you do not know and then continue to recite from the "do not know" pile. You can also carry some cards with you and look at them whenever you have a few extra moments. To create your own set of cards, simply write the term on one side of the index card and the definition on the other:

Index Card

PEDAGOGY *text p. 22 or notes 5/17*	*the art or method of* *teaching* *or how a teacher teaches*
side one	side two

Depending upon the course and the material you are studying, you may want to include other information on the cards. For example, you might want to include a cross-reference to the textbook page or your lecture notes (see the previous example). On the definition side of the card, you should write the formal definition as well as your own definition because that will make it more meaningful to you. Side two could also be used to write examples or simple memory tricks or associations (discussed in Chapter 8). You might even draw a diagram or a picture which describes the term. These flash cards are your learning tools: include anything that would help you master the material.

There are five major benefits to using 3 x 5 cards. First of all, they are highly visual and tactile; that is, you can easily see the words and can handle and manipulate the cards. Second, you can use them yourself or have someone help you study: a friend, a spouse, a child—anyone who can read. Third, you can test yourself using either side of the card: Look at the word to recite the definition, or look at the definition to recite the term and spell it correctly. Fourth, they are sturdy, extremely handy, and portable. And finally, you can reshuffle them into any order so that you learn them all, not just the first or final terms.

Learning New Terms by Using the Back Side of Notes

You may want to keep your new vocabulary words with your notes. If you take notes on one side of the page, then you can use the back side of the page for your new terms. If your terms and definitions are added next to and parallel with the relevant notes, you will be able to study your terms more easily. See the following example:

Back Side for Terms   Front Side for Notes and Questions

| terms listed | definitions of terms, corresponding to notes | your questions | class notes |

Summary Paper

You can enter terms on the back side of your notes during class as you hear the words or after class when you Edit or Ask questions in your notes. Write the word in the three-inch margin and the definition in the five-inch space of your summary paper. Thus, you can cover one side or the other to recite your terms and definitions out loud. Simply looking over the list or rereading the words is not an effective way to learn the terms.

Learning New Terms by Making Your Own Glossary

Just as textbooks often have a glossary of terms at the end of each chapter or at the end of the book, so might you want to keep your own glossary for each course. Determine how you want to record your definitions: handwritten on summary paper or on your computer. Then, you need to decide where you want to file the terms and definitions in your binder: two logical places might be at the beginning or at the end of your notes for a class. The terms, of course, will be listed in the order they occur in your lecture notes or by chapters in the textbook. If you use a computer to make your glossary, you may leave them in that order or sort them alphabetically. You should make a hard copy of your computer glossary so that it can be filed in your binder. The format will be just like that of terms on the back side of notes (terms on the left, definitions on the right), but now you will have all terms together in one place. Your self-made glossary can be removed from your binder, which enables you to study your terms at any time and almost in any place.

Exercise 3-D

Directions: Now that you know three methods for learning terms, you need to use one or more of those methods to master the terms in this chapter and the remaining chapters assigned to you in this textbook. Also, incorporate a system for learning terms into all of your other courses.

Summary

In this chapter, you have been introduced to one of the most powerful tools for succeeding in college: note taking. By examining the Ebbinghaus Forgetting Curve, you have learned that new information is forgotten within a relatively short period of time unless you take steps to ensure that you will remember it.

In order to understand what true classroom listening means, you should be aware of the differences between the actions and attitudes of power listeners and passive listeners. Power listeners are those students who are *actively* involved in listening. Passive listeners, on the other hand, do more physical *hearing* than actual mental listening.

Next, the steps of the GREAT note-taking system were explained. GREAT is an acronym that stands for the five steps involved in the note-taking process:

Get ready
wRite
Edit
Ask questions
Test yourself

When you practice these steps, you will see them as a powerful process that allows you to write classroom notes and create a study guide for yourself to review and help you remember the information.

Finally, this chapter described three systems for organizing and studying new terms. Using a systematic way to learn vocabulary words and technical terms in all your courses is essential because every discipline has its own language. The recommended methods of mastering vocabulary are creating 3 x 5 flash cards, using the back side of your notes, preparing a glossary, or choosing a combination of these systems.

List of Terms

Ebbinghaus Forgetting Curve
power listeners
passive listeners
GREAT (Get ready, wRite, Edit, Ask questions, Test yourself)
cues, signal words, or transitional words
study buddy

literal questions
critical-thinking questions
creative questions
Quality Questions Pyramid
summary question or statement
sensory learning

In this box, write your summary question or statement for this chapter.

4 The Power of Reading for Meaning

"I don't have any trouble reading," the college student said emphatically to his professor. "I just don't know what I've read when I get to the end of the chapter!"

Oops! The logic here seems to be a little off, to say the least. Sincere as this student may be, the statement about reading does indicate a problem . . . and a big one. Such a statement is like saying, "I don't have any trouble water skiing; I just can't stand up on the skis!" Probably this student is confusing reading for meaning with simply recognizing words. The two are not the same.

In this chapter, you will learn what true reading actually involves, and you will understand why you should adjust your reading speed. In addition, you will distinguish topics from main ideas and recognize differences between major and minor details. You will increase your comprehension by understanding the use of transitions and patterns of organization. Finally, you will discover how to read and interpret visual aids, such as graphs, tables, diagrams, and pictures.

WHAT IS READING?

Some people think that reading means recognizing words. True reading, however, requires critical thinking and an understanding of the author's message. Certainly, words—just like eyes and good lighting—are necessary reading tools. But more importantly, when you truly engage in the process of reading, you must focus on the *meaning* of the words in order to understand a writer's ideas. Reading is a process, and a process always involves change: True reading changes words on paper into meaningful thoughts that the reader understands and evaluates.

A good way to illustrate reading for meaning is by comparing three lists like the ones in the following exercise.

Exercise 4-A

Directions: Take a few seconds to look at the following sets of information.

Set 1: s t d k l f r n g p w

Set 2: far able date high true ore yet only from sort

Set 3: blind readers use their fingertips as tools for reading

Which set of information is the easiest for you to recall in the shortest

period of time? _____   Why? _____

You probably took only a few seconds to realize that Set 3 is the easiest to recall. Even though it is longer and actually involves more letters, it is the easiest to read because your natural desire to understand makes you cling to the set of letters that makes the most sense!

True reading involves understanding. If you do not already do so, you should read phrase by phrase, not word by word, because this will enable you to grasp the meaning much more easily and quickly. For example, compare the two readings of President Lincoln's "Gettysburg Address" written below. Force yourself to pause at each of the slash marks (/) and notice the difference in your reading comprehension.

"Four/score/and/seven/years/ago/our/fathers/brought/forth/ on/this/continent/a/new/nation,/conceived/in/liberty/and/dedi- cated/to/the/proposition/that/all/men/are/created/equal."

Stopping after each word makes for jerky reading, doesn't it? Now, read the version below, which is set off phrase by phrase:

"Four score and seven years ago/our fathers brought forth on this con- tinent/a new nation,/conceived in liberty/and dedicated to the proposi- tion/that all men are created equal."

No doubt you can feel and understand Lincoln's message much better in the second version. The first version stops your thoughts at every word; the second one groups your thoughts into meaningful phrases.

ADJUSTING READING TO DIFFERENT PURPOSES

Wherever you go, whatever you do, you are constantly surrounded by printed words. Much of what is written can be read either for enjoyment or for information, and pleasure and learning can even be combined. You need to consider that *what* you are reading and *why* you are reading it determine *how* you should read.

What we read definitely affects *how* we read because we read for many different purposes. For example, would you read a murder mystery the same way you would read a recipe? Would you read an article on exercising the same way you would read a poem? Would you read the information on the sports page of a newspaper the same way you would read the comics? Or, for that matter, would you read the comics the same way you would read a textbook assignment? If you answered any of these questions with a yes, then you may need to learn how to adjust some of your reading habits. If you answered no to all of these questions, then you are well on your way to understanding the various demands of reading.

Whether you love to read or find it difficult to read, the only way to improve your reading skills is to read, read, and read some more. If you have not formed the habit of reading, begin by choosing magazine or newspaper articles that interest you. High interest in a subject provides the best motivation for reading. At a minimum, you should set aside thirty minutes a day to read for fun. As you acquire the habit of reading, your skills and pleasure in reading all kinds of information should increase.

Reading for Pleasure

When reading for pleasure, you have complete freedom as to how, when, and what you read. You can skip information, skim through the story, or even stop reading if you become bored. For example, when reading a novel full of intrigue and suspense, you might skim through long descriptive passages and just concentrate on the plot. However, when reading about a country that you have never visited, you might slow down to visualize the unfamiliar places and scenes. In contrast, if you are reading a sexy book, you might skim the plot very quickly, but slow down and savor the juicy parts. The point is, when you read just for entertainment, you can read any way you please.

Reading for Information

Newspaper and magazine articles are usually read to obtain general information. The format is very different from that of a novel. Headlines and titles are strategically placed to tempt you to read the whole article. Often, in these types of writing, the first paragraph gives you the most pertinent information—who, what, when, where, and why. Then, depending on your interest in the story, you can decide to read the article completely or skip to another headline that catches your eye.

In contrast to fiction, newspapers, or magazines, a "how to" book or a recipe needs to be read very carefully because you want to be certain that you accurately get all the information you need. Omitting a step or misreading the directions could be disastrous. For example, imagine tasting a cookie made with one *tablespoon* of salt instead of one *teaspoon* because the baker misread the directions. Those would be memorable cookies!

You should also be aware that in addition to textbook assignments, you could have outside reading assignments, such as novels, nonfiction books, and journal articles. Reading any of these outside reading assignments for a course differs greatly from reading them for pleasure because

you need to read them more seriously, more slowly, more carefully and thoughtfully, and take notes. You must understand how this information fits into the course.

Finally, reading a textbook requires an even more specialized approach. Your primary purpose in reading a textbook is to learn information. However, unlike reading a magazine or a recipe, reading your textbook is usually a mandatory task required to pass most college courses. Thus, you cannot skim your textbook, skip through it, or read it passively. Your goal is to learn as much as you can as efficiently as you can by being an active reader.

The above examples illustrate that your reading is influenced by the type of reading, your purpose, and the printed format. Therefore, the way you read (quickly or slowly, lightly or thoroughly) is determined by whether you are reading for pleasure or for information.

Critically Thinking in Writing

In a journal entry, describe your attitudes about reading. Do you think of yourself as a good reader or a poor reader? Why? Describe what you currently read for pleasure and for educational purposes. Tell how you feel about reading in general as compared to required reading. What frustrates you the most when you are reading?

Reading Speed

Students often ask reading teachers, "How fast should I read?" There is no single answer to this question. Because you are striving for a flexible reading speed with adequate comprehension for your purpose, your speed should depend on *what* you are reading and *why* you are reading it. For example, if you are reading a word problem in math, you may read at fifty to one hundred words per minute, a very slow pace. In contrast, when you first look at your personal mail, you may skim each piece at a thousand words per minute to decide whether you really want to read it or trash it.

Some speed-reading courses promise that their graduates can read at well over a thousand words per minute. Such promises can be misleading because the application of those speeds is very limited. These high speeds are helpful only if you need to skim ten to twenty newspapers per day or if you just want to identify the plots of novels. Speed reading is merely a skimming technique; it can be useful, but it should not be applied to reading textbooks. Your reading speed should always relate to your purpose.

WEB SITE INFORMATION

To learn more about reading quickly and effectively, visit our web site.

<http://college.hmco.com/success/>

FINDING THE STATED MAIN IDEA IN A PARAGRAPH

At the heart of reading for meaning is the skill of finding the main idea in a paragraph or, more often, in a longer passage. The *main idea* is the major concept the author wants you to understand.

The Paragraph

Think of a good piece of writing as a unified structure, somewhat like a perfectly constructed building. All parts of the piece of writing, that is, the paragraphs, fit nicely together and contribute to the whole. In a written passage, paragraphs contribute to the whole piece of writing just as rooms contribute to a building's whole structure.

A paragraph usually expresses its own main idea in a sentence, called a topic sentence. The *topic sentence* announces the *topic* or subject of the paragraph and then states the *point* the author wants to make about that topic. A *topic* is simply the person, place, thing, or idea that an author is discussing. It can be expressed in one word or a few words, but it is unfinished all by itself. For example, here is a topic:

the ozone layer

This topic has possibilities, but it doesn't tell you much. By itself, it actually might raise all kinds of questions in your mind. Now, here is that topic expanded into a topic sentence:

The ozone layer [topic] has become dangerously thin, which could threaten all organic life.

If the topic is "the ozone layer," what is the point the author is making? Easy: Organic life may be endangered because of damage done to the ozone layer. Notice that a topic is only a word or a few words, but the topic sentence (because it is the main idea of a paragraph) is always a complete sentence.

A topic sentence may be anywhere in a paragraph—it may be the first sentence, the second, the third, somewhere in the middle, or even the last sentence. Sometimes the thought is actually stated twice. In such a case, the main idea is usually stated in the first sentence and repeated, in different words, in the last sentence.

Most writers want readers to comprehend the message right away, right up front; therefore, they usually make the topic sentence the first or second sentence. You can take advantage of this tendency on the part of writers. For example, you may want to read all first sentences before you thoroughly read an article, which is a method of previewing (see Chapter 5). Furthermore, when you wish to review or summarize information, you might also want to reread first sentences.

Exercise 4-B

Directions: Based on the definitions of topic and topic sentence, read the following paragraph, and find the topic and the topic sentence.

Long-distance telephone companies seem to be plotting to keep their customers confused. Several times a week, telephone patrons receive unsolicited calls by operators of this or that long-distance company offering free long-distance calls for the first so many months, free remote calling cards, free calls to friends and neighbors, free prizes, gifts, and rental cars. One company sends checks in the mail for anywhere from $50 to $100; if you endorse the check to spend on anything your heart desires, you have agreed to hook up to their long-distance services. The endorsed check is your signed agreement. Some of the ten-cent-per-minute rates actually do apply, but the solicitor fails to mention the fine print: an expensive "switch-over" fee, "an out-of-country-calls-only" clause, and calling certain times only on the odd days of the even months, or something to that effect.

(continued on the next page)

Exercise 4-B (continued)

1. What is the simple topic of this paragraph? _____

2. In your own words, what is the point the author is making about this topic?

   _____

   _____

3. What sentence states this point? _____

Unstated or Implied Main Ideas

Most paragraphs, but not all, contain topic sentences. Sometimes writers do not state the main idea in a sentence; they expect you, the reader, to understand the main idea from the details given. Main ideas that are not stated, but hinted at through the other sentences, are called unstated or *implied main ideas.*

Critically Thinking Together

Divide into small groups. Individually read the following paragraph which has an implied main idea, and then, as a group, answer the following questions.

   I followed the line of cars into the parking lot. Before long, I found a parking place. I grabbed my backpack and followed the crowd, walking quickly to the big building on the right. As I entered the doors, I hesitated. "Is this really what I want to do?" I silently asked myself. "Of course," a little voice in my head replied. "Keep moving! You're looking for Room 145." I proceeded down the hall to the last room on the left. As I entered, I could see that most of the desks were occupied, so I had to walk clear over to the windows to find a seat. I looked around only to see strangers, who looked at me with no signs of friendliness. I took a deep breath and tried not to be nervous. I was

(continued on the next page)

beginning to get out some paper and a pen from my backpack, when the door opened again. A determined older-looking man with a beard and mustache walked to the front of the room, stood behind the lectern, and said gruffly, "This is Chemistry 101."

1. What is the topic? _____

2. What is the point (the implied main idea) the author is making?

   _____

   _____

3. What would be a good title for this paragraph?

   _____

The Main Idea in Longer Readings

Most readings are much longer than a single paragraph, of course. But once you know the structure of the paragraph, you will be able to expand this knowledge to the larger structure of an article, essay, chapter, or book.

The main idea in a longer reading goes by another name, but the basics are the same as in the single paragraph. The main idea in a longer reading is usually called the *thesis* or the *thesis statement*. Just as the topic sentence is usually the first sentence of a paragraph, so, too, the thesis statement is almost always found early in a longer reading. In most essays, for example, the thesis is stated in the first paragraph. Many times, this main idea is repeated in the last paragraph of the essay as well. Knowing this, you would benefit by paying close attention to the first and last paragraphs of an essay, article, or chapter.

MAJOR AND MINOR SUPPORTING DETAILS

You can count on experienced writers to back up or reinforce their main ideas adequately with additional information. These supports or proofs are called supporting details. *Supporting details* include reasons, examples, facts, statistics, definitions, testimonials, and other information that supports or proves the main idea. *Major supporting details* are larger, more general proofs that directly support the main idea. *Minor supporting details* are smaller, more specific bits of information that strengthen the major supporting details. Here is an illustration of the structure of an essay:

Introductory paragraph

Thesis statement

Body Paragraph #1
Topic sentence
    Major support #1
      minor support
    Major support #2
      minor support
    Major support #3
      minor support

Body Paragraph #2
Topic sentence
    Major support #1
      minor support
    Major support #2
      minor support
    Major support #3
      minor support

Body Paragraph #3
Topic sentence
    Major support #1
      minor support
    Major support #2
      minor support
    Major support #3
      minor support

```
                    Concluding paragraph
```

Of course, not all essays are the same length as this example. Essays can be of any length. This diagram simply illustrates how the major supporting details and minor supporting details develop the topic sentences. The topic sentence of each paragraph, in turn, develops one aspect of the thesis statement, the main idea of the essay.

The following paragraph is taken from an economics textbook. This paragraph explains one aspect of gross domestic product (GDP). The first two sentences are introductory sentences. The topic sentence is in bold print, and the major supporting details are underlined. The remaining sentences are minor supporting details used to back up the major supporting details.

> The *market value* of final goods and services is their value at market price. The process of determining market value is straightforward where prices are known and transactions are observable. **However, there are cases where prices are not known and transactions are not observable.** For instance, illegal drug transactions are not reported to the government, which means they are not included in gross domestic product (GDP) statistics. In fact, almost any activity that is not traded in a market is not included. For example, production that takes place in households is not counted . . . , nor are unreported barter and cash transactions. For instance, if a lawyer has a sick dog and a veterinarian needs some legal advice, by trading services and not reporting the activity to the tax authorities, each can avoid taxation on the income that would have been reported had they sold their services to each other.
>
> (Boyes & Melvin 139)

Transitions Connecting Ideas

Another way to promote good reading comprehension is to develop an awareness of transitional words. *Transitions* are words that connect one idea to another and show relationships between ideas. They may be small, but they are extremely powerful words that help you distinguish between main ideas, major supporting details, and minor supporting details.

The following are examples of the most common types of transitions:

1. Some transitions that show *additional* information

first, second, third	next
also	furthermore
another	finally
in addition	moreover

2. Some transitions that show *time* relationships

first	before
next	after
later	until
then	during
often	when
while	meanwhile

3. Some transitions that show *comparison or sameness*

just like	equal
like	equally
alike	in the same way
likewise	almost identical to
similar to	comparable to
similarly	the same as

4. Some transitions that show *contrast or differences*

in contrast	although
on the other hand	even though, even if
however	yet
but	instead
differ	unlike
different from	despite

5. Some transitions that show *examples* will follow

for example	including
for instance	such as
to illustrate	one such

6. Some transitions that explain *why or cause and effect*

because	the result of
since	as a result

reasons for	therefore
is caused by	thus
if . . . then	so

So, how can these transitional groupings help you read for meaning? The answer is simple: As you become aware of transitional connectors, you should become aware of your powers of prediction. Transitions help you, as a critical thinker, follow a writer's train of thought and predict what he or she will say next.

Exercise 4-C

Directions: Read each of the following unfinished sentences, and predict an ending by finishing the statement. Then circle the most important transitional word and identify what type of transition it is. The first one is done for you.

1. "My sister and I have a lot in common; (however),
   <u>we definitely disagree on anything related to politics.</u>"

   Kind of transition: <u>*Contrast*</u>

2. "To open a new document on the computer, first, click on the icon called 'Microsoft Office' . . ." _____

   _____

   Kind of transition: _____

3. "The doctor said the man was a heart attack waiting to happen. I know, for example, that he smoked too much, ate mostly junk foods, and . . ." _____

   _____

   Kind of transition: _____

4. "While I was playing golf, the thunder and lightning began. As a result, . . ." _____

   _____

   Kind of transition: _____

(continued on the next page)

Exercise 4-C (continued)

5. "The feeling I experience when I get an A on a test is just like . . ."

   _____

   Kind of transition: _____

6. "The new sporting goods store that opened last week has a wide variety of items for young children, including . . ."

   _____

   Kind of transition: _____

As you discovered from doing Exercise 4-C, using transitions to predict what is coming can help make you comfortable and confident with your reading. You can also better understand how major and minor supporting details fit together.

Patterns to Show an Author's Organization

So far, you have examined transitions within sentences. In addition, you will find it useful to be able to recognize transitions when they link a sentence to another sentence or a paragraph to another paragraph.

When certain types of transitions are repeated within a paragraph, you are seeing what is called a *pattern of organization*. In this sense, a pattern means a repetition of something. Patterns of organization occur when a writer uses several transitions from one category (addition, time, contrast, comparison, example, or cause and effect). Although patterns of organization are not always present, when they do exist, they are a powerful means of enhancing your comprehension.

Patterns of organization can easily be recognized once you understand transitions. Below you will find some common patterns of organization that are based upon the types of transitions you saw earlier.

Listing Patterns   Listing patterns occur when an author uses addition transitions (first, second, also, in addition, moreover, etc.) to list details in any order the author chooses. The following is an example of a paragraph using the listing pattern of organization. The addition transitions that create this pattern are underlined.

IMPROVING CONCENTRATION

If you have trouble concentrating when you study, you may want to try some of the following suggestions. <u>First</u>, make sure you are not hungry or sleepy or wearing uncomfortable clothes. <u>Another way</u> to keep focused is to eliminate external distracters. You should turn off the radio or television and take the phone off the hook or turn on the answering machine. <u>Next</u>, study at your "peak time," when you are most mentally and physically alert. <u>In addition</u>, make sure your study area is organized, fully equipped, well lighted, and comfortable in terms of temperature. <u>Also</u>, study your hardest or least enjoyable subject first, and take short breaks when your concentration begins to lag. <u>Moreover</u>, plan to reward yourself when you finish a task. These are just a few of the many ways to improve your concentration.

Time Order Patterns   Time order occurs when an author is setting up steps or stages in a process or is describing chronological events. The steps, stages, or events are fixed in a certain order (first, second, then, next, finally, etc.). The following is an example of a paragraph using time order as its pattern of organization. The time transitions that create this pattern are underlined.

HUMAN GROWTH

Once human beings are born, they go through six rather obvious and important stages. <u>First</u>, newborn babies begin to adapt to the external world in the first two weeks of life. <u>Then</u>, as infants up to about fifteen months, babies grow considerably in both height and weight. <u>Next</u>, as children, bone formation and overall growth continue. This lasts up to the age of twelve or so. Puberty begins for girls between twelve and fifteen and for boys between thirteen and sixteen, <u>during which time</u> secondary sexual characteristics develop. Adolescence follows puberty. <u>At this time</u> teenagers mature physically, mentally, and emotionally. <u>The final stage</u> in human growth is adulthood. Between the ages of eighteen and twenty-five, bone formation and growth come to a stop. <u>After that</u>, any changes in adults occur very slowly.

Comparison and Contrast Patterns   Comparison and contrast patterns occur when an author uses comparison (similarly, like, likewise, etc.) and contrast (in contrast, on the other hand, but, etc.) to show how two or more subjects are similar and/or different. The following is an example of a paragraph using the contrast pattern of organization. The contrast transitions that create the pattern of organization are underlined.

THE CREDIT CARD VS. THE DEBIT CARD

Many banks are now offering a plastic card called the debit card. This card goes by various names, but it is essentially the <u>opposite of</u> a credit card. When you use a credit card, you make the purchase at one moment but are billed later, usually within a month. <u>On the other hand</u>, when you use the debit card, your payment is immediate because a computer approves immediate withdrawal from your checking account. Credit cards have an approved charge limit, up to say $3,000 or $10,000 depending upon your spending and credit history. Should you try to charge more than that amount, your credit will not be approved by the card issuer, and you will go home empty-handed. Also, if you do not pay the full amount due each month, interest of roughly 12 to 20 percent will be charged on the balance. <u>In contrast</u>, debit cards have the limit of your own bank account balance. Should you go over that amount, you may have to pay a penalty for overdrawing your account. A final <u>difference</u> lies in bargaining power or guaranteed satisfaction. If you charge on a credit card and something is wrong with the merchandise, you can withhold payment from the store and explain this in writing to the credit card company. Your payment is deferred until the situation is settled. <u>In contrast</u>, with the debit card, your bill is completely paid and you have no leverage for complaining.

Cause-and-Effect Patterns   Cause-and-effect patterns occur when an author uses cause-and-effect transitions (because, as a result, resulting in, etc.) to show how one event leads to another. The following is an example of a paragraph that uses a cause-and-effect pattern of organization. The cause-and-effect words that create this pattern are underlined.

BEING LATE TO CLASS

Being consistently late to class can <u>cause</u> several unpleasant <u>results</u> for you and for others. <u>If</u> you arrive late, <u>then</u> the <u>consequence</u> could be that you miss a quiz or miss hearing about a change of assignments. You might also feel disoriented <u>because</u> you walked in on the middle of a lecture. In addition, your late arrival disturbs the rest of the class. <u>Because</u> they look at you instead of listening to the instructor, you have momentarily made some students lose their concentration. You might even make the instruc-

tor lose his or her train of thought. The <u>resultant</u> scowl on the instructor's face indicates a reaction of anger and frustration. In the long run, the <u>result</u> of habitual lateness is a clear demonstration that you lack respect for both your peers and the professor.

Definition-Example Patterns   Definition-example patterns occur when an author defines a term and then explains it through examples or illustrations (for example, for instance, to illustrate, including, such as, one such). The following paragraph illustrates a definition-example pattern of organization. The transitions that indicate examples are underlined.

CLICHÉS IN WRITING

Clichés are phrases or sentences in writing that are overused or trite [definition]. Often they are comparisons (similes) that were clever the first time they were used, but have been repeated so many times that they have lost their freshness. <u>For instance</u>, some common clichés refer to varying degrees of heat or cold, such as "cold as ice," "hot as Hades," "cool as a cucumber," or "warm as toast." <u>Other examples</u> of clichés include "pretty as a picture," "red as a rose," "big as a house," or "dead as a doornail." <u>To illustrate</u> how easy it is to come up with clichés, finish these sentences with the first words that pop into your mind: "I'm so hungry I could eat a _____." "The child was as quiet as a _____." "He was faster than a _____." Chances are, your responses were "cow," "mouse," and "speeding bullet," or similarly trite words. Good writers avoid clichés and create new, bright images of their own as they write.

In conclusion, as you saw previously, transitions can help you understand and predict what is coming in a sentence. When transitions are repeated into patterns of organization, you can understand and predict an author's message in a paragraph or an essay. Often main ideas seem to stand out more readily when details settle themselves into recognizable patterns.

READING VISUAL AIDS

College textbooks, and many magazines and newspapers as well, contain not only printed information, but also *visual aids,* such as graphs, tables, diagrams, and pictures. These visual aids are not simply page decorations, something you can skip. The general purposes of visual aids are to explain processes, condense detailed information, compare related ideas, show change over time, or otherwise support the text.

You would do well to follow some general guidelines in order to understand visual aids. Here are some helpful tips:

- Get an overview of the entire visual aid by observing the printed title, caption, units of measurement, terms used, years covered, etc.
- Now carefully read all printed information. This may include what is called a legend. A *legend* is an explanatory caption, table, list, or chart found on or next to the visual aid. The legend gives information that helps you interpret the meaning of the visual aid.
- Next, carefully study the actual visual aid for details.
- Try to see what relationships exist between the words and pictures.
- To check your understanding of the visual aid, try to summarize the information in a few sentences.

Reading Graphs

Graphs are visual aids that show comparisons and/or contrasts between two or more items. Three popular types of graphs often used in textbooks are line graphs, bar graphs, and pie graphs.

Line graphs are visual aids in which information is plotted using horizontal and vertical axes. The major use of a line graph is to show changes over time and/or trends. The following is a line graph plotting the amount of information a person retains over periods of time.

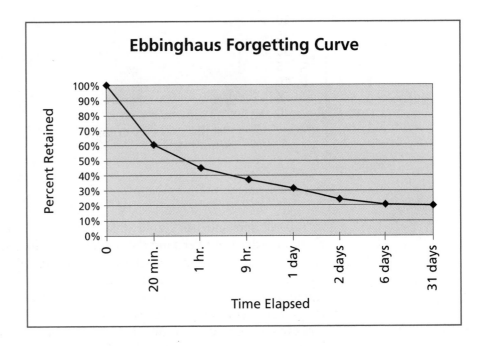

To read a line graph, take a point on the line, and trace down to the information on the horizontal axis and across to the information on the vertical axis. This will tell you how the two variables are related (in this case, the time elapsed and percent retained). Two pieces of paper, or other straightedges, placed across the two directions may help you clearly see the point of intersection.

Bar graphs are graphs that use thick lines, or bars of various lengths, arranged either horizontally or vertically, to show comparisons among quantities or amounts. Sometimes bar graphs are stacked; that is, the whole concept being examined is broken into its various parts. Often different colors or shadings are used to represent these different parts of the larger category. The following is an example of a bar graph.

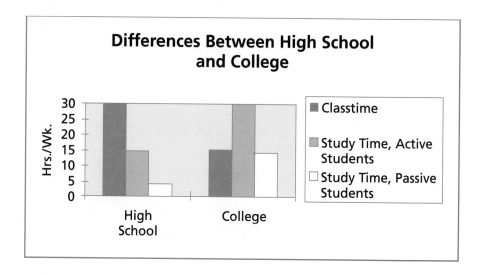

To understand bar graphs, first read the title and any explanation given in order to understand the main idea of the bar graph. Then look at the vertical and horizontal labels to determine what is being measured and the units of measurement. In the above example, for instance, the legend to the right indicates what the shaded bars represent. Using this information, you can see how each bar is related to hours per week. Then you can compare and contrast the different uses of learning time among high school and college students. Using a piece of paper or a ruler for a guide, you can look at the value in the horizontal column and see where it intersects with the vertical column. That intersection tells you how the two relate to each other.

Pie graphs or *circle graphs,* unlike the other two types of graphs, are in the shape of a circle. Each slice of the circle or pie represents a percentage, with the whole pie representing 100 percent. Pie graphs quickly show you how each part relates to the whole. The following graph shows the percentage of time one student spends on each activity during a typical school week.

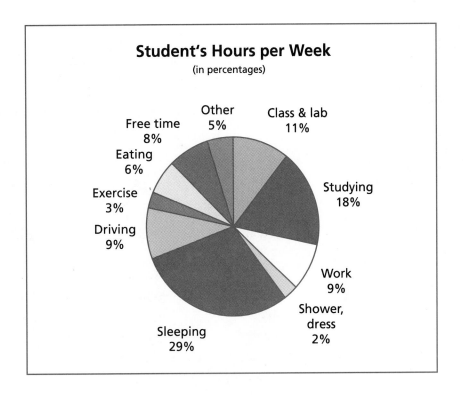

Student's Hours per Week
(in percentages)

To read a pie graph, you simply see how large each slice of the pie is (what percentage) compared to the whole pie (100 percent). In the case of the student above, the percentages represent this much time during a week (168 hours).

Class & lab	11 percent	=	18 hours
Studying	18 percent	=	30 hours
Work	9 percent	=	15 hours
Shower, dress	2 percent	=	4 hours
Sleeping	29 percent	=	50 hours
Driving	9 percent	=	15 hours
Exercise	3 percent	=	5 hours
Eating	6 percent	=	10 hours
Free time	8 percent	=	13 hours
Other	5 percent	=	8 hours

When you read any pie graph, the larger the pie slice, the more value, time, or weight an item represents.

Reading Tables

Tables are lists of percentages, facts, numbers, or other related information set up in rows and columns. This arrangement allows you to see comparisons easily. The following table, taken from a biology textbook, shows what it takes to burn calories from four different foods.

What It Takes to Burn Calories

Food	Activity	Calories/minute	Time to Burn (minutes)
Milkshake	Resting	1.1	289
318 Calories	Walking	5.5	58
	Swimming	10.9	29
	Running	14.7	22
Corn, 2 pats butter	Resting	1.1	155
	Walking	5.5	31
170 Calories	Swimming	10.9	16
	Running	14.7	12
Corn, unbuttered	Resting	1.1	63
	Walking	5.5	13
70 Calories	Swimming	10.9	6
	Running	14.7	5

(Levine & Miller 738)

To understand a table, first read the general title in order to determine the subject under discussion, in this case "What It Takes to Burn Calories." Then read the labels at the tops of the columns; these will tell you how the subject was broken down for analysis. In this table, the labels are "Food," "Activity," "Calories/minute," and "Time to Burn (minutes)." Next, read the descriptive information under the labels from left to right. You may want to use a ruler or a piece of paper under each line of information in order to keep your eyes accurately focused as you read across the line.

Reading Diagrams

Diagrams include drawings or illustrations used to represent processes, ideas, the operations or working parts of a physical object, a system of the human body, plans for the future, or any other such information. The following diagram illustrates the parts of the human eye.

Human eye

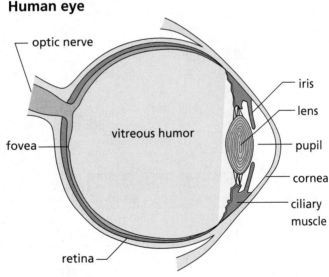

(Levine & Miller 928)

To read a diagram, look at the title or heading first. Then read the labels and view the pictures to get an overall idea of what is represented in the diagram. Next, study the diagram, trying to see how each part fits into the whole picture or system. For instance, in studying the diagram of the human eye, you will want to know the parts of the eye and their locations. You may also need to know the function of each part. If the diagram is one you will have to reproduce or label on an exam, one way to study it is to trace it and try to label your tracing with the names of the parts. Then you can compare your reproduction with the one in the text to check your accuracy. Another way to study a diagram is to mark the textbook diagram by inserting the particular function of each part.

Another type of diagram is called a flow chart. A *flow chart* shows step-by-step procedures or the top-to-bottom line of command in an organization. Diagrams of this type are usually read from top to bottom, although at times they are set up to be read from left to right. Connecting lines and arrows usually guide you as you move through the process of reading the diagram. Often boxes or circles represent the stages or steps in the process. The following flow chart, which is read from top to bottom, shows the functional divisions of the human nervous system:

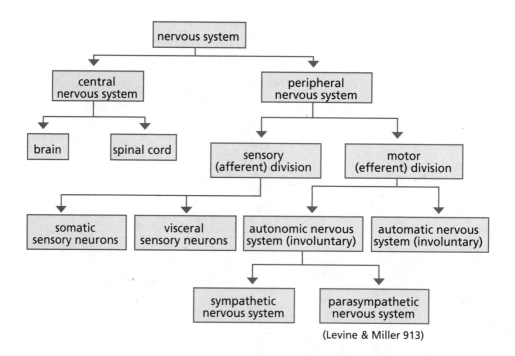

(Levine & Miller 913)

Critically Thinking Together

Find a visual aid in one of your other textbooks and bring it or a photocopy to class. In your group, explain to the other members what type of visual aid it is and how to read it.

Observing Photographs, Pictures, and Cartoons

One more category of visual aids that you will encounter in textbooks consists of photographs, pictures, and cartoons. The general guidelines for reading and understanding these visual aids are similar to those for graphs, tables, and diagrams: Get an overview, read the printed details (if any), and study the picture details. However, with a photograph, picture, or cartoon, your main goal is to understand the picture, connect it to your experience, and draw a conclusion about it in relation to the subject you are studying. Your conclusions are drawn from your observations of the picture itself within the context of the chapter, as well as your own background and logic. In this sense, understanding pictures is more personal and less exact than interpreting graphs, tables, and diagrams.

Summary

In this chapter, you learned how reading, by definition, requires that you think critically and read for meaning. Because reading is an individual and unique process, your approaches to reading and reading rates must be adjusted to accommodate varying purposes and types of reading materials.

You also learned how to recognize main ideas, which are the topic sentences of paragraphs and thesis statements of essays. These main ideas can be stated or implied. In addition, you examined major and minor supporting details and the importance of recognizing transitions. Transitional words link sentences to sentences and paragraphs to paragraphs, and they create patterns of organization within a paragraph.

Finally, you discovered ways to read and understand visual aids, which include graphs, tables, diagrams, and pictures.

List of Terms

reading
main idea
topic
topic sentence
implied main idea
thesis statement
supporting details

visual aids
legend
graphs
line graphs
bar graphs
pie or circle graphs
tables

major supporting details   pattern of organization
minor supporting details   diagrams
transitions   flow charts

In this box, write your summary question or statement for this chapter.

5 The Power of STUDY-READING

"Some books are to be tasted, others to be swallowed, and some few to be chewed and digested." Although you may think it is unusual to compare books to eating, Sir Francis Bacon classified books in this manner way back in the 17th century, in order to illustrate that the manner in which books are read must be adjusted for different purposes. Some books can be taken lightly; others must be taken very seriously because of the value of their contents to the reader.

If you were to ask Sir Francis today (and of course you can't), he would most likely put college textbook reading into the most serious "chewed and digested" category. Because information from textbooks is so vital to your college education, you must read them very carefully and critically in order to understand, learn, and apply the information they contain.

In this chapter, you will first learn how to examine your textbooks at the beginning of each course to familiarize yourself with the contents. Next, you will learn a powerful way to make your textbooks work for you: the STUDY-READ method. This method will allow you to read each chapter critically, turning your textbook chapters into personal study guides.

EXAMINING AN ENTIRE TEXTBOOK

Before beginning the intense reading of individual text chapters, you need to get an initial overview of the whole book. This means much more than just thumbing through the book to see how many pages it has and if there are any pictures. Surveying or previewing a textbook is a way to make yourself familiar with it, to see where you are going before you get there, to understand the parts and the whole. Most instructors never mention the various aspects of the textbooks they use, but they expect *you* to take the initiative to investigate what your text contains so that you can use all of its resources. The more you know about the text before you start any class, the easier it will be for you to read each chapter and to understand how it will fit into the entire course.

In examining a textbook, look at the following features:

- Title (on the cover and the title page)
- Publication date (on the reverse side of the title page)
- Edition (on the cover and the title page)
- Author(s)
- Foreword, Introduction, or To the Student
- Table of Contents
- Index
- Appendix(es) (at back of book)
- Glossary (at back of book or end of chapters)
- Answer key
- Additional information (keys, charts, lists) on inside covers

These features will be found in most college textbooks. A quick survey of all your textbooks will provide you with an understanding of the features of each of them.

Examining your textbooks gives you an opportunity to learn about your courses and helps you to understand what you will be expected to know. During your survey, you may have discovered that the text was written by a very distinguished person in that particular field of study, maybe even your own instructor. The date of publication and the edition tell you how recently the book was printed or revised. If it is a revised edition, the foreword or introduction will usually tell you how the book has been improved or updated as well as explain the major purposes or concepts of the text.

By looking at the table of contents, you will gain an overview of what material is included in the text and how the information is organized. The chapter titles should indicate whether the information will be familiar to you or not. The subheadings for each chapter give you an outline of the chapter itself. In addition, some books are divided not just into chapters, but into larger sections or parts. These larger units provide you with an understanding of the major divisions of the text.

Investigating information contained in each of your textbooks will familiarize you with all of their resources. Appendixes, glossaries, answer keys, and charts on the inside covers of the text provide you with quick ways to find information. Knowing all the special aspects of each of your textbooks gives you the power to use them wisely.

Exercise 5-A

Directions: This exercise shows you how to examine a textbook. Answer all the questions as they relate to this study skills book.

1. What is the title? (Look at the cover or the title page.) _____

_____

2. When was it published? (See the reverse side of the title page.)

_____ What edition is it?_____

3. Name the author(s). _____

4. Read the introduction. State one important fact that you learned

from this section._____

_____

5. Next, look at the table of contents. How many chapters are listed?

_____

6. Do most of the chapter titles look familiar? Yes _____ No_____

7. Does the book have an index at the back? Yes _____ No_____

8. From your preliminary preview, do you think this will be an easy

text to read or a difficult one? _____ Give a reason for your

answer. _____

_____

Critically Thinking in Writing

Preview one of your other textbooks. In a journal entry, describe your initial reactions to the text by considering the following questions.

1. Is your "gut reaction" positive or negative and why?

2. What is your comfort level with this book? Try to predict if it is going to be easy or difficult to read based on your previous knowledge and background.

3. Are you discouraged or encouraged by any aspects of this book— the subject matter, the resources, the length, or other aspects?

4. What discoveries did you make that you were not expecting about any aspects of the book? Explain.

READING A TEXTBOOK CHAPTER: STUDY-READ

Have you ever finished an assignment, congratulated yourself for finishing, and realized that you don't remember a word of what you just read? Have you ever been so bored you thought you would never finish? Have you ever actually fallen asleep while trying to read an assignment? How frustrating those experiences are, and how terribly time-consuming it is to reread the entire assignment. You might, on the other hand, read the assignment and think you know what it is all about, but when you take quizzes, you get only Cs. By midterm, you are not doing as well as someone else who seems to put in less time than you do.

If you fall into one of these categories or for some other reason are not achieving the grades you expect or want on quizzes and tests covering textbook content, you need to develop a more effective method of completing your reading assignments. You need STUDY-READ.

STUDY-READ, a critical-thinking process for reading, marking, and studying textbook chapters, consists of three parts:

- Preview
- Read and mark
- Review by reciting

This system evolved from two sources: the learning theories of experts in the college study skills field and the actual study habits of successful students.

By using STUDY-READ, you can become a more active reader, instead of a passive reader. Active readers use *sensory learning*, engaging as many of their senses as they can—sight, sound, touch—as they study in order to understand and remember the information. They are thinking about what they are reading and trying to make ideas and concepts meaningful. Active readers read critically for meaning and understanding and make their study time worthwhile. Passive readers often only go through the motions of reading without really grasping the meaning; the words just travel in front of their eyes.

With a little effort and practice, STUDY-READ will provide you with a new habit that will make learning easier and more enjoyable. You will be putting in quality time and getting quality results. The rewards you will gain will include a much better understanding of the material and, most likely, better grades. Using STUDY-READ will make you feel as though you have been to a two-for-one sale: You will read with depth and understanding, and you will create your own study guides at the same time. Once you master the system, it will make preparing for classes and exams easier and more effective.

The three parts of STUDY-READ—preview, read and mark, and review by reciting—are all integral to the system, although they are performed separately. The following diagram presents an overview of the STUDY-READ method. At the center of the STUDY-READ process is the familiar activity of reading, combined with text marking. In this system, reading is preceded by the mental warm-up of previewing; thus the arrow is pointing toward the reading. Once you have read and marked your chapter, your final step is to review by reciting; thus the arrow points back to the read-and-mark stage. Reviewing allows you to store information in your long-term memory and later retrieve it.

Step One: PREVIEW ➡️

Previewing or *surveying* the chapter is the first step in STUDY-READ; it provides your brain with a systematic overview of the new information discussed in the chapter. Just as you examined or previewed your whole textbook, now you will take a close survey of the chapter.

1. First, read the *title* of the chapter to determine what clues the title provides to predict the chapter content.
2. Next, if the chapter begins with an *introduction* or chapter *objectives*, read them.
3. Then, quickly thumb through the chapter and read all *boldfaced headings*; they will give you an outline of the main ideas of the chapter. If your textbook has no boldfaced headings, you can skim the first sentence of the larger paragraphs. Since the first sentence is often a topic sentence, it may act as a substitute for a boldfaced heading.
4. Another item to notice as you preview the chapter is all *nonverbal information*. This includes maps, charts, graphs, diagrams, pictures, and cartoons. As you examine these visual aids, read any captions that accompany them.
5. When you reach the end of the chapter, read the *summary* or *conclusion* if there is one.
6. Finally, if the chapter ends with *questions*, read them. End-of-chapter questions are usually sequential, so reading them will give you an

added picture of the chapter's organization as well as a summation of what the author thinks is important.

Exercise 5-B

Directions: Preview the next chapter you will be reading in this text, timing yourself as you do so. Then answer the following questions without referring back to that chapter.

1. How long did it take you to preview the chapter? _____

2. What are the *major* points in the chapter?

   _____

3. What information seems familiar? _____

   _____

   _____

4. What information seems new? _____

   _____

   _____

5. What is another feature, idea, or aspect of the chapter that you noticed? _____

   _____

Reading and understanding the explanation of the six steps in previewing a chapter probably took you longer than actually doing a preview. In fact, it should take you approximately five or, at the most, ten minutes to preview most chapters.

The few minutes it takes to preview a chapter are a good investment of time. Looking over the chapter as you preview stimulates your critical thinking and helps you understand the organization of the material. This will greatly increase your comprehension and will also make your reading easier.

The short time spent in surveying definitely pays for itself. Once you begin to preview all your reading assignments and adopt previewing as a habit, the task will become easier and easier. Previewing is just the beginning of STUDY-READ, but it adds extra power to activate the next step.

Step Two: READ-and-MARK

The second step in STUDY-READ is actually reading the textbook chapter, and reading it in such a way that you are systematically and actively engaged in learning. Reading merely to finish the chapter and reading to understand the material are two entirely different approaches to reading. The first way will leave you dissatisfied because you will remember very little of what you have read. The second way, reading to understand and marking the text as you read, will leave you with a feeling of accomplishment and a good start on remembering what you have read because you are actively involved in the reading. After all, textbook reading is intense reading for knowledge and understanding. You, therefore, must employ critical thinking and reading skills.

In step 2 of STUDY-READ, called the *read-and-mark* step, you will read each paragraph or each section set off by a boldface heading, one at a time. Your goal is to find the main idea, which is usually the topic sentence, and then find the supporting details, facts, reasons, or examples. You are actively reading with an inquiring, questioning mind. What is the major point? What details support this point? You are reading to find answers.

To begin the read-and-mark step of STUDY-READ, you should read one whole paragraph or section completely *before* marking. Ultimately, you need to determine what question(s) the material in the paragraph answers. Determine your questions by second-guessing what your instructor might ask in a class discussion, on a quiz, or on a test or final exam. Make your questions complete sentences that cannot be answered with yes or no. Use questions like "what," "when," or "how much," but strive for higher-quality questions like "how" and "why," as well as comparisons, contrasts, and explanations. Just as you want good questions in your notes, you want to strive for quality questions in your textbooks (see the Quality Questions Pyramid in Chapter 3).

Then for each paragraph or, at most, each section, actually write your question(s) in the margin of your text and mark key words or phrases that will answer your question(s). You mark your text by highlighting or underlining. The rule of thumb when highlighting is "less is more." In other words, be very selective about what you highlight.

Novice or beginning highlighters tend to overkill by highlighting whole paragraphs and whole pages. Such textbook pages are colorful, but they are not very useful when it comes time to study.

Highlighting Tips

Do highlight	Avoid highlighting
key words	whole pages
key phrases	whole paragraphs
main ideas	whole sentences
supporting details	bold-faced headings
terms, definitions, and equations	bullets or numbers without key words when you have no
answers that correspond to your questions	corresponding questions
key word items in a list	math problems
formulas, principles, rules	

Besides writing questions, you may also need or want to add other marginal notes—numbers 1, 2, 3, etc., for lists of items, stars (*) for very important information, def. for definitions, and ex. for examples. Marking your textbook makes it a working tool for you.

Complete this read-and-mark step for a paragraph or section before you go on to the next paragraph or section. Then follow the same procedure for the next paragraph or section, and the next, and the next. As you read, you are creating a series of questions in the margins of your book, with key words highlighted as answers to those questions. You will know what you have read, and you will be more likely to be ready to take tests.

Note: For an example of a textbook page illustrating the read-and-mark step of STUDY-READ, see the example "Understanding the Art of Concentration" (Patterson 17–18) in this chapter.

When you have completed the whole reading assignment or chapter, challenge yourself to write one more question or statement at the end of the chapter: a summary of the whole chapter. Granted, writing a summary question may seem difficult at first, but it will help you put the parts back into the whole and give you an overview of the chapter. (See

UNDERSTANDING THE ART OF CONCENTRATION

MENTAL ABILITIES

What 3 mental abilities are involved in concentration?

Concentration involves a series of three mental abilities: ① the ability to sustain <u>focus over a period of time</u>, ② the ability to <u>focus at will</u>, and ③ the ability to <u>focus on one task at a time</u>. These three separate abilities each need to be explained, but since they work together, they need to be considered as an interactive and connected whole.

Sustaining Focus Over a Period of Time

The first mental ability is sustaining focus over a period of time. Do you have trouble settling down with a complex problem because your mind keeps shifting to another topic? Do you start a conversation with a friend, then remember the math problems that are due the next day? As soon as the math problems are started, do you decide to take the dog for a walk? Are you usually busy but don't seem to get that much accomplished?

How long can a typical student concentrate?

For challenging or <u>difficult mental tasks</u> (which include much of college work), the optimum concentration <u>span is 10 to 50 minutes</u>. In one study, college students reported concentration spans from 1 to 105 minutes with an average concentration span of 16 minutes for textbooks (Patterson, 1993). The implications of this study are that <u>15-20 minute study periods enable us to read</u> in a textbook <u>with maximum concentration</u>.

How can I vary my studies and increase concentration?

Instead of giving up studies when your mind wanders, however, try <u>breaking up</u> your <u>study</u> periods <u>with a variety of activities</u> so you can <u>sustain focus over a longer period of time</u>. For example, Mike, an Emergency Medical Technician student, tries to concentrate on an anatomy text but finds his eyes looking at words without really understanding, even though he's just two hours into an eight-hour study day. He could vary the task by <u>reading for 20 minutes</u>, <u>studying anatomy charts for the next 20 minutes</u>, and <u>testing</u> himself over <u>what he's read for the next 20 minutes</u>.

<u>A short break</u> will also <u>keep concentration to a maximum</u>. Mike's concentration will be better if he sets 20-minute study goals and <u>intersperses</u> these <u>study periods with a relaxation exercise</u>, an <u>eye break</u> which consists of focusing on something in the distance, or a <u>short aerobic workout</u>. Taking a short break every hour gives him the energy he needs to sustain focus for longer periods of time.

What other factors influence my focus-over-time abilities?

Give examples.

The ability to <u>sustain focus depends</u> on both your ① <u>motivation</u> and on the ② <u>task</u>. Concentration spans vary according to people's motivation to do the task. Those who are <u>highly motivated may maintain focus for hours</u> at a time. Learning to motivate yourself thus becomes an important ability, enabling you to increase your concentration span. Concentration spans also vary according to the task. If you are <u>working at the computer</u>, you may <u>pay attention for three hours</u>, yet a <u>difficult physics textbook</u> may only keep your <u>full attention for five minutes</u>. Some of my students reported better concentration in difficult material because the text was challenging, they couldn't let their minds wander at all. One goal of this book is to increase your amount of sustained concentration by increasing your motivation and learning how to concentrate in a variety of tasks.

Focusing at Will

Explain the signs of a person who cannot "Focus at Will."

A second concentration skill is the <u>ability to "focus at will" rather than being at the mercy of interest</u> or a good <u>mood</u>. Jennifer is a college junior who gets good grades but suffers from a series of <u>stress-related illnesses</u>. She needs advice about how to concentrate on a school paper when it is assigned rather than <u>waiting to write</u> it the <u>night before it is due</u>. She <u>isn't</u> in the <u>right mood to write</u> on Monday, Tuesday, or Wednesday, and has to stay up all Thursday night in order to turn the paper in on Friday. Are you like Jennifer?

Chapter 3 for more information about summary questions or statements.)

Here is an example of a summary question based on the information in the "Art of Concentration" excerpt:

Summary Question: Name the three mental abilities necessary for concentration and tell how they affect each other.

By using the physical and mental process of actively reading and marking a textbook, you are reading critically rather than reading passively. The reader who uses read-and-mark will discover that this method has many advantages:

- By deriving questions from the answers that are already there (i.e., the text itself), you keep your mind actively on your reading and avoid daydreaming.
- By writing the questions and marking key words, you are using sensory learning, engaging your senses of sight and touch in the process of reading and learning.
- By marking, you are actively creating your own study guide.
- By reading and marking, you may spare yourself having to reread all of the material when you review.

- By using this method, you can easily take a break at any point instead of doing the entire reading at one sitting. If you have marked your text and written questions, it is easy to find your place to continue when you return to the assignment.

When you have finished this step, you have provided yourself with an easy way to review your material.

An Alternative: Using Summary Paper

If you have borrowed a book or magazine or are using one from the library, of course you should not write in it. However, you can still use the read-and-mark step of STUDY-READ. Also, some people feel that they learn better when they write down information themselves rather than marking a textbook. In either case, you can follow the STUDY-READ method, but instead of marking the textbook, use your summary paper just as if you were taking notes.

On your summary paper, first title the page with the subject of the reading assignment and any other pertinent information you might need, such as the title of the book, the author(s), the publication date, the edition, and so on. You need to title only the first page of a group of notebook pages that are all from the same source. See the following example:

Ch. 4 (pp. 64–84), "Growth and Diversity, 1720–1770," in *A People & a Nation: A History of the US.* Brief, 4th ed. Vol. A, by Mary Beth Norton, et al., pub. Houghton Mifflin (Boston), 1996.	
Write your	Write the
questions	key-word answers
in the three-inch margin.	in the five-inch column.

Then, after previewing the assignment, as you read each paragraph or section, write your questions in the three-inch margin, and write your key-word answers in the five-inch column. You should include the page number(s) for each key-word answer in case you need to go back to your source later for more information.

Step Three: ⬅━━ **REVIEW BY RECITING**

Once you have finished reading and marking the chapter assigned, you are ready to complete the learning process by transferring the information into your long-term memory. This third step in STUDY-READ is called *review by reciting*. As the arrow in the heading above indicates, you will be going back to the questions in your text and reciting the marked information. As you review, you will be able to determine what you know and what you need to review in more depth. This step allows your long-term memory to retain the valuable answers you have marked in step 2. Your recitation should be done aloud so that you use sensory learning—engaging your sense of hearing, along with your senses of sight and touch.

To accomplish this last step, review by reciting, return to the beginning of the chapter, and cover the text with a piece of paper or gently fold the page over to cover everything except your questions. Look at the questions you have written in the margins and recite the answers aloud, in your own words. Do this as soon as you finish reading and marking the chapter, while the answers are still fresh in your mind. If you mark your chapter without the follow-up recitation, you are likely to *think* you know the answers, but when you have to take a test, you may not *remember* the information.

Next, check the accuracy and thoroughness of your recited answer by looking at the key words or phrases you marked. If you are unable to answer your own question, then you need to look at the answer once more and recite aloud again, or even do this several times. This review-by-reciting step should be done as often as necessary until you feel confident that you know all the material.

STUDY-READING CLASS HANDOUTS

Many professors provide handouts either in class or on their web sites that give additional information about a particular topic being discussed in class. The instructors consider these handouts essential extensions of their textbooks. However, many students treat these handouts as if they are unimportant—they file away in their notebooks and may not look at them again. Students may visit the web sites, but they may fail to print a hard copy of the information.

Information on a handout typically gives an outline or overview of a certain topic, or it may go into greater depth and detail than the textbook itself. Sometimes handouts contain diagrams, maps, charts, or other visual aids. In any case, once you receive a handout, instructors usually feel that they have "covered" the topic well. It is then up to you to deal seriously with that printed information.

When the teacher discusses the handout in class, use your active listening skills. Active listening always requires careful note taking: Take as many notes as possible using summary paper.

You should consider class handouts and web-site information as valuable as your textbook or lecture notes. Apply the STUDY-READ method to reading all class handouts. You may do so by using the following guidelines or procedures :

Preview

If the instructor explained the handout in class, that explanation serves as your preview. If the instructor gave you the handout without an explanation, you must do a preview of the handout yourself by looking over titles, major headings, nonverbal information, captions or labels, or first sentences.

Read-and-Mark

After class, in order to read and mark the information on the handout, you have a choice of two methods depending upon how much space there is to write on the handout or how much detailed information the handout contains.

Method 1: If the handout has wide margins and plenty of white space to write directly on the handout *and* the information is not overly-detailed, then highlight the major ideas and supporting details and write questions in the margins of the handout. This is the same approach that you would use for marking a textbook page.

Method 2: If you have little space to write on the handout, *or* if the information is so complex and detailed that common sense tells you that you need more room to deal with the handout, then use summary paper to do the read-and-mark step.

When using summary paper, follow these steps:

a. Put summary paper next to the handout in your binder as in the following illustration.

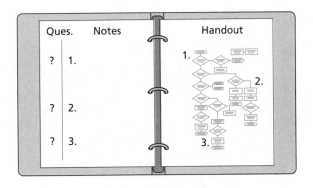

Figure 1: Open Three-Ring Binder

    b. If your handout is printed on the front side of the paper, then you would actually take notes on the back side of your notebook paper (see Fig. 1).

    c. If your handout is printed on both sides of the paper, then you would take notes on the back side, then the front side of two pieces of notebook paper (see Fig. 2).

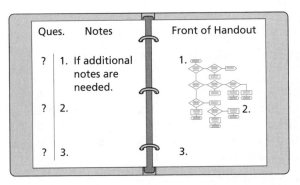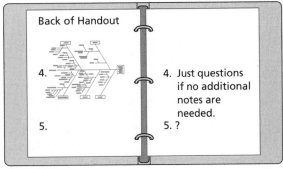

Figure 2: Back-to-Back Pages in Open Three-Ring Binder

    Remember to keep notes and questions opposite each other, even if that means skipping lines on the notebook paper.

Review by Reciting

In order to place information into your long-term memory, cover the information on the handout, ask yourself your questions, and recite the answers until you know them.

Exercise 5-C

Directions: Now that you are familiar with STUDY-READ, go back to the beginning of Chapter 5 and write questions in the margins (use a pencil at first), then highlight or underline key words in each paragraph or section. Continue using STUDY-READ as you read your texts. (Feel free to return to previous reading assignments to read and mark your texts so that you can review by reciting.)

Creatively Thinking Together

After you have completed Exercise 5-C, compare your questions in the margins and your highlighting with those of other members of your group. Help each other to improve questions or highlighting as needed. Consider some of the following questions when you give feedback to members of your group:

- Does the highlighted information actually answer the question in the margin? If not, how can the question be reworded?

- Does every bold-faced section have at least one question and highlighting?

- Has any information been overlooked that should have been marked with a question and highlighting?

- Has too much information been highlighted?

STUDY-READ IN VARIOUS DISCIPLINES

The STUDY-READ method is the most effective way to read your textbooks. As a critical reader and thinker using STUDY-READ, your goal must be to go well beyond factual reading. You are reading in order to gather, analyze, synthesize, and apply information to your course work, your daily life, your career, and your future.

Once you have mastered the basic steps of STUDY-READ, you can begin to adapt the system to books or assignments that do not follow the *typical* textbook format. Following are some suggestions for adjusting the method when you are studying courses in literature, the humanities, mathematics, and the sciences.

Reading Literature

When you are taking literature courses in college, you will be expected to read different genres, such as poems, novels, short stories, or dramas, not just for enjoyment, but also to think critically about the literary work, to participate in discussions about the selection, and to write about various aspects of it.

Reading Novels, Short Stories, and Drama   Novels, short stories, and drama are written in prose usually without the help of headings or subheadings. Thus, you have to adjust your previewing to just a few items instead of previewing the whole selection. Besides, most people certainly do not want to know the end of a story or play before they read it!

First, as part of your preview, you should read the introduction to the story or information about the author, if these are included. Many times your instructor will not tell you to read this information, but will expect you to read and be familiar with it so that you can relate it to the selection.

Second, if study questions are given at the end of the story, read all of them *before* you begin reading the assignment. It is a good idea to put a bookmark at the place where the questions appear. Because study questions in literary anthologies are usually sequential, keep the first question in mind as you begin to read. When you find the answer to that question, write in the margin a question similar to the question at the end of the story, and then highlight the key words that answer it. Also, as a cross-reference, write the page number(s) of where you found the answer next to the listed question at the end of the story. Read the second question and continue reading the story to find the answer, and so on.

If your instructor gives you study questions, you should follow a similar process. Write your own questions in the margins and highlight key-word answers. Then write page numbers next to your study questions and jot down key words on that piece of paper.

Once you have previewed, you are ready to read and mark the literary piece. The read-and-mark step will be used to identify important aspects of the work, such as ideas relating to the theme, traits of the major characters, significance of events, and so on. You most likely will discuss the assignment in class and write about characters, theme, and setting. Your marginal questions should include references to these major aspects

of literature. Finally, writing *why* questions in the margins is very important. You will need to know more than just the plot; you will need to interpret why events are happening and why characters do what they do.

As you are reading, you may be confused about what happened in the story or be unable to explain why a character makes a certain statement or acts in an unusual way. Jot questions about aspects you don't understand on another piece of paper (noting the page numbers). Then bring these questions to class to get them answered during class discussion. If you have questions, other students most likely will, too, and if you do not write your questions down, you may not remember what they are.

The last step in STUDY-READ, review by reciting, also differs from most textbook chapter recitations. For quizzes, essay questions, discussions in class, and critical analysis or essay writing, you will have to know the various aspects and details of the literary work. Your review by reciting should include answers to study questions and knowledge of names and traits of characters, development of plot, theme, setting, and any other aspects of the story that are important.

Furthermore, each genre or type of literature has its own vocabulary. You need to learn these terms and definitions so that you can recognize and understand them as you read the assigned selections. If you are using an anthology in the course, it will generally have a glossary of literary terms at the end of the book, to which you can and should refer for the terms and their definitions.

Reading Poetry

Because the format in which a poem usually appears on a page differs from that of prose, some people think it should be read line by line. On occasion, this method of reading might work, but rather than reading

line by line, you should concentrate on reading a poem aloud, *sentence by sentence*, using the *punctuation* as a guide indicating when to pause or stop. In addition, poetry is usually much more condensed in meaning than prose, so you need to read a poem several times and think about the significance of almost every word.

As mentioned in the preview step of the discussion on reading fiction and drama, be sure to read any explanatory information about the poet and the poem, questions at the end, and any footnotes. Also, keep a dictionary handy to look up unfamiliar words or references. Poets often use allusions, which are references to other works of literature, mythology, history, or the Bible. You may even need to go to the library to use a dictionary of mythology or a dictionary of the Bible to clarify some meanings if the text does not have footnotes explaining unfamiliar references.

Read the following untitled poem by Emily Dickinson, in which she praises the delight and benefits of reading. Look up any unfamiliar words in your dictionary.

> There is no frigate like a book
>   To take us lands away,
> Nor any coursers like a page
>   Of prancing poetry:
> This traverse may the poorest take
>   Without oppress of toll:
> How fragile is the chariot
>   That bears the human soul!

Anyone who tries to read Emily Dickinson's poem line by line may not be able to understand it. The poem, like most poems, is packed with images and verbal pictures. You need to read the poem aloud more than once, grouping the words and phrases according to punctuation, not according to lines, and replacing unfamiliar words with familiar ones. Sometimes, too, it is necessary to change the word order to clarify the meaning. Here is Emily Dickinson's poem transcribed into prose:

> There is no ship [frigate] that can take us to foreign places the way a book can (because we can go anywhere in time or space or distance by reading), nor any horse [courser] fast enough to match the pace and rhythm [prancing] of a poem.
>
> This (ability to read books and poems) is a road or a way to travel [traverse] that even people without money [the poorest] can take because they do not have to worry [without oppress] about paying a toll.
>
> How delicate [fragile] is the vehicle or body [chariot] that either holds, contains, or gives birth to [bears] a person's soul!

In the first six lines, Emily Dickinson is explaining the joys of reading prose and poetry, using several images of, and comparisons or contrasts to, traveling—frigate, courser, and paying tolls. The last two lines of the poem are the most complex because the verb *bear* has so many possible meanings and the meaning goes beyond the simple act of reading a book.

You might think of reading a poem as being similar to working a jigsaw puzzle: All the pieces are there; you just have to fit them together properly. Your marginal questions for the read-and-mark step will relate both to the meaning of the poem and to the poetic techniques that are used. Reading poems can be just as enjoyable as reading prose if you use your critical-thinking skills and your knowledge of *how* to read a poem to get meaning out of it.

Reading in the Humanities

STUDY-READ, as explained earlier, works well in subjects like history, psychology, and sociology because the textbooks for these courses are usually easy to mark. However, instructors in these subjects often assign outside reading, such as books, biographies, or articles to supplement or even to replace a text. These readings, most likely, will not follow the typical textbook format. In particular, they may not have introductions, headings, and summaries.

In approaching these outside readings, first make sure you understand the instructor's reason for assigning them. For example, in a history course, you may be assigned a biography or novel to get some background on the historical period you are studying. If that is the case, you may not need to read in great detail because you just want to get the

general idea. On the other hand, if you are going to be tested on the information, ask your instructor what kinds of information you need to know. The way you read and mark will be very different depending upon your goals. If you need to learn specific dates and names, you will have to take careful notes and write questions about as many facts and details as you can. If you just need to learn background information or get an overview of the topic, you will be looking for and writing questions relating to major ideas and trends. If the sources are library books or articles on reserve, you will need to do your read-and-mark step on summary paper.

Reading Mathematics

STUDY-READ should certainly be used for a math text, but some special considerations are necessary for math reading. Math is much more than computation, the simple act of solving problems. It is a language whose symbols must be understood. Learning the concepts and principles behind the formulas and techniques is equally important. There is a very big difference between just reading a mathematical expression or statement and actually understanding what it means. You need to visualize the technique and verbalize the steps required to solve a problem. For example, if you have to find the distance traveled at a certain rate of speed, the mathematical statement or formula is $d = rt$. However, knowing the formula is helpful only if you know what the symbols in the formula mean. In this case, the formula means "*d*istance is equal to *r*ate times *t*ime." So if a train travels at a rate of 90 miles per hour for 6 hours, you need to multiply the rate (90 miles) by the time (6 hours), or d = 90 x 6, which is 540 miles. The more complex formulas become, the more important it is that you focus on the *meaning* of the formula instead of just being able to repeat it.

Usually math teachers assign only one section of a chapter at a time. Because math courses are organized in a sequential way, with one concept leading to the next, it is very important that you understand each section before you go on to the next. In addition, you should always review the previous section or sections right before you preview the current assignment.

Your preview in math will be much more extensive than in other courses. In your preview, read the boldface print and new terms. But, in addition, quickly read the paragraphs of explanation the first time you actually read through the new section. Always read the introduction and summary during your preview. You may not understand everything, but be sure you read everything *before* you go to class.

In class, when the instructor works problems on the board, the explanations may seem crystal clear at the time, but when you get home, that clarity may fade unless you have good notes. So take *lots* of notes. Good notes include not just the problems copied from the board but, more importantly, the explanations, the reasons, and the logic behind them. So write down as much as possible of the instructor's information.

You have read each section quickly during your preview; now you are ready to read and mark in depth. When you perform the second step in STUDY-READ, be prepared to read a section several times. Then, when you read and mark, concentrate on the explanatory information, asking yourself questions concerning definitions of terms and the main concepts, principles, or properties. This can be done in the text or on summary paper. Since you have already taken good class notes, you can refer to them as you read your text. Your goals as a critical thinker are to understand the underlying concepts and principles and to follow the appropriate steps, not just to get the correct answer for an individual problem.

Most math chapters contain many problems for students to solve. Work all the problems assigned, using your marked text to help you understand the new concept. If you are to select the problems yourself, be sure to do a sampling of problems throughout the section and not just the first several problems. If you have time to do only a few problems, be sure to include application as well as computational problems. Really understanding a few well-selected problems is more valuable than mechanically working through many problems just to arrive at the correct

answers given at the back of the textbook. Remember, your goal is to *understand the concepts*, not merely to get correct answers to specific problems. Try to reason through the examples so that you understand the elements in the problem. As you come across new terms, add them to your vocabulary.

Sometimes students who otherwise understand mathematical concepts are a bit puzzled by the reading of a word problem. When you are trying to solve a word problem, you need to be concerned with organizing the information in a way that allows you to form a plan for solving the problem. Although there is no one way to solve all word problems, the following four steps provide a method for reading a problem critically and then working through it.

1. *Read.* Analyze the problem until you understand the situation and identify the question(s) you are being asked to answer.
2. *Organize.* Identify the knowns and unknowns. Using actual words, write out the relationships in the problem. Look up any unfamiliar mathematical terms or formulas needed to solve the problem. Make a chart, diagram, or picture if it will help you visualize your task.
3. *Model.* Form a mathematical model for the problem. When beginning word problems, this usually consists of translating the words into an algebraic statement such as an equation. To form the model, you must define mathematical vocabulary such as variables and expressions to represent words in the problem.
4. *Solve.* Find the solution to the mathematical model, and use it to answer the question in the word problem. Check the reasonableness of your answer, and state it in an English, not a mathematical, sentence.

The following example illustrates how to use these guidelines: A student's grades on three tests are 82, 94, and 75. What must the student score on the fourth test so that the average of the four tests comes out to 83?

First, you *read* the problem and learn that you are being asked to find the score on the fourth test. Second, you *organize* your facts. You already know the scores on the first three tests, and you know that you want the average of all four tests to be 83. You need to know how to find the average of four numbers. You may have to look in your textbook or notes to find the correct steps to take in order to make your model. Third, you can then form a *model* by defining a mathematical symbol, such as x, to represent the score on the fourth test. To find the average of four numbers, you add them up and divide by 4. You make a model of the needed relationship of "the average of the four tests is 83" with these mathematical symbols and numbers:

$$\frac{82 + 94 + 75 + x}{4} = 83$$

Finally, you need to use your knowledge of algebra to solve this equation. You find that $x = 81$. Since x represents the score on the fourth test, you can answer the question after checking that your result is reasonable. Your statement of the answer is, "The student must score 81 on the fourth test to get an average of 83 on all four tests." Following these four steps will allow you to reach the solution for most word problems.

In the review-by-reciting step of STUDY-READ in math, you should review groups of similar problems you have worked and recite specifically *how* to do each step. To be sure you know how to work each type of problem, make up your own examples. It is imperative that you review both your notes and the chapter sections continually until you are certain that you understand the concepts and know the technical terms.

Reading in the Sciences

Reading science textbook assignments is very similar to reading math texts. Both require careful and detailed problem-solving skills as well as analytical and critical reading. Previewing the text is especially important because it gives you background information, which allows you to read the text with an understanding of how each detail fits into the whole structure of the chapter. Pay particular attention to nonverbal materials. The diagrams, graphs, charts, and pictures found in all science texts illustrate details of processes, formulas, or reactions.

After the preview step, you are ready to read-and-mark, remembering that you must account for all diagrams, as well as new terms and the information in the paragraphs. In order to read diagrams in science, you must follow several steps. First, to get an overall idea of what the diagram is illustrating, read the general description in the text. An example of a scientific diagram, entitled "Figure 2.4" (Mader 20), is provided on page 132. In this diagram, the general description is found below the drawings: "Ionic Reactions: Gain/Lose Electrons." As you read the description, identify the special terms, which in this case are *ions* and *ionic reaction.* If these terms are not in your vocabulary at this time, you may need to take notes or create 3 x 5 cards.

After reading the general description, carefully read the information in the specific description, found in this illustration at the top of the page. Read this description step by step. As you read, follow the steps of the diagram, matching the written words with the visual picture. Try to visualize what is happening, making sure you understand how one step leads to or is related to the next. Continue with this procedure until you reach the last step of the process. Depending on the complexity of the material, you may have to repeat these steps until you clearly grasp the meaning of the diagram.

Finally, the best way to make sure you understand the concept depicted in the diagram is to make your own. As you make your diagram, explain the process aloud. Use your diagram to study the process, always visualizing what is occurring as well as reciting the steps.

In science textbooks, as you read and mark, another focus will be to learn the terminology and formulas. It is essential that you look for new terms and definitions as you read and that you highlight them and use a system to keep track of them (see Chapter 3).

When reading the information in the paragraphs, you should read-and-mark only one paragraph at a time, rather than a section, because each paragraph is packed with information. In fact, the information is so dense that you cannot depend on key words because most words are key words. Thus, if you mark the text too quickly, you will tend to mark everything. To avoid overmarking the text, read each paragraph until you understand it. Try paraphrasing what has been said or, better yet, writing it in your own words. You will need to mark in the text and write information on a separate notebook page or the back side of your class notes. Because the sciences are so precise and the white space in the text

Figure 2.4

Ionic reactions. **a.** When the neutral atom sodium (Na) becomes an ion, it loses an electron. It then has 8 electrons in the outer shell. The sodium ion (Na⁺) has a positive charge because it has one more proton than it has electrons. **b.** When the neutral atom chlorine (Cl) becomes an ion, it receives an electron. It then has 8 electrons in the outer shell. The chloride ion (Cl⁻) has a negative charge because it has one less proton than it has electrons. **c.** When sodium reacts with chlorine, sodium gives an electron to chlorine, and sodium chloride (Na⁺Cl⁻) results. The 2 ions are held together by their opposite charge in an ionic bond.

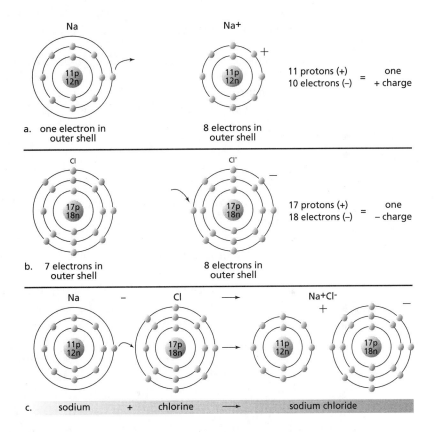

Ionic Reactions: Gain/Lose Electrons

In one type of reaction, atoms give up or take on electrons in order to achieve a completed outer shell. Such atoms, which thereafter carry a charge, are called **ions**, and the reaction is called an **ionic reaction**. In ionic reactions, atoms lose or gain electrons to produce a molecule that contains ions in a fixed ratio to one another. For example, figure 2.4 depicts a reaction between a sodium (Na) and chlorine (Cl), in which chlorine takes an electron from sodium. The resulting ions in sodium chloride (Na⁺Cl⁻) have 8 electrons each in the outer shell. Notice that when sodium gives up an electron, the second shell, with 8 electrons, becomes the outer shell.

is usually inadequate for all the information you need to learn, you should employ both methods simultaneously—highlighting pages in the text and writing questions and answers separately on paper. Be sure you put the textbook page numbers on the pages of your notes. The textbook marking can be used for major questions and highlighted answers. In addition, the separate notebook page or the back side of your class notes can be used for more detailed questions and answers and your own illustrations.

The following paragraph from a biology book illustrates how packed full of information a science textbook can be.

CHLOROPLASTS: WHERE IT HAPPENS

The interior of a chloroplast contains stacks of membranous compartments called grana (sing. **granum**). The individual flattened sacs within each granum are called **thylakoids.** The green pigment **chlorophyll** is found within the membrane of the thylakoids, and it is here that solar energy is captured. Surrounding the grana is a fluid-filled space called the stroma. The **stroma** contains enzymes that participate in photosynthesis. (Mader 84)

As you read and mark this paragraph, you will realize how full of information it is. Your questions in the margin might be a pair of factual ones ("What is inside chloroplasts?" "What does each of these structures do?"), or you might choose to write a higher-level question ("Describe the structural arrangement of granum, thylakoids, chlorophyll, and stroma within a chloroplast."). With a paragraph like this one, you could easily fill the margin with questions and highlight almost every word! Thus, you would be wise to supplement text notations by using summary paper—either a separate notebook page or the back side of your class notes—so that you have room to write your questions and answers.

Additionally, your instructor will hold you accountable for all the terms. Whether you use 3 x 5 cards, the back side of your notes, or your own personal glossary, you will have to learn these terms. For example, the "Chloroplasts" paragraph includes the following words that a student in the course should know how to define and spell: chloroplast, granum (pl. grana), thylakoids, chlorophyll, stroma, and photosynthesis.

In the read-and-mark step, in addition to writing questions and identifying technical terms, you should draw your own representation of the structure you are reading about—in this case, the inside of the chloroplasts. The drawing does not have to be perfect, nor do you have to be an artist: Just draw a picture (lines, stick figures, or whatever) of how you visualize the structure. Here is an example of what your drawing might look like.

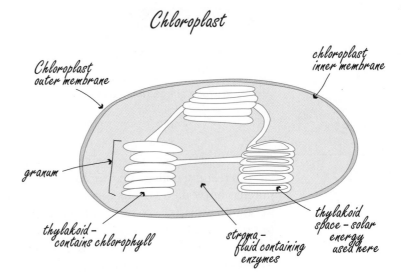

Chloroplast

Chloroplast outer membrane

chloroplast inner membrane

granum

thylakoid – contains chlorophyll

stroma – fluid containing enzymes

thylakoid space – solar energy used here

As you read any chapter in a science text, look for relationships such as cause and effect, comparisons and contrasts, processes, cyclic activity, patterns, or groupings. When you find such relationships, your questions in the margins or on summary paper might be phrased to show how structure relates to function, temperature to state of matter, or pressure to volume. Whenever you can, draw pictures showing these relationships and practice visualizing them in your mind. Your picture could even be a chart that would allow you to see similarities and differences or relationships in time or cause and effect (see Chapter 9 for examples).

In both the read-and-mark stage and the review-by-reciting stage, break the task into manageable segments. Do not try to overload your brain with too much material at one time. Also, because of the density of the information, you will want to review frequently by reciting manageable portions of the chapter until you have mastered the material. As in math, much of what you learn in the sciences is cumulative. You will be expected to understand the information so well that you can confidently apply it to the next process you are learning. You need to master one concept before you go on to the next, so review of previous material is a must.

Exercise 5-D

Directions: Begin using STUDY-READ in all your classes.

WEB SITE INFORMATION

For more information about studying humanities, mathmatics, social and natural sciences, and foreign languages visit our web site:

<http://college.hmco.com/success/>

Summary

In this chapter, you focused on the power of reading, specifically as it relates to reading college textbooks. Each quarter or semester, shortly after purchasing your textbooks, you should thoroughly examine each textbook to familiarize yourself with the contents of each course and the layout of each textbook. This quick survey will give you an overview of the contents, the organization of the information, and the additional resources each textbook contains.

For reading assignments, you can master your textbook chapters by using the STUDY-READ method. This method of reading and studying a textbook involves three steps: preview, read-and-mark, and review by reciting. STUDY-READ is useful for all college textbook reading assignments, as well as for class handouts and web site information. Some adaptations may be necessary in specific subjects, such as literature, the humanities, math, and science. By using this three-step method, you will be reading critically, understanding what you read as you go along, creating your own study guide, and storing information in your long-term memory.

List of Terms

STUDY-READ	previewing or surveying	review by reciting
sensory learning	read-and-mark	non-verbal
examining a textbook		information

In this box, write your summary question or statement for this chapter.

6 The Power of Critical Thinking

Like all people, your understanding of the world is based on your experiences. To illustrate how experience plays a large part in our basic knowledge, consider this old, well-known Hindu fable titled "The Blind Men and the Elephant":

> Six men of India, blind from birth, were led to an elephant to "see" what an elephant looks like. The first blind man accidentally ran into the elephant's side and concluded the elephant was like a solid wall. The second blind man, carefully reaching out his hand, touched an ivory tusk and decided that certainly an elephant was most like a spear. The third blind man, with both hands outstretched, felt the trunk of the elephant and resolved that obviously this elephant was mostly like a snake. The fourth blind man, grabbing a solid bumpy knee of the elephant, concluded that the elephant was like the trunk of a tree. The fifth blind man, reaching out, encountered one of the elephant's large ears and determined that this animal called an elephant must be very much like a fan. The sixth blind man reached out and grasped the elephant's swishing tail and knew instinctively that this animal was very much like a rope.

Like all fables or folk tales, this story of the six blind men was told to make a point: that our perceptions are sometimes limited, so we must think *beyond the obvious*. Critical thinking can help us do this. Critical thinking is a process that enables us to see separate parts, as the blind men did, but more importantly *to relate those parts, interpret what is found, re-assemble ideas into a new whole, and make a judgment or draw a conclusion.*

Critical thinking is the process of thoughtfully and deliberately gathering, analyzing, and evaluating information. Critical thinkers are not born; they are made.

WHY IS CRITICAL THINKING SO IMPORTANT?

By now you might be saying, "Most people are able to get by okay in their daily lives without mastering critical thinking, aren't they?" Yes, probably so. However, by asking such a question, you are revealing that critical thinkers like yourself want more out of life than just to "get by."

Critical thinking can help you to: (1) gain control over your life; (2) make sound judgments; (3) activate your creativity. The first, and perhaps most basic, reason to foster your critical-thinking skills is to know that you can withstand difficulties by *thinking through them*, not running or hiding from them. Thus, you need to be able to evaluate what you hear, read, or see through skillful attention to actual evidence and implied messages. In other words, you need to know how to "read" between the lines. You can then control your life better, knowing that you have weighed the facts and made appropriate decisions.

A second reason to cultivate your critical-thinking skills is that it allows you to make sound judgments. A *judgment* is an opinion that is reached after considering relevant facts. On a daily basis, you are expected to make many important judgments about products and people. Here are some examples of day-to-day situations calling for informed judgments:

- You must judge the worth of a product in order to decide whether or not to buy it.
- You must read persuasive arguments and determine whether you agree or disagree with the writer.
- You must judge the behaviors of others to decide if you will join them or if you will challenge them because their actions are harmful or dangerous.
- You must judge what is right and wrong by your conscience and values.
- You must know when to conform and go along with the crowd or when to be an individual and be yourself.
- You must know how to solve problems that may significantly impact your goals and your future (see Chapter 2).

A third reason to nurture critical thinking is that it stimulates your creativity. Maybe you think of yourself as a creative person, maybe not. Creativity is not only possible, but necessary for everyone. *Creativity* is the ability to put ideas together in a unique way. It often involves playing with an idea until you hit upon the perfect discovery. After pondering a problem, when you finally reach the point of saying, "Yes!" or "Aha, this is it!! This is the answer I've been looking for!" Then you know the satisfaction of a creative moment.

HOW TO APPROACH CRITICAL THINKING

To become a critical thinker, you should begin with an awareness of your own background and biases. *Bias* is the mental tendency to lean in one direction or to favor one side over another. Personal biases can keep you from making fair, impartial decisions. Our biases stem from our backgrounds—where we live, what we know, how much money we have, what our culture is, what our religious beliefs are, and everything else that makes us who we are.

Everyone has biases; it's only natural. Problems occur, however, when you believe, because of your biases, that you are always right, that your way of thinking or doing is the only way or the best way for everyone in every circumstance. Think of an instance when you hear a person give

an opinion similar to yours. You readily agree with that person. Why? Because the person's information and logic agree with your own opinions
and biases. On the other hand, when a person states something you disagree with or are unfamiliar with, you might tend to view that opinion as
wrong or useless because it challenges your personal biases. In fact, you
may totally shut down and not even listen to the argument.

Recognizing your own biases should help you understand that
everyone else has biases, too. Thus, people who come from different
backgrounds or cultures are going to have different opinions or beliefs.
Several different opinions may all have merit, and, as you become more
aware of these differences, you will learn to respect more fully others'
opinions and ideas. For example, in the well-publicized shootings at several high schools across the United States, everyone thought he or she
knew *the* reason why these shootings occurred. Some blamed it on television violence, others on video games; some on parents, others on the
media; some on ineffective gun control laws, others on the schools
themselves; and some blamed it solely on the social rejection felt by the
shooters themselves. In reality, no one cause is *the* answer to such
tragedies because there are numerous causes and effects for complex situations. By listening to others' opinions and filtering through their natural biases, you can develop a broader knowledge base and a deeper
understanding of all aspects related to an issue.

As a critical thinker who recognizes your own and others' biases,
you learn to welcome new ideas. This open-mindedness may not always
be easy to achieve, because sometimes it means that you need to change
the way you think. It is human nature to resist change, even when that
change could have positive results. However, in order to grow intellec-
tually, you must be willing to change your ideas and approaches when
better ones come along. For example, you may have arrived at college
thinking that you have all the study skills you need to succeed. Then you
discover that some of your methods are not as effective as you had hoped
they would be. Instead of rejecting new approaches to learning, you
should try to be receptive to them. New techniques could broaden, en-
rich, and add to your own knowledge and success.

UNDERSTANDING COMMON FALLACIES

In addition to biases, you should also be aware of fallacies in your own
and others' thinking. *Fallacies* are mistakes in thinking that produce incorrect conclusions. Logical fallacies occur in writing as well as in speech,

and they are direct enemies to critical thinking. If a statement contains a logical fallacy, it may seem reasonable at first, but upon reflection, it does not make sense. Following are some of the most common fallacies.

Hasty Generalization   A *hasty generalization* occurs when someone makes a general statement without enough evidence to back it up.

> **Example:** "Our local college must be the best college in the state because almost 60 percent of my high school graduating class is enrolled here."

> **Reason:** There is not enough evidence to prove that this college is the best. For example, it might be the closest and/or have the lowest tuition.

A common type of hasty generalization is stereotyping. *Stereotyping* occurs when a person makes a broad generalization about a religious, political, racial, ethnic, or other group of people.

> **Example:** "That guy in my computer class must be a biker. He just looks the part."

> **Reason:** The student in question is a burly man with a ponytail and scraggly beard, wearing a black leather jacket and boots. The speaker in this example sees this person and immediately classifies him as somebody who "typically" rides a motorcycle. However, this man should be seen first and foremost as an individual. Furthermore, all kinds of people with different hair styles and dressed in a variety of ways ride motorcycles.

Either/or Fallacy   The *either/or fallacy* states that there are only two possibilities when, in fact, several options could exist.

> **Example:** "My program is a two-year program, so I must complete it in two years or quit school."

> **Reason:** Dropping out of school or going through the program nonstop are not the only choices. A student could, for instance, go part-time and take three or more years to complete the program.

Attacking the Person   A *personal attack* fallacy ignores the issue and criticizes the person or people involved in the issue.

> **Example:** "My psychology teacher should not be teaching this course because I heard that her son is serving time in a juvenile detention center."

> **Reason:** Even if this rumor is true, the son's behavior has no bearing on whether or not the professor is an effective psychology teacher.

Circular Reasoning   In *circular reasoning,* a person tries to prove a point by repeating the same idea in different words. This fallacy is also called *begging the question.*

> **Example:** "Whenever I try to study, my little brother Dante is annoying because he is a nuisance."

> **Reason:** The words "annoying" and "nuisance" basically have the same meaning and do not explain why Dante is a pest.

Red Herring   A *red herring* fallacy means talking about something that really has nothing to do with the issue. (This hunting term comes from the ploy of dragging a red herring across the trail to distract hounds from the scent of a fox or other animal.) This fallacy is also called *ignoring the issue.*

> **Example:** "I shouldn't be required to take calculus. The calculus professor is a foreigner."

> **Reason:** Where the professor was born has nothing to do with why calculus is required or with the teacher's qualifications.

False Comparisons   A *false comparison* tries to show similarities between two items or ideas that are more unlike than they are alike.

> **Example:** "Letting your children watch violent television programs is like putting guns in their hands."

> **Reason:** Neither watching violence on television nor holding guns is healthy for children, but the two actions are very different.

False Cause   When using a *false cause* fallacy, a person believes that because one event follows the other, the first caused the second. Superstitions are often based on false cause. For example, some people believe that a broken mirror will cause seven years' bad luck.

> **Example:** "I never should have sold my 20 shares of IBM. Ever since I did, the value of IBM stock has gone up steadily."

> **Reason:** The fact that this person sold a small amount of stock is not going to affect IBM's stock value one way or another.

If you are aware of and understand these common fallacies in thinking, then you recognize how these fallacies are opposed to logic and critical thinking. This knowledge will guide you in making reasonable evaluations and decisions about important issues in your life.

Exercise 6-A

Directions: Read the following sentences and name the logical fallacy; then explain why the statement is illogical.

1. If you work hard in college, you will certainly get good grades.

   Fallacy: _____

   Reason: _____

   _____

2. Unless schools provide a very strict code of discipline, no one will be able to learn anything.

   Fallacy: _____

   Reason: _____

   _____

3. Smoking is not good for your body because it is bad for your health.

   Fallacy: _____

   Reason: _____

   _____

4. We should not read George Bernard Shaw's plays. Everyone knows he was homosexual.

   Fallacy: _____

   Reason: _____

   _____

(continued on the next page)

Exercise 6-A (continued)

5. I don't know why anyone should be worried about saving the manatee when we really should be concerned about recycling.

Fallacy: _____

Reason: _____

_____

6. Ever since we put satellites in space, we have had more rainfall in the United States. I think we should take them all down so the weather can get back to normal.

Fallacy: _____

Reason: _____

_____

7. Driving at 100 miles per hour is just like gambling $100.00 in Las Vegas—you are taking risks in both cases, but risks can be thrilling.

Fallacy: _____

Reason: _____

_____

RECOGNIZING PROPAGANDA AS USED IN ADVERTISEMENTS

In the preceding paragraphs, you learned how logical fallacies can distract you, making it difficult to separate genuine reasons from illogical reasons. In this section, you will discover that sometimes advertisers also try to distract you in different ways. Instead of telling you the whole truth, some advertisers try to deceive you by using propaganda techniques.

Propaganda techniques are deliberate attempts to convince people of something by using emotional appeals rather than logic and objective facts. Advertisers are not the only group who use propaganda techniques; propaganda is also used by some special interest groups and by politicians. However, by recognizing and understanding propaganda techniques in advertising, you should be able to evaluate messages by these other groups and individuals as well.

Advertisements are part of our daily lives. They appear everywhere—on television, on the radio, on billboards, in newspapers and magazines, and on the Internet. The following examples, using made-up products and companies, demonstrate several well-known propaganda techniques.

Bandwagon or Everyone's Buying It   The propaganda technique called *bandwagon* basically says that everybody else likes and wants this product, so you should want it, too.

> **Example:** "More than 20 million people are wearing Stylex watches. Shouldn't you?"

Testimonials   A *testimonial* uses a famous person to endorse a product. Because you admire this person, you are supposed to want to buy the product.

> **Example:** "Sammy Sosa says, 'Start each day with Cubby Crisp cereal.'"

Plain Folks   In the *plain folks* technique, an ordinary person—just like you—says this is a good product. Because you, too, are just a plain, ordinary person, you are expected to identify with and trust the ordinary person's advice.

> **Example:** "Just like you, I'm a college student. I have a family, a part-time job, a term paper due, and two tests coming up. So what do I take for my headache? X-Stress tablets—they x out my headaches due to stress."

Image Appeal   *Image appeals* are positive images that advertisers associate with their products, but the association really has little or nothing to do with the actual product. The person hearing or seeing the advertisement is supposed to relate to the message: "If you buy this product, you will be more relaxed, sexier, happier, richer, more patriotic, more popular, etc."

Example: "Are you tired of fast food? Make tonight's dinner a dinner to remember with candlelight, soft music, and Dinner-for-Two Meals. Stir up some passion in your life every night by trying all seven varieties."

Glittering Generalities   *Glittering generalities* are words like "great," "wonderful," "exciting," or "fabulous" used by advertisers to make a product sound good, but these words are too general to have much meaning. The words glitter, but they don't tell you anything specific about the product.

Example: "This new stereo by MusiSound will give you heavenly music."

Name Calling   *Name calling* is a propaganda technique that tries to make a product appealing by putting down a competitor's product.

Example: "Try our new Mellow Yellow Mustard. It's twice as mellow as New Style Mustard."

Card Stacking   Sometimes advertisers purposely leave out or hide important details that, if they were known, might make you change your mind about buying a product. This technique is called *card stacking* because it is like a dishonest card dealer stacking the deck.

Example: "To save on your long-distance calling, it's simple. Just dial 3610-1234-00 before you dial your long distance number, any time, any day for 6 cents a minute for interstate calls."

What is hidden in fine print in this kind of message is that many restrictions apply: a $4.99 monthly access fee, $1.99 monthly service charge, $25.99 one-time-only customer hook-up fee. After 60 days from your first completed call using the code, interstate calls will be billed at 8 cents a minute.

Along with these propaganda techniques, advertisers often use appealing pictures to enhance their products. On radio, television, and the Internet, ads may also include music or other sound effects that help promote the product. Because the pictures on television and the Internet are usually animated, this aspect adds another element seducing the viewer into buying the product. As a critical thinker and intelligent consumer, you should be able to analyze an advertisement to determine what specific value a product actually has and whether or not it is something you want to buy.

Exercise 6-B

Directions: From magazines, television, radio, billboards or the Internet, find examples of three different propaganda techniques. If possible, bring in the picture from the magazine or Internet, or, on a piece of paper, write a brief description of each advertisement. Name the propaganda techniques used.

Critically Thinking Together

Bring your assignment from Exercise 6-B to class to share, and discuss these propaganda techniques with your group. Here are some possible questions you might consider:

- What is the advertiser really trying to sell in addition to the product?

- Is the advertiser appealing to a fear? If so, what?

- Is the advertiser appealing to a certain desire? If so, what?

- Is there any other hidden message in the ad? If so, what?

ANALYZING A PERSUASIVE MESSAGE

When listening to or reading another person's argument, your critical thinking powers need to be sharp. Whether you agree or disagree with an argument, it is important to remain open-minded until you have evaluated it. This will keep you from jumping to a hasty conclusion.

To begin your evaluation of someone's argument, you must discover the major point. In other words, what is the speaker or author trying to convince you to believe or do? In reading an argument, you are able to go back and reread any information. If you are listening to a speech, however, this is not possible, so you must take notes during the talk in order to recall the information and analyze it.

In both instances, pay careful attention to the introduction given by the writer or speaker. Here, the major point may be stated most concisely in a thesis statement, the main idea of the whole speech or essay. The main idea is also likely to be found in the conclusion.

Once you have determined the major point of the argument, you should examine what evidence is included to prove the point or thesis. Evidence includes reasons, facts, examples, and statistics supporting the argument's conclusions. A useful way to clarify what evidence is being offered to you is to informally outline the argument. To do this, list the thesis, and under that, list the major supporting details. Under those points, you may want to list any minor details.

One note of caution: In examining the evidence given, you should pay particular attention to the use of statistics. Because statistics are based upon exact numbers and percents, they seem to be unquestionably true. But this is not always the case. People using statistics might manipulate the words or numbers to *prove* what they want you to believe. As a critical thinker, you should view statistics skeptically. First of all, ask yourself, is the source of the information reliable? For example, if a statistic shows how good a particular television set is, you would trust the numbers from *Consumer Reports* as more reliable than the statistics given by a television manufacturer because *Consumer Reports* does not sell televisions and is, therefore, not biased. Second, determine if the statistics are representative of a large enough group to be significant. For example, if someone says, "Eighty percent of the students surveyed said this college needs a new student center," then examine the number and type of people surveyed before accepting this conclusion. How many students were surveyed: 5? 10? 100? 1,000? Were the students representative of the campus in terms of population: male and female, ethnic groups, year in school, age, and so on? As these examples indicate, you cannot take statistics at face value because they might need further clarification to be useful.

After you have made an outline of the argument, you should have a clearer picture of what the writer or speaker is saying. You are then ready to evaluate all of the evidence.

- Is enough evidence given to prove the point?
- Are the reasons, facts, statistics, and examples true?
- If you are not sure whether a piece of information is true, can it be validated through research?
- Is all the evidence actually related to the topic?
- Has the writer used any logical fallacies?
- Are propaganda techniques used?
- What important information, if any, is omitted from the argument?

Once you have thoroughly examined the evidence, you should be able to state what the person is saying (the point or thesis), why he or she is saying this (evidence or support), and whether or not it is logical and reasonable. Thus, having thought critically about the argument, you can determine if you agree or disagree.

Exercise 6-C

Directions: Clip or photocopy an editorial from a current newspaper. On another piece of paper, make an informal outline of the argument. Then, in writing, evaluate the thesis and supporting evidence using the questions above. Your instructor may ask you to hand in this information.

RELATING CRITICAL READING TO CRITICAL THINKING

As you have read, correct knowledge and accurate information are at the heart of critical thinking. Correct knowledge comes from reading carefully and critically. Critical reading involves more than just understanding words on a page. It also includes understanding the difference between facts and opinions; considering the author's purpose, tone, and biases; and knowing how to make inferences.

Facts and Opinions

Facts are objective statements that can be proven true at a certain point in time. Factual evidence is not always perfect "proof," however, because facts that are thought to be accurate at a certain point in time can later be contradicted. For example, ancient people thought that the earth was flat. Only later, with more exploration, was this proven to be false. At that point, the "fact" died because the world was proven to be round.

Opinions, on the other hand, are subjective statements that cannot be proven true or false. They express personal beliefs, feelings, or evaluations about something. Opinions are sometimes stated directly by words such as "I believe," "I think," "I feel," or "you should," "you ought to," "you must." For example, you might say, "I believe our city is 'safe' (or clean or beautiful or dangerous or dirty)." This statement is obviously an opinion. This same opinion can be disguised to sound like a fact: "Our city is safe," but it is still a subjective opinion. The word "safe," like many other descriptive words, can be defined in various ways according to whose opinion it is.

Much of what you read or hear will be a mixture of facts and opinions. Newspaper editorials, commercial advertisements, and persuasive arguments provide many examples of how facts and opinions are combined. As a critical reader and thinker, you must recognize the differences.

Critically Thinking Together

Your instructor will provide your group with an editorial. Choose a recorder for the group who will write down which information in the editorial is fact, which is opinion, and which is a combination of both fact and opinion. Be ready to discuss your findings with the rest of the class.

Purpose, Tone, and Bias of an Author

When reading critically, besides differentiating between facts and opinions, you must also understand an author's point of view. An author's point of view includes his or her purpose, tone, and bias. By observing an author's point of view, you are trying to size up the author's reliability to determine how much value to place on that writer's opinions.

To grasp an author's viewpoint and attitudes, you should first determine the purpose or intention of the writer, in other words, why the author wrote the particular essay or text. Does the author intend to inform, entertain, or persuade you? Or is the writing a combination of these? The purpose will definitely affect the organization, type of evidence given, and word choices.

To identify an author's point of view, you should also consider the author's tone. In a conversation with another person, you can tell a great deal about the person's feelings and intentions by the tone of voice and facial expression. Similarly, you can carefully observe an author's word choices to determine the author's underlying feelings and intentions. Because writers communicate with you only in words, not sounds, they let word choices express their attitudes. Most experienced writers choose their words very carefully and are aware of denotations and connotations of words. *Denotations* of words are the dictionary definitions of words, the exact definitions. *Connotations* of words, however, are the emotional reactions that people attach to words. Reactions to some words may be positive, negative, or neutral. For example, observe how the verb in each of these sentences changes your attitude about Miguel as he eats.

- Miguel *savored* the wine and cheese. (positive)
- Miguel *gobbled up* the wine and cheese. (negative)
- Miguel *tasted* the wine and cheese. (neutral)

Authors will deliberately use words with certain positive or negative connotations when they want to influence your reactions to their messages. When you consider the word choices of an author and the writer's tone, you are critically evaluating how much emotional influence he or she is trying to have on you.

In considering the viewpoint of an author, you should also be aware of a third influence, bias. Bias in writing is the strong attempt to influence a reader by forcefully giving only one side of an argument. Biased writing gives certain favorable facts that the writer hopes will persuade you to accept his or her point of view.

Exercise 6-D

Directions: Before class, read the following "Letter to the Editor." As you read, underline words that have strong connotations.

To the Editor:
I have long suspected that people who recycle must be either retired and bored or just plain idiots. My smug and self-righteous neighbors think they are superior when their trash collection, including the recycle bins, is displayed curbside once a week. Despite the ugly stares I get from my neighbors, I will not play the recycling game with these radical do-gooders.

Here are my reasons why recycling is ridiculous: 1) I have to work long and hard for a living, so my precious time should not be squandered doing the disgusting, dirty work of rinsing foul, smelly bottles and cans and separating newspapers from glossy, nonrecyclable paper that leaves me with grubby print-stained

(continued on the next page)

Exercise 6-D *(continued)*

hands. 2) The exorbitant expense we pay for the pickup kills any mindless fantasy of saving the planet. If this country is so concerned about saving the environment, then why don't the Big Brother Feds pay *us* for the privilege of recycling? 3) I've paid my hard-earned money for those products and containers, so I have the right to do anything I want with the empties and old papers. 4) Recycling is a putrid, unsanitary mess that can breed loathsome roaches, ants, flies, and other disease-carrying vermin.

It's about time my goody-goody neighbors woke up and smelled the garbage: Recycling is a waste of time and money. It is a national joke.

Sincerely,

A Concerned Citizen

Critically Thinking Together

In a small group, compare your underlined words from Exercise 6-D with those of the other members of your group. Discuss what you think are the author's purpose, tone, and biases. Have one person record your group's conclusion, and be ready to share them with the class.

Making Inferences

Closely related to tone and bias in critical reading and thinking is the concept of inferences. *Inferences* are conclusions drawn from the facts you know or observe. You make many inferences in your everyday life. For example, you arrive at school for your 9:00 a.m. English class, and your watch says exactly 9:01 when you enter the room. You immediately realize that no one is in the room. What inferences might you draw from this? The class was canceled? Your watch battery has died? You forgot to change your watch to Daylight Savings Time last night, so you are an hour early? You are in the wrong room? This is Tuesday instead of Monday? Everyone else, including the professor, is ill? Maybe your English class is meeting in a different room today? Aha! Something jogs your memory, and you make a correct inference on this last attempt. Now you must rush down the hallway to the college computer lab where your class is meeting today to do peer reviews of students' essays.

As you see in this example, inferences may be correct or incorrect. Often we go through many incorrect inferences before we arrive at correct ones. However, the process of making correct inferences usually includes several steps:

1. When making inferences, first, consider the evidence or facts as you know them. (The classroom is empty.)
2. Then, think about those facts and how they relate to your experiences and general knowledge about that topic or situation. (My English class is held in Room 222 every Monday at 9:00 a.m. There are 20 people in the class, plus the instructor.)
3. Finally, apply logic to the facts and your personal knowledge in order to draw a correct and logical conclusion. (My day and time are all correct; probably everyone is not ill; therefore, the students and professor must be holding class somewhere else.)

WEB SITE INFORMATION

If you would like more information on critical thinking and reading, visit our web site:

<http://college.hmco.com/success/>

EVALUATING SOURCES OF INFORMATION

When a friend, relative, acquaintance, or business person verbally tells you something, your natural, sometimes automatic, inclination is to consider the source before deciding how much you value or even believe that information. This evaluation of a source is natural and sometimes necessary. Likewise, when other kinds of information are presented to you, they need to be evaluated to decide how much credibility each has. In addition to advertising, information that attempts to influence you includes printed materials and on-line sources, as well as television programs and movies. As a critical thinker, you should know how to evaluate each of these sources of information.

Evaluation of Printed Materials and On-line Sources

Since printed information and on-line or Internet sources are written, you can ask several key questions to evaluate them both. Often, articles and books in print have already gone through some form of evaluation before they are published. For example, an article that appears in a professional journal is usually screened by professionals in that field before it is allowed to be published. This is not true, however, for on-line sources. Literally anyone can post information on the Internet. Many sites on the Web are informative and valid, but others are full of misinformation. Here are some questions to consider when evaluating printed materials and on-line sources.

What is the authority of this author?   Determine who wrote the article and if that writer is really an authority on the subject. Some suggestions to do this include:

- looking at biographical information;
- noticing the author's title or position in a company or institution;
- determining whether an author has other publications on this subject;
- noticing if other established authorities on the topic refer to this person as an authority; and
- checking the author's knowledge-base by viewing his or her bibliography, or when reading on-line, by looking at the bibliography or links to other Web documents.

(*Note:* With an Internet document, searching for the author's name on the Web might give you his or her home page.)

What is the quality of the writing?   The care a writer puts into his or her document can be a good indication of the validity and accuracy of that information.

- Is the purpose and organization of the writing clear and easy to follow?
- Is the document written with few or no grammatical, spelling, or other errors?
- Does the writer give clear references to works cited or consulted?

Is the publishing body reputable?   A publishing body is an organization that stands behind an author's work. For example, you can expect most articles printed in a well-respected journal, like the *Journal of Psychology,* to be reputable articles. On the Internet, the publishing body is really the server or computer where the document originated. An informational Web page that is sponsored by educational institutions or government agencies will typically have a URL address that ends in .gov or .edu. (A URL is the string of letters, dots, and slash marks that identifies a unique page of information on the Web.) Chances are, URLs with these endings might be good sources of information; however, a server can never guarantee the reliability of its stored information.

How biased is the information?   As mentioned before, biased writing attempts to influence you by giving only one point of view, the one favorable to the writer's arguments. With print and on-line sources, you will want to notice if the information is associated with a corporation, a certain product, a specific interest group, or political organization. Such information will likely be biased in favor of promoting that group's particular interest. With on-line sources, if you look at the URL of the document, you might be able to determine what group or organization is sponsoring the information.

How current is the information?   Often, in order to be valuable, the information must be current. To evaluate how up-to-date a source is, you should:

- Check printed sources and on-line sources for the date of publication or most recent copyright date.
- With on-line sources, look for the "last updated" date or "last revision or modification" date, often found at the top or bottom of a page. If no date is given in the document, you might be able to find one in the directory by returning "back" down the path you took to find the document.
- Check to see when any research was gathered to decide if it is still relevant.

WEB SITE INFORMATION

If you would like more detailed information about evaluating on-line sources, visit our web site:

<http://college.hmco.com/success/>

Critically Thinking in Writing

Describe how much experience you have had using the Internet and how useful the Internet is to you academically and personally. Give some of your positive and negative reactions to using the Internet.

Evaluation of Movies and Television Programs

Some criteria used to evaluate printed materials and advertisements can also be used to evaluate movies and television shows. For example, a major question to ask when examining television shows or movies is: "What is the purpose—to inform, to entertain, or to persuade?"

Movies and television programs such as soap operas (daytime and nighttime), sitcoms, mysteries, drama, music, game shows, and cartoons primarily provide entertainment. But as a critical thinker, you might want to evaluate these programs in terms of the *quality* of the entertainment. As you view programs that attempt to entertain you, consider the following questions.

- If this movie or program is humorous, what kind of humor is used, and is it in good taste?
- Who is the main audience (children, teenagers, young adults, older people, a specific ethnic group, men, women)? Is the movie or program appropriate for that audience?
- If it is supposed to imitate "real" life, how realistic is it?
- What kinds of stereotypes, if any, are presented?
- What kinds of biases are shown?
- Besides providing entertainment, do these shows contain hidden messages about people's behavior?

Although talk shows can be entertaining, they often include persuasive and informative elements. Frequently, these talk shows have celebrity guests and so-called authorities who speak out on a variety of issues. As a critical thinker, you should not assume that the talk show guests are always qualified to give advice on the topics being discussed. Here are some questions you might consider when viewing talk shows.

- Is the topic of this talk show worth discussing?
- Are the guests and hosts qualified to speak as authorities on the subject?
- What biases do they express?
- Are they speaking from factual evidence or are they giving personal opinions?

Some talk shows are indeed very informative and worth watching. On the other hand, some talk show hosts and their guests pretend to be informative, but in reality these shows are forums for airing public violence and exploiting people's private lives. Most likely, such talk shows are not worth your time.

All of the major networks have daily local and national news shows whose purpose is primarily to provide information. Although local and national news programs report almost all the same news, you probably have a preference for which channel you regularly watch. Consider why you watch one station rather than another. News magazines and investigative journalism, such as *60 Minutes, Meet the Press, Date Line,* and *48 Hours,* tend to go into more depth than news broadcasts. All are informative, but some are slanted and try to justify a certain cause or point of view. As a critical thinker, you should be able to recognize biases in a story and evaluate the information accordingly.

Summary

Critical thinking, the process of thoughtfully and deliberately gathering, analyzing, and evaluating information, is a skill that helps make all aspects of life more meaningful. Three reasons why you should become a critical thinker are that you will feel more in control of your life; you can make sound judgments; and you will become more creative.

Becoming a critical thinker requires that you become aware of your own and others' biases. Biases are personal ways of viewing ideas based on one's background, including culture, experience, income, ethnicity, and religious beliefs. As a critical thinker, you will realize that you are not always right, so you must be open to other people's ideas. Critical thinking makes us aware of common fallacies, that is, mistakes in thinking that produce incorrect conclusions, as well as propaganda in advertising. Propaganda is a deliberate attempt to convince people of something by using emotional appeals.

To evaluate others' arguments, you must find and understand their major points. Outlining an argument is a good way to do this. If you are listening to a speech, taking notes can help you to analyze the information later.

Critical thinkers are also critical readers. They distinguish facts from opinions and determine the author's intended audience. As a critical reader, you are aware of purpose, tone, and biases, and that authors select words with emotional appeals. Finally, as a critical thinker and reader, you are able to make inferences by drawing your own conclusions based upon the facts you know or observe.

As a critical thinker, you must also evaluate sources of information in printed materials and on-line. Your evaluation of sources is based on the authority of the author, the reputation of the publishing body, the possible bias of the information, and the date of publication. Because television and movies can greatly influence you as well, you should be able to judge these media forms by evaluating their purposes and content.

One other application of critical thinking is your ability to evaluate movies and television shows. This will help you to become an informed and, therefore, a selective viewer.

List of Terms

critical thinking
judgment
creativity
bias
fallacies:
  hasty generalization
  stereotyping
  either/or fallacy
  attacking the person (personal attack)
  circular reasoning (begging the question)
  red herring (ignoring the issue)
  false comparisons
  false cause

propaganda techniques:
  bandwagon (everyone's buying it)
  testimonials
  plain folks
  image appeals
  glittering generalities
  name calling
  card stacking
facts and opinions
denotation
connotation
inferences

In this box, write your summary question or statement for this chapter.

7 The Power of Time Management

One of the popular misconceptions about college is that success depends solely upon intelligence. Certainly brain power is necessary, but you do not have to be a genius to do well in college. You do, however, need to know how to study and how to budget your time.

Walter Pauk, one of the earliest college study skills experts, states in *How to Study in College,* "Your success or failure in college depends directly upon your use of time" (35). Your success depends upon your *wise* use of time, and your lack of success could relate directly to your poor use of time.

This chapter will focus on how to be realistic about the time you have so that you can plan adequate time to study, go to classes, work, eat, sleep, live, and even have fun. Since procrastination affects all students (actually, almost all people), it will receive special attention—later in the chapter, of course.

REALITY CHECK

Often you may catch yourself saying, "I don't know where the day has gone." Yet each day has twenty-four hours, no more, no less. Time—you can't buy it, you can't sell it, and you can't inherit it. The following exercise will help you to gain some insights into how you use your time.

Once you have completed Exercise 7-A, you can begin to assess your results.

Exercise 7-A

Directions: Approximate the number of *hours per week* you spend engaging in the following activities.

1. Eating meals _____
2. Sleeping _____
3. Attending classes and labs _____
4. Studying _____
5. Working (job outside the home) _____
6. Working at home (laundry, fixing meals, cleaning, etc.) _____
7. Driving to school and work _____
8. Keeping appointments (doctor, dentist, haircut, etc.) _____
9. Watching TV, reading, listening to music, relaxing _____
10. Exercising _____
11. Attending religious services and/or other meetings _____
12. Showering, dressing _____
13. Socializing or talking on the phone _____
14. Taking care of children _____
15. Fulfilling other responsibilities _____

Total _____

A week has 168 hours. If the total number of hours you identified in Exercise 7-A was less than 168, then either you have good control of your time and obligations or you may be underestimating the amount of time necessary to fulfill all your responsibilities.

If the number of hours you identified in Exercise 7-A totaled more than 168, it is time for you either to clone yourself or to reassess your priorities. You cannot realistically duplicate yourself, and you cannot do the work of one and a half or two people. If you try to overextend yourself, you may pay for it in some significant way. Your body may rebel in the only way it knows how: by getting sick. Or you may be forced to neglect something, such as your studies, your job, or your family.

Being realistic about how much time you have is important. In high school, every hour of your school day was structured for you with classes, study hours, and other activities. In college, however, although your classes are scheduled, you are responsible for determining when and how much you study. The rule of thumb for study time in college is that for every hour you spend in class or lab per week, you need to spend *twice* that amount of time *studying and doing homework* outside of class. For example, if you are in class and lab twelve hours a week, then you should be studying approximately twenty-four hours a week. This means that you will be devoting thirty-six hours a week to meeting your college obligations; this amount of time is equivalent to a full-time job. If you are taking a particularly difficult subject, you may have to allow for more study time. A challenging course, for example, may require that you study three to four hours for every class hour.

If you are enrolled as a full-time student, you need to balance your class and study times with your other obligations, such as a job and family. As a general rule, if you are a full-time student, you should not work more than twenty hours a week. Likewise, if you have many family obligations, a full-time class load may not be appropriate.

Despite your best efforts to balance available time and meet your obligations, you, like most people, may occasionally feel overwhelmed. Learning to schedule your time is a key factor in time management.

Critically Thinking Together

In small groups, brainstorm the differences between high school and college. Analyze this list of differences, and then write at least three changes or adjustments in attitude, behavior, and time management that college students need to make. Be ready to share your list of suggestions with the class.

Critically Thinking in Writing

In your journal, jot down your personal and academic goals. Then look at your responses to Exercise 7-A. Without strictly counting hours, which activities *seem* to take priority in your life? According to

(continued on the next page)

Critically Thinking in Writing (continued)

your goals, which activities *should* take priority in your life? Explain how your goals and your priorities either fit together or don't. For example, if your goal is an education, but you are working 40 hours a week and do not have sufficient time to study, your goals and priorities are at odds. If your goals and priorities don't match, describe some changes or steps you can take to make them compatible. If your goals and priorities do match, explain how you are going to keep yourself motivated to achieve your goals.

PEAK TIME PREFERENCES

Everyone's body has its own internal clock. That is why some people say, "I'm a night person," while others say, "I'm a morning person." The time when you are best able to perform physical and mental activities is called your *peak time*.

You probably already know when you are most alert, but you may need to explore your own time clock in more detail.

Exercise 7-B

Directions: Answer the following questions in order to determine your peak time.

1. If you did not set your alarm, what time would you get up in the morning? _____

2. If you did not have any responsibilities tomorrow, how late would you stay up tonight? _____

3. If you have the chance, would you take a nap? Yes? _____ No? _____ What time of day? _____

4. What time of day do you prefer doing something mentally stimulating, like reading a book, writing a letter, balancing your checkbook, or making a decision? _____

5. What time of day do you prefer doing a physical task or activity, such as exercising, cleaning the house, washing the car, walking, swimming, or doing yard work? _____

If you answered the first question by giving a time before 9 a.m., indicating you get up early even without an alarm clock, you probably are a morning person. If possible, you should schedule classes early in the day or set aside morning hours to study. If you are not a night person but are forced to study late at night, you will not get as much accomplished as you would have if you had studied during your peak time. Early birds should also avoid enrolling in a night class.

In response to the second question, if you generally go to bed at 11 p.m. or later and enjoy staying up into the wee hours of the morning, you are a night person. You might have so much energy at 2 o'clock in the morning that you find yourself buzzing around the house doing a load of wash, cleaning your room, or fixing a pizza. Although in most colleges you cannot take a class at 2 a.m., you can harness this nighttime energy to work on a paper, review your notes, or study your vocabulary or terms. It would also make sense for late sleepers to avoid scheduling an 8 a.m. class.

If your response to the third question about taking naps was "no," then you can skip the rest of this paragraph. If, on the other hand, you answered "yes," you need to keep reading. You may find yourself feeling drowsy or dozing off at a time when you are at your physical and mental low point, the opposite of your peak time. If possible, do not schedule classes at that time or try to study difficult subjects because that would be counterproductive.

Your responses to questions four and five, indicating when you prefer to be mentally and physically active, should give you clear evidence of your peak time. Some circumstances at school, at work, at home, and in social situations can interfere with your using your peak time to its best advantage. However, even if you cannot use your peak time to study, to take a class, to work productively, you can at least understand why you are more alert and effective at certain times and less so at other times.

SCHEDULING YOUR TIME

Schedules, calendars, checklists, planners—these are the tools of busy, successful, determined people. If you have never kept a schedule before, now is the time to learn how. Look at most successful professionals at work each day. More often than not, some kind of planner sits atop their desks to guide their daily and long-term actions and decisions. Since college is much like the professional world in its expectations of you, you should be aware of the types of schedules available so that you can make use of them.

Three popular types of schedules are:

1. A *time planner*, which gives you a broad overview of the whole term, plus a detailed look at your activities for the week
2. A *weekly study schedule*, which indicates specific study hours for each course
3. A *daily to-do list*, which outlines all your tasks for the day

Each of these three schedules serves a different purpose in your life and, used together, they provide a complete system of time management for your whole life.

Time Planners

The purpose of a time planner is to give you an overview of important dates and obligations. This overview allows you to juggle and balance your activities and helps you to avoid unpleasant surprises or conflicting events. Time planners are usually month-at-a-glance or week-at-a-glance planners. They are readily available in your college bookstore, as well as in discount stores and office supply stores. Your time planner should have enough room to write down both college, personal, and work-related activities. By updating your planner frequently and referring to it often, your time planner can serve as an invaluable tool for balancing school, family, work, and social commitments. It can also prevent the embarrassment of missing an appointment or of scheduling two activities for the same time.

To set up your time planner, copy important dates from your official school calendar. These may include such items as registration dates, tuition payment dates, holidays, last day to withdraw, and final exam week. Once you have the college dates on your planner, go through your syllabi and record all major test dates, due dates for papers, and due dates for any other major assignments. Then record such items as birthdays and various appointments or events that you will be attending. That way you can see an overview of your commitments at a glance, and you are less likely to forget when a paper is due or an appointment is scheduled. As time passes, you will need to update the planner as you become aware of new responsibilities and activities, such as additional test dates, personal and family appointments, conferences, meetings, and social occasions.

Exercise 7-C

Directions: If you have not already started keeping and using a time planner, do so now. Your instructor may ask you to photocopy and hand in sample pages from your planner.

Weekly Study Schedule

The second kind of time organizer is called a weekly study schedule. The purpose of the weekly study schedule is to provide you with definite study times for specific courses that will fit in with your other obligations and activities each hour of the day for a week at a time. A completed one may look like the example on the next page.

During the weekend, prepare your next week's study schedule. When making your own weekly study schedule, write down all the commitments that you are obligated to meet at specific times, such as classes and labs, work, or other fixed activities in the appropriate boxes. These are called *inflexible times,* that is, times that you are required to be somewhere or do something. Then fill in the remaining boxes with your flexible activities. *Flexible times* are the hours that remain, in which you can make choices about when to study and do other activities. One of the most important reasons for keeping this schedule is that you can plan your study time. To make sure you include sufficient and specific study hours, use the two-for-one rule—for every hour you spend in class or lab, you need to spend two hours studying and doing homework. Notice how the sample study schedule shows the student indicating specific times for studying specific courses. Also, the student has made good use of time for studying before and after classes. The student has abbreviated the words to keep notations as brief as possible to fit within the boxes. Time for meals, transportation, recreation, and relaxation are also indicated. Finally, when an activity lasts for more than an hour, arrows indicate the length of time. Your schedule is complete when you have accounted for every hour of the day. The major advantage of the study schedule is that it identifies specific times for studying specific courses during each day of the week.

A shortcut you can use to prepare a study schedule is to fill out a schedule with your inflexible activities and then photocopy the schedule for each week of the term. Then all you have to fill in each week are the flexible activities. If you fill them in with erasable pen or pencil, you can still make minor changes as the need arises. For example, if you have decided to study from 7 to 10 P.M. on Tuesday, but someone calls to invite you to a movie you are dying to see, you can reschedule your studying for a time when you had planned to watch TV or do some other flexible activity. Just erase it and write it in somewhere else. If you adhere to your revised schedule, you will not feel guilty about going out, and you will still get the studying done that you had planned.

Time	Sun.	Mon.	Tues.	Wed.	Thurs.	Fri.	Sat.
7-8 a.m.	sleep		dress	eat			sleep
8-9 a.m.			drive	time			
9-10 a.m.	church	Biology	Bio	Bio	Sdy	Bio	free
10-11 a.m.		StSkills	lab	StSkills	Bio	SS Lab	time
11 a.m. - 12 p.m.		sty Psyc	Psyc	sty SS	Psyc	sty Psyc	gym
12-1 p.m.	eat	sty Psyc	free	sty Bio	free	sty Psyc	eat
1-2 p.m.	gym			Lunch			Eng hw
2-3 p.m.	free	English	sty Bio	Eng.	sty Psyc	Eng.	sty SS
3-4 p.m.		sty Eng	sty SS	English — essay — draft			sty Bio
4-5 p.m.				driving			sty Psyc
5-6 p.m.				dinner			
6-7 p.m.	sty Psyc			Work			
7-8 p.m.	sty Bio			Work			free time
8-9 p.m.	sty SS			Work			
9-10 p.m.	TV		driving	Gym	driving		
10-11 p.m.	Rec	sty Psyc	sty Bio	driving	sty Bio	free	
11 p.m. - 12 a.m.	read		sleep			time	

For your own use, you can photocopy the following blank weekly study schedule form.

Time	Sunday	Monday	Tuesday	Wed.	Thurs.	Friday	Sat.
7-8 a.m.							
8-9 a.m.							
9-10 a.m.							
10-11 a.m.							
11 a.m. - 12 p.m.							
12-1 p.m.							
1-2 p.m.							
2-3 p.m.							
3-4 p.m.							
4-5 p.m.							
5-6 p.m.							
6-7 p.m.							
7-8 p.m.							
8-9 p.m.							
9-10 p.m.							
10-11 p.m.							
11 p.m. - 12 a.m.							

> ## Exercise 7-D
>
> ***Directions:*** Make two photocopies of the blank study schedule (one to keep and one to hand in), and fill in your inflexible times and flexible times for the upcoming week.

Daily To-Do Lists

The purpose of a daily to-do list, as its name implies, is to provide you with a list of tasks, assignments, errands, or projects you need to accomplish on a given day. In a sense, it is a commitment to do the very specific tasks listed. It is action-oriented because it motivates you to complete each item before the day is over. Every evening or early in the morning, you should make a list of what needs to be accomplished during the day. You can make your list on a 3 x 5 card, on a piece of paper, or in a special notebook—whatever works for you. You don't need to include everyday occurrences that you won't easily forget, like eating lunch or driving to work or school. Some people divide their to-do list into three sections: must, should, and would if I had time. Others divide it into A, high priority; B, important; and C, can be delayed. Or you might rank the most important three or four items on your list. Don't forget to add last-minute appointments, obligations, and items or activities if they occur during the day. As you accomplish each task, check it off or cross it out.

Read the following true story to get a sense of the value of to-do lists (Usova 23).

> ## *First Things First*
>
> One day a management consultant, Ivy Lee, called on Schwab of the Bethlehem Steel Company. Lee outlined his firm's services briefly, ending with the statement: "With our services, you'll know how to manage better."
>
> The indignant Schwab said, "I'm managing as well now as I know how. What we need around here is not more knowing but more doing, not knowledge but action. If you can give us something to pep us up to do the things we **already know** we ought to do, I'll gladly listen to you and pay you anything you ask."
>
> *(continued on the next page)*

First Things First (continued)

"Fine," said Lee, "I can show you something in twenty minutes that will step up your productivity at least 50 percent."

"OK," said Schwab. "I have just about that much time before I have to catch a train. What's your idea?"

Lee pulled a blank 3 × 5 card out of his pocket, handed it to Schwab, and said: "Write on this card the six most important tasks you have to do tomorrow." That took Schwab about three minutes. "Now," said Lee, "put this card in your pocket, and the first thing tomorrow morning look at the first item. Concentrate on it until it is finished. Then tackle item two in the same way, then item three. Do this until quitting time. Don't be concerned if you finish only two or three, or even if you finish only one item. You'll be working on the important ones. The others can wait. If you can't finish them all by this method, you couldn't with another method either. And without some system, you probably would not even decide which are most important.

"Spend the last five minutes of every working day making out a 'must' list for the next day's tasks. After you've convinced yourself of the worth of this system, have your men try it. Try it out as long as you wish, and then send me a check for what you think it's worth."

The interview lasted about twenty-five minutes. In two weeks, Schwab sent Lee a check for $25,000—$1,000 a minute. He added a note saying the lesson was the most profitable from a money standpoint he had ever learned. Did it work? In five years it turned the unknown Bethlehem Steel Company into the biggest independent steel producer in the world, making Schwab 100 times a millionaire and the best-known steel man of that time.

Admittedly, making a daily to-do list does not mean you will become a multimillionaire as Charles Michael Schwab did, but you should be able to get done what needs to be finished every day.

If you have not made to-do lists before or your lists tend to be much too long to accomplish, you may want to "guesstimate" how long each task will take and then write down how long it actually did take to do it. Knowing how long a given project usually takes can help you write more realistic lists.

At the end of the day, a typical to-do list, not including the student's classes or work schedule, might look like the illustration below. The two items that were not checked off can be added to the next day's to-do list.

10/16 To-Do List

- ☑ *Study for biology test. Ch. 8 & 9*
- ☑ *Mail Visa bill*
- ☑ *Lunch with Carolyn 12-1—cafeteria*
- ☑ *Conference with Prof. Luther about Eng. paper 10:00*
- ☐ *Go to library to find books on W.W. II paper*
- ☐ *Get haircut*
- ☑ *Study-read Ch. 4 in Psych.*
- ☑ *Do 20 calculus problems*

As you complete the items on your list, you will not only have each task accomplished, but you will also have the psychological satisfaction of checking each item off as you finish it. By the end of the day, you will feel as if you have "moved mountains" as your checkmarks mount up and your day's tasks come under your control.

Exercise 7-E

Directions: Starting tonight or tomorrow morning, make a daily to-do list every day for the next five days (omit weekends if you choose to do so). Anything you do not accomplish during a given day, add to the following day's list. Be prepared to turn in these lists (or a photocopy).

Summary of Schedule Information

Time Planner
Purpose: To give you an overview of important dates and obligations.

- Important dates from college calendar
- Major test and due dates from syllabi
- Personal records and appointments

Weekly Study Schedule
Purpose: To provide you with definite study times for specific courses that will fit in with your other obligations and activities each hour of the day for a week at a time.

- Inflexible times and activities
- Study hours (two-for-one rule)
- Flexible activities

Daily To-Do List
Purpose: To provide you with a list of activities you need to accomplish on a given day.

- Tasks
- Assignments
- Errands
- Projects

Additional Scheduling Tips

Time planners, study schedules, and daily to-do lists are the keys to getting control of your time in college, as well as in your whole life. In addition to these basic tools, here are some other useful tips for scheduling your time in college.

- Determine which courses are easy and which are hard for you. Study your hardest subject first.
- Study your hardest course every day.
- Consider your peak time. Study for your hardest course during your most mentally and physically alert period.
- Study as soon after class as possible. Remember that the Ebbinghaus Forgetting Curve clearly indicates that most forgetting happens immediately after hearing or reading information.
- Prioritize: What needs to be done now? Attack the most urgent task right away.

- Study dissimilar subjects back to back. For example, if you are taking sociology and psychology, study a math course in between. Or if you are taking statistics and a math course, separate these courses in your study time with English or history. On your study schedule, insert *specific subjects* to study.
- Use *distributed effort;* that is, breaking a large task into several manageable steps, and spacing your work time over a period of days. For example, if you have an essay to write, you could begin by brainstorming, then starting a rough draft, and so forth.
- Note due dates and allow yourself plenty of lead time to get long projects finished.

Getting the Most Out of Your Time

Even though you have only twenty-four hours every day, you can sometimes bend or stretch those hours to your advantage.

- Make use of portable study materials. For example, carry with you 3 x 5 cards with terms and vocabulary or loose pages from your notebook.
- Record information on cassette tapes to use in the car.
- Use stolen moments of time to study—for example, standing in line or waiting for an appointment or class to start.
- Do two tasks at once. Everyone has routine, repetitive chores to do, such as making the bed, washing and folding clothes, mowing the lawn, or exercising. While you are engaged in these activities, let your brain work, too, by studying.
- Study in a regular place, and be sure it is equipped with everything you need: pens, paper, books, dictionary, etc. If you always study in the same place and have a well-equipped study area, you will get to work faster and have better concentration when you are there because you will develop a conditioned response. *Conditioned response* means that the habit of study will be triggered automatically when you sit down in your study environment.
- Get into the habit of using positive self-talk. Replace "I have never been good in math" with "One by one, I can do these problems." A positive attitude will actually make studying easier.
- Reward yourself when you have completed an assignment or task. In advance, plan your rewards, whether they are large or small. Your reward could be a snack, a phone call, a break to watch TV, exercising, a trip to the mall, or whatever will help motivate you to resume studying later.

- When you have finished a task or a study session, do one more small task before you stop. You might do one more math problem or prepare tomorrow's to-do list. One more item accomplished today is one less item to complete tomorrow.

WEB SITE INFORMATION

For information about evaluating your place of study and some general time management and scheduling guidelines, visit our web site:

<http://college.hmco.com/success/>

PROCRASTINATION

Most people, despite their best efforts, lapse into periods of procrastination—for some just now and then, some more often, and some almost all the time. *Procrastination* is the tendency to needlessly put off jobs, tasks, or assignments. Planners, study schedules, and daily to-do lists are useful in helping you to solve the problem of procrastination, but only if you *use* them after you make them. At times, the consequences of procrastination are not too serious. If you don't clean your room, it can wait another day or two. However, if you don't do your assignments before they are due, you have a more serious problem. Missing due dates in college can have serious consequences. Procrastination that jeopardizes your success or interferes with your goals must be overcome, and it *can* be if you take positive steps.

In order to overcome the habit of procrastination in school-related tasks, you first need to analyze your reasons for procrastinating.

Reasons for Procrastination

Although many reasons for procrastination exist, four of the most common ones indicate that "procrastinators finish LAST."

L = Lack of motivation
A = Afraid of failure
S = Start-up problems
T = Task is too overwhelming

L = Lack of Motivation   One major reason some students procrastinate is that they lack the basic motivation to take control of their goals and their lives. Although goal setting (Chapter 2) and internal locus of control (Chapter 1) were discussed previously, they both deserve further mention here because they are essential to motivation and, in turn, to overcoming procrastination. *Motivation* may be considered the driving force that makes you act. If your motivation is weak or lacking, you may not accomplish much.

The following are strategies to overcome procrastination caused by lack of motivation.

- Examine your long-term goals. Are they clear? If not, reexamine your reasons for attending college, and clarify your long-term goals. If your career goals are uncertain, you might consider visiting the career counseling center for guidance.
- Focus on several short-term goals because they are much more visible and more easily accomplished than long-term goals. For example,

short-term goals might be completing a writing assignment on time, reading an assignment, or doing twenty math problems.

- Put your short-term goals on your daily to-do list, keep the list in sight, and check off each accomplishment.
- Operate through internal locus of control only (see Chapter 1). Just because you think an assignment is boring or useless, you are still responsible for completing the work to the best of your ability. Whether you like an assignment or not is irrelevant; it is only one piece of a whole course. You might try reading the course objectives or discussing the purpose of the assignment with your instructor or a classmate to clarify the purpose. As a person exercising internal locus of control, you are taking ownership of your own education.
- When you *think* about having to do something, stop thinking and *do it!*
- Offer yourself a reward for completing a task.

A = Afraid of Failure   A second major reason for procrastination is being afraid of failure. Procrastination caused by fear of failure is a psychological game many people play, either because they lack self-confidence or because they are perfectionists. In fact, perfectionists sometimes lack self-confidence because they equate achievement with self-worth. They want everything to be perfect, and so they put off challenging tasks. Whether fear of failure stems from perfectionism or simply from a basic sense of not measuring up to the task, the result is the same: The student postpones doing an assignment until it is too late to do it well or even at all. Then the student does not need to face the fact that he or she couldn't do an acceptable job. Often people will say after the fact, "Well, I could have done it, and done it well, if I'd had more time."

If you use such an excuse, you are setting yourself up for failure and creating a self-fulfilling prophecy. In other words, you fail because you have set out to fail by not living up to either your own standards or the standards that have been set for you.

To overcome procrastination caused by fear of failure, try the following approaches:

- Remind yourself that you are only human. You do not have to be perfect; just try to do your best.
- Plan your time wisely in order to finish the project without using the "if-only-I-had-more-time" excuse. Use your time planner, weekly study schedule, and daily to-do list to stay on track.
- Maintain a positive attitude. Even though you may not have done well in the past, put that behind you. If you work hard and encourage

yourself with positive self-talk, you should be able to avoid procrastination and tackle the assignment.

- Talk to a friend or counselor about your fears. With that person's help, devise a plan to overcome your fears.

S = Start-up Problems

A third reason for procrastination involves the problem of getting started. If you find yourself making excuses as to why you are not ready to start a project or assignment, then you have start-up problems that you need to face.

Start-up problems are usually based on excuses rather than reasons. Maybe you are not sure how to do the task, or you may be waiting for that "magic moment." Maybe you are just plain tired. Whatever your reason for procrastinating by not starting an activity, try the following suggestions.

- If you are not certain about how to do an assignment, reread the assignment, jot down some specific questions about what needs to be clarified, and then see or call your instructor or a classmate or get help from the math lab, writing lab, tutor service, etc. As soon as you have learned the answers to your questions, take action.
- On your weekly study schedule, write down specific tasks in blocks of times that you will need in order to do the task. Follow your schedule, beginning the first task right away.
- Write down specific tasks on your daily to-do list, and check them off as you complete them.
- Study in your regular place of study, free from distractions, because you will be using a conditioned response to help you get started.
- Study at the same times every day, if possible, because this could make studying become a habit.
- Do the task now; don't wait for inspiration. This is just another delaying tactic. The truth is that inspiration is 90 percent perspiration. In other words, get to work!

T = Task Is Too Overwhelming

A fourth reason for procrastination involves the large size or importance of the task. If your assignment seems overwhelming, use the following strategies to complete it.

- Break down the task into small, manageable segments. A large assignment does not have to be completed all at one time. Do the task bit by bit.
- Use small segments of time every day to whittle away at parts of the large task.

- As soon as you get any assignment, budget your time by putting specific, manageable segments of the task into your time planner and daily to-do list. Then follow your schedule until the whole task is completed.
- Start early. Begin the first segment of your assignment immediately. Reading a thirty-page chapter might seem formidable; reading five pages at a time is easier, but you need to read the first five pages as soon as possible.
- Reward yourself when you have completed a segment of the assignment.

Regardless of your reasons for putting off something, learn to recognize when you are procrastinating. Then take active steps to change your avoidance tactics. If you are inclined to procrastinate, think of it as a bad habit. Habits can be broken and can be replaced with more positive approaches.

WEB SITE INFORMATION

For information about perfectionism and procrastination, visit our web site:

<http://college.hmco.com/success/>

Critically Thinking in Writing

In a journal entry, describe a typical situation in which you procrastinate about doing an assignment. Using the suggestions above as well as your own ideas, devise a plan to overcome your procrastination.

Summary

Managing your time well means being realistic about your available time and how you use it. It is essential that you adopt a method of scheduling your time so that you can accomplish everything that needs to be done without forgetting appointments or other responsibilities. Whenever possible, use your peak time to the best advantage.

Three types of schedules available to you are the time planner, which gives you a broad overview of your whole term, plus a detailed look at your activities for the week; a weekly study schedule, which indi-cates specific study hours for each course; and a daily to-do list, which outlines your tasks for the day. Whatever schedules you use, begin by de-termining your inflexible times, when you have fixed responsibilities, and your flexible times, when you can choose what activities to do. Once you have a schedule, use it.

As you create your schedules, take into account the scheduling and timesaving tips listed in this chapter. These tips will help you be more productive and time-efficient.

Finally, this chapter discusses some reasons why people procrasti-nate. Procrastinators finish LAST because they Lack motivation, are Afraid of failure, have Start-up problems, or think the Task is Too over-whelming. Most importantly, the chapter provides you with solutions to overcome procrastination.

List of Terms

peak time
time planner
weekly study schedule
daily to-do list
inflexible times
flexible times

distributed effort
conditioned response
procrastination
LAST
motivation

In this box, write your summary question or statement for this chapter.

---

8 The Power of Memory

Everyone forgets something sometimes, and almost everyone wishes he or she could remember more. You probably already have some methods to help you remember. What do *you* do to jog your memory? The classic (and probably the corniest) way to remember something is to tie a string around your finger. Today Post-it Notes have become a popular means of sparking memory because they are conveniently sized and adhere to most surfaces. Some people even use the human element to help them remember: "Hey, Jess, would you remind me to tell so-and-so such-and-such when we get to class?"

How often do you accuse yourself of having a "bad" memory? At times, we all do. The good news is memory is neither "bad" nor "good." Rather, it is untrained or trained, and everyone has the power to train his or her memory. With training and practice, you can remember almost anything you want.

This chapter will show you ways to train your memory. It opens with an explanation of short-term and long-term memory, followed by a description of the process of remembering. The chapter then explains concentration and its role in the improvement of your memory. Finally, you will learn about several well-recognized memory techniques to help you increase your memory power and make sense out of hard-to-learn material and "slippery" facts.

SHORT-TERM AND LONG-TERM MEMORY

All memory begins with the senses because the five senses are the channels through which information comes. However, although you are bombarded by vast numbers of sights, sounds, touches, tastes, and smells twenty-four hours a day, only certain impressions and information actually go into your short- or long-term memory.

Short-term memory is the ability to recall bits of information for a very brief time, usually from twenty to thirty seconds unless you make a special effort to remember the information longer. For example, if you look up an unfamiliar telephone number in the phone book, you can remember that number until you have dialed it; after that you usually forget it. You may remember more familiar items somewhat longer. For example, you are likely to remember what you wore to school yesterday, but you have probably forgotten what you wore a month ago unless the date, clothing, or occasion was memorable. These two examples illustrate that short-term memory is limited in endurance and capacity. In fact, short-term memory can store only between five and nine items at a time. We can easily learn a phone number (seven digits) or a social security number (nine digits divided into three, two, and four numbers). But to get those numbers into long-term memory, we have to use them or repeat them until they are firmly in place. That takes time and effort. Thus, as another illustration, if you just listen to a lecture without taking notes, your short-term memory is bombarded by much more information than it can handle. It is way over that five-to-nine limit.

Long-term memory, as the name implies, is the ability to recall information for days, months, and even years after you have learned it. In fact, long-term memory can last a lifetime. Unlike short-term memory, long-term memory is unlimited in its capacity to store information. Examples of items that may be in your long-term memory are your own phone number and those of your closest friends, your social security number, and the multiplication tables, which you learned in grade school. Besides items composed of numbers, you also probably have nursery rhymes, lyrics to songs and commercials, and the general rules for your favorite sporting events stored in your long-term memory. Items you are able to retrieve from your long-term memory did not get there by magic. Either you made a conscious effort to put them into long-term memory or you heard them over and over for an extended period of time, as with the McDonald's commercial. If you hear the opening words, "Two all-beef patties . . . ," you can probably finish that ditty all the way to the sesame seed bun.

If you can retain all these commonplace items, you can certainly train your memory to store both the basic and complicated information you need to learn for your courses, your job, and your everyday life. Using what you know about short-term and long-term memory, you will realize, for example, that just listening to a lecture is not sufficient to remember all the major points and details. Storing information in your long-term memory requires that you take GREAT notes (see Chapter 3) and study them until you have mastered the material. The unique feature of the human brain is that the more you learn, the more you are capable of learning. Bits of information in your brain are like magnets: they attract and hold more and more information. Unlike a computer disk, which finally gets full, your memory has an unlimited capacity to take in information, store it, add to it, make connections, and permanently remember it.

THE PROCESS OF REMEMBERING

Unfortunately, in terms of memory, the human brain is not like a tape recorder or VCR: It cannot take everything in and then automatically repeat it all. As stated previously, moving information from short-term to long-term memory takes time and effort, as well as organization.

The human memory works in a way that is similar to that of a computer. A computer, like the human brain, deals with information in three stages: *input, storage,* and *output.* Input takes place when you sit down at a computer keyboard and enter information by pressing the right keys to create a meaningful document; at this point, the information is displayed on a screen and entered into what you consider to be the computer's short-term memory. Storage occurs when you want to have a more lasting record of your efforts: You enter the "save" command and name your file. Output happens when you retrieve that information for later use: You simply open the saved document and enjoy immediate recall of the information previously saved.

Like the computer, you initially have to use your senses, your power of observation, and your curiosity so that new information can enter your brain (input). When you preview a textbook chapter, for instance, you are carefully setting up a background so that you can connect and predict and make sense of your reading. Again like the computer, your brain needs a direct "save" command in order to put information into long-term memory (storage). When you mark sections in a textbook, write questions, and recite aloud over a period of time, for example, you are making a conscious and direct effort to "save" or store information in your long-term memory. Your brain will more readily and efficiently store information that is organized or structured. All of the memory techniques discussed in this chapter are effective ways to organize and structure information for storage. Finally, when you take a test later, you should be able to respond to the questions easily and accurately (output) because you have a permanent record in your long-term memory. You realize then that your study time and concentrated efforts have paid off.

The following chart lists and defines the three parts of the memory process—input, storage, and output. The chart includes a numbered list of learning techniques that you can use to enhance your memory process.

Enhancing Your Memory Process		
Input How to take in information.	**Storage** How to put information into long-term memory.	**Output** How to recall information later.
1. Become more observant.	1. Make a conscious effort to remember.	1. Use positive self-talk.
2. Control distractors, if possible.	2. Use your preferred learning style.	2. Focus and concentrate on test questions.
3. Understand concepts before learning them.	3. Mark texts and take notes in class.	3. Let memory techniques act as cues for recall.
4. Use sensory learning.	4. Review and recite frequently.	4. Mentally picture your personal visual organizers.
5. Be actively curious.	5. Use memory devices.	5. Use relaxation exercises to fight stress.
6. Get ready before listening to lectures.	6. Organize material personally.	
7. Preview before reading.	7. Make your own visual organizers.	

Realizing that you need time and effort to train your brain to remember, you can probably see why cramming has earned its bad reputation. If you cram (truly a four-letter word in this sense!), you are overloading the capacity of your short-term memory. Then, by magic, you expect to retrieve that information from long-term memory the next day. Such a procedure seldom works. In essence, it creates stress, which actually interferes with your ability to process information. Cramming is not an effective shortcut to putting information into your long-term memory. Instead of cramming, you should recite by repeating information out loud until you can quickly and comfortably recall it.

CONCENTRATION AND MEMORY

Have you ever found yourself lounging on your bed looking at the words in a textbook, but your mind has wandered a thousand miles away? If you are nodding your head "yes," then you realize how easy it is to get off-track or become distracted.

To enhance your memory and to achieve quality study time, you will benefit from understanding concentration and developing techniques to strengthen your own concentration. *Concentration* means focusing your attention on the task at hand.

Distractions include thoughts, people, surroundings, and other factors. At times, distractors can be interesting and even enjoyable. However, when you are studying, distractions can undermine your efforts. In general, distractions can be divided into two categories: environmental and personal.

Environmental and Personal Distractions

Environmental distractions include any outside conditions or interactions with others that interfere with your focus of attention. Noises of all kinds—music, TV, radio, telephones, and overheard conversations—create distractions. Interactions with friends, spouses, siblings, children, and even pets may become distractions. Some conditions that could interfere with concentration might include poor lighting, poor temperature, an uncomfortable chair, and unhealthy air quality. Even a beautiful day can lure you away from concentrating on your studies.

Personal distractions include any internal conditions that interfere with your focus of attention. One major distraction in the personal area is daydreaming, which occurs when you are not interested or are bored with the task at hand. Worry and stress of all kinds—an unresolved problem, a recent argument, lack of self-confidence, relationships, money difficulties, grades, jobs, and so on—can also interfere with your concentration. Other internal distractions include hunger, thirst, tiredness, lack of sleep, or physical illness.

WEB SITE INFORMATION

If you wish to take a Study Distractions Analysis, visit our web site:

<http://college.hmco.com/success/>

Solutions to Distractions

Identifying the types of distractions is not nearly as important as finding solutions. Generally, environmental distractions are easier to overcome than personal ones; you can often change or control your environment. However, because many personal distractions are complex and intense, you may only be able to develop coping strategies to deal with them.

One of the steps you can take to improve your concentration is to have a regular place to study. A regular study place allows you to concentrate better because it promotes the mental habit of studying. Ideally, you should have a private work space, free from most distractions, where you keep all your supplies—books, paper, pens, dictionary, computer. This study area should include a comfortable chair (but not so comfy that you begin to lounge!), adequate lighting, pleasant temperature, and good ventilation. Another way to promote concentration is to set up a study schedule (see Chapter 7).

The following chart provides some other possible solutions to common distractions.

Distractions	Solutions
1. CDs, radio, or TV	1. Turn them off.
2. Telephone	2. Ignore it; let the answering machine pick up, turn off the ringer.

(continued on the next page)

Distractions	Solutions
3. Outside noises (people talking, others' music or TV, sirens, etc.)	3. Move to a quieter place; wear ear plugs; consciously focus on your task.
4. Friends interrupting	4. Reason with them by explaining your goals/needs; set aside special times to see them.
5. Spouses/significant others	5. Same as above. Ask them to watch children, do chores, or entertain themselves while you study.
6. Children	6. Find something to amuse them (TV or VCR); study with them if they are in school; get someone to watch them; study during their naps or school hours.
7. Pets	7. Put them in another room; give them a treat; tune them out.
8. Nice day outside	8. Focus on your task; reward yourself for keeping on track; study outside.
9. Daydreams or wandering thoughts	9. Stop what you are doing as soon as you find your mind wandering and take a short break. Train yourself to get back on track. Write down your thoughts and get back to your task.
10. Boredom	10. Analyze why you are bored. Find ways to become interested; break task into smaller segments; take short breaks.
11. Worry	11. Try to solve the problem before you begin to study. Jot down your problem and deal with it after studying.
12. Stress	12. See guidelines in Chapter 2.

(continued on the next page)

Distractions	Solutions
13. Tiredness	13. Take a short nap; follow a regular sleep schedule, exercise; eat a moderate, well-balanced diet; have a moderate amount of caffeine.
14. Illness	14. Take the necessary steps to get well. Accept your limitation and adapt to the situation.

Critically Thinking in Writing

In a journal entry, name at least two distractions that keep you from concentrating while studying. Instead of saying something like, "I worry a lot," make it a specific statement, such as, "I'm worried about having enough money to make my next car payment." Provide at least three solutions for each distraction that should work for you. Make an effort to go beyond the suggestions in this chapter, and come up with your own creative solutions.

CLASSIC MEMORY TECHNIQUES

Everyone uses some memory strategies. But whatever memory devices you already use, you may want to train your memory further by adopting some of the following techniques: observation, association, clustering, imaging, and mnemonics. These five methods and their variations are called the classic memory techniques because they are well-established ways to increase memory and are used in education, businesses, advertising, organizations, and in all aspects of everyday life.

Observation

Much of your ability to remember is based on careful observation. *Observation* involves a conscious effort to pay attention, be alert, listen attentively, and notice details. If, for example, you have ever lost track of your car in a public parking lot, it was probably because you did not make a conscious effort to pay attention or to notice landmarks. Likewise, you need to employ basic observational skills both in the classroom and in your studying before you can apply any other memory techniques.

Exercise 8-A

Directions: Complete this exercise on observation without looking at any of these objects or people.

1. How many separate parking lots are on the campus? _____

2. What is the speed limit in the college parking lot(s)? _____

3. Describe a student who sits behind you in one of your classes.

_____

_____

_____

4. Describe how one of your teachers enters his or her classroom and begins class.

_____

_____

_____

_____

5. Name and briefly describe one unusual thing you saw on campus yesterday or today.

_____

_____

_____

_____

_____

Observation is not only fun, it is also essential to learning. For example, when you are listening to lectures, taking notes, and studying textbooks, you must make a conscious effort to notice and remember pertinent information. When you are taking notes in class, besides recording the obvious—information on the chalkboard or an overhead transparency—you should be noticing the teacher's body language, his or her vocal emphasis, and transitions and organizational cues. Careful observation of these details allows you to determine what information is of major or minor importance and what you should emphasize in your notes, that is, what is important to remember.

Exercise 8-B

Directions: Carefully observe one of your instructors. Note how he/she uses body language, facial expressions, or voice to indicate important points.

1. What kinds of body language are used by your instructor to emphasize major points?

   _____

   _____

   _____

2. What facial expressions does he or she use to emphasize major points?

   _____

   _____

3. How does the teacher use his or her voice to emphasize major points?

   _____

   _____

   _____

Association

The second memory technique, learning by *association,* is based upon a simple principle: Learning something new is always easier if you can associate or connect it with something you already know. For example, if you are just beginning to use a computer, you might not understand what is meant by "windows" until you realize that windows on computers are very similar to windows in buildings: When you look into them, you can see what exists in the computer and in the environment. Or, in a biology class, if you are learning about the structure of neurons in the brain, you might associate one part of the neuron, the dendrites, which grow as you learn new information, with the roots of a tree, which grow when they are watered.

When you encounter new information in, for example, a math or science course, you can often relate it to some previously learned concepts because many such courses are arranged sequentially. However, if you find new information puzzling, make an extra effort to associate it with information you already know, such as the previous example of associating dendrites with tree roots. You might also try to relate what you are learning in one course with what you are learning in another. For example, what you learn in a psychology class about people's behavior might help you to better understand the actions, motives, and personality of a character you are reading about in your English literature class.

A practical application of remembering by association is learning people's names. The association can be either direct or silly. For example, suppose the new nurse in your doctor's office is named Karen. You discover that she is a very helpful, caring person, so you could remember her name by thinking of her as being a *caring* (Karen) person. Also, the person at the information desk at the college is named Shirley, so you think to yourself, *surely* Shirley knows everything. These are examples of direct and logical associations. Other associations might be a bit silly, but they will still help you to remember a name. For instance, if you meet someone named Marcia at a party, you might picture her hair crowned with big white marshmallows. Marshmallows remind you of the sound of her name, Marsh-a.

Critically Thinking Together

Name the dean or president of your college or university. Write it below. As a group, write the name below and find several ways to associate the name with the title. Write your best association in the blank below, and share it with the rest of the class.

Name: _____

Best Association: _____

_____

Clustering

Clustering, the process of grouping a large number of ideas into subgroups, is another handy memory device. This technique is based on the fact, mentioned earlier, that you can remember several groups of five or so items more easily than a large number of separate items. If you have thirty items to learn, try to organize them into groups. For example, you might try clustering new terms or vocabulary you have to learn.

Clustering can also be useful as a method for prewriting or organizing an essay or research paper. If your ideas, information, or material cannot be arranged chronologically (relating to time, from first to last) or spatially (relating to area, from top to bottom, side to side, etc.), you can cluster to find categories or groupings of ideas that will provide you with a logical method of organization.

Clustering is also useful as a study technique when you have to learn a number of items. For example, in Chapter 7 on time management, eight "Additional Scheduling Tips" are listed in random order. Here is what the original list looks like:

- Determine which courses are easy and which are hard for you. Study your hardest subject first.
- Study your hardest course every day.
- Consider your peak time. Study for your hardest course during your most mentally and physically alert period.
- Study as soon after class as possible. Remember the Ebbinghaus Forgetting Curve, which clearly indicates that most forgetting happens immediately after hearing or reading information.

- Prioritize: What needs to be done now? Attack the most urgent task right away.
- Study dissimilar subjects back to back. For example, if you are taking sociology and psychology, study a math course in between. Or if you are taking statistics and a math course, separate these courses in your study time with English or history. On your study schedule, insert *specific subjects* to study.
- Use *distributed effort;* that is, breaking a large task into several manageable steps, and spacing your work time over a period of days. For example, if you have an essay to write, you could begin by brainstorming, then starting a rough draft, and so forth.
- Note due dates and allow yourself plenty of lead time to get long projects finished.

If you were required to learn these eight tips for a test, you might cluster them into the following three categories:

Hardest-Class Cluster	How-To Cluster	Early-Bird Cluster
Hardest first	Dissimilar back to back	ASAP after class
Hardest every day	Distributed effort	Prioritize: first things first
Hardest at peak time		Plenty of lead time for big projects

Notice how the three clusters logically combine the information as well as condense it; both processes will make it easier to learn. The cluster titles may seem silly, but even that silliness can help to prompt your memory. So when you are clustering ideas, use headings to group them that will be memorable to you.

Exercise 8-C

Directions: If you were moving away from home to go to college, you might go shopping for the following items. Determine how you could cluster them.

(continued on the next page)

Exercise 8-C (continued)

1. On a piece of paper, rearrange related items by clustering them into groups.

2. Give each group a heading that indicates what the items have in common. Try to place every item into a group.

3. If you are desperate, put any leftover items into a group called "Miscellaneous."

   Your goal is to make logical groups with as few leftovers as possible (or none).

backpack	shoes	hammer
CDs	lamp	phone card
wastebasket	pliers	textbooks
sheets	pencils	salt & pepper
microwave	journal	futon
soft drinks	comb	snacks
Walkman	soap	computer disks
bath towels	Frisbee	paper towels

Imaging

Imaging, or using a picture to represent something, can be an excellent way to remember a fact, process, definition, or concept. For example, most of us know the geographical shape of Italy because its image resembles a boot. If you can add pictures to whatever it is you are learning, you will be enhancing your learning because you are using your imagination, your visual sense, and your sense of touch (tactile). You may even want to consider drawing your pictures in various colors and visualizing them as three-dimensional shapes. Colors and shapes in themselves can spark your visual memory. Pictures can make words and ideas become more real and physical, thus more memorable.

You may already have discovered how to reinforce ideas, definitions, or other material that you need to learn by drawing pictures. If you have not done so yet, try this method with something that you are having trouble remembering. You do not have to be a great artist. Stick figures to represent people, boxes to represent ideas, lines to show relationships—all these simple illustrations are fine. These pictures are for your eyes only, so however they look, you will know what the picture is supposed to represent. The picture will be imprinted on your mind because *you* drew it!

Exercise 8-D

Directions: Select a term or concept that you need to learn for any one of your courses.

1. Name the term or concept and give its definition. _____

   _____

   _____

   _____

2. Draw a picture that will provide you with an image of the term and definition.

Mnemonics

Mnemonics is a catch-all category of memory tricks. Mnemonic devices include acronyms and abbreviations, made-up sentences or phrases, rhymes or songs, and physical techniques.

Acronyms and Abbreviations   An *acronym* is a mnemonic device formed from the first letters of words in a list or phrase; these letters are pronounced together as a word. GREAT (Chapter 3), SOLVE (Chapter 2), and LAST (Chapter 7) are examples of acronyms in this textbook. Some acronyms have become so popular that they have taken on a life of their own. You are all familiar with Light Amplification by Stimulated

Emission of Radiation printers and Light Amplification by Stimulated Emission of Radiation surgery, but you call them laser printers and laser surgery. The acronym *laser* (originally in capital letters) and other words like *radar, sonar,* and *scuba,* all originally acronyms, have become actual words in the English language. *Abbreviations* are composed of initials pronounced as letters like USA, FBI, SAT, and IBM that have replaced words. People have used acronyms and abbreviations for ages, but in our rapid high-tech world, they are becoming more and more common.

In college, you can create your own acronyms and abbreviations to help you remember information. Some acronyms are well known. For example, HOMES stands for the Great Lakes—Huron, Ontario, Michigan, Erie, and Superior. SAGE is a "wise" way to remember the four different kinds of context clues: Synonyms, Antonyms, General sense of the sentence, and Examples. SKILL represents the excretory organs of the body—Skin, Kidneys, Intestines, Liver, and Lungs. RICE is the first-aid treatment for a sprain—Rest, Ice, Compression, and Elevation. Some abbreviations are also commonly used. ASAP is used commonly in business and stands for As Soon As Possible. ADA stands for American Dental Association as well as the American Disability Act. URL is a computer term for Uniform Resource Locator. ESL is English as a Second Language. CD-Rom couldn't decide whether to be an abbreviation or an acronym—Compact Disc-Read-Only Memory. In your studies, you can borrow useful acronyms and abbreviations, and you can benefit even more by creating your own.

Made-up Sentences or Phrases   Making up sentences or phrases, either nonsensical or serious, can be an effective way of learning and remembering material. The spellings of difficult words can often be learned easily with mnemonics. For instance, saying "A Rat In The House May Eat The Ice Cream" is an easy way to teach a child how to spell *arithmetic* because the sentence is silly (making it memorable), and the first letters of the words, taken together, spell *arithmetic.* For adults, mnemonics can be applied to remember more difficult or confusing spellings. For example, do you spell attendance with an *ance* or *ence*? It's easy to remember the correct spelling if you think of attending a dAnce. Likewise, FeBRuary is a very cold month—brrrrr!

Sentence mnemonics can help you learn very complex information. For example, students in biology class have to know all the basic elements of living things. The sentence to remember is "K. P. COHN'S CaFe (has) Mighty good salt." The elements this sentence helps you remember are, in order, potassium (symbol K), phosphorus (symbol P), carbon (C), oxygen (O), hydrogen (H), nitrogen (N), sulfur (S), calcium (Ca), iron (Fe), magnesium (Mg—Mighty good), and sodium and chlorine (Na and Cl), which make up salt. (The word *has* is in parentheses because it does not have any meaning in terms of the elements in this sentence.) Thus, by learning one sentence, you can recall the eleven elements you need to know as well as their symbols.

There are several well-known sentences used in biology and medical courses. To remember the classification of living things (Kingdom, Phylum, Class, Order, Family Genus, Species, Variety) say, "Kings Play Cards On Fairly Good Soft Velvet." If, for example, you needed to learn the eight categories in the Myers-Briggs Type Indicator (MBTI) (Extravert, Introvert, Sensor, iNtuitive, Thinker, Feeler, Judger, and Perceiver), you might say, "Ed and I Snuck North To Find Juicy Plums." As you make up your own sentences to remember information, keep in mind that the sillier you make the sentence, the easier it might be to remember it.

Rhymes and Songs   *Rhymes* and *songs* are popular mnemonics because they help you learn through rhythm and sound. Probably the first "learning" song you encountered was the ABC song. Another popular jingle enables us to remember which months have thirty days and which ones have thirty-one: "Thirty days hath September, April, June, and November, all the rest have thirty-one; excepting February alone, which hath but twenty-eight in fine, till leap year gives it twenty-nine."

At times, using rhymes can also help you in practical situations. If you need to do any maintenance around the house, such as putting a washer in a faucet, attaching a hose to a spigot, or changing a light bulb, and you are relatively inexperienced, you may wonder which way to turn the wrench, hose coupling, or bulb. Although experts know that all standard threads turn clockwise to tighten, all you need to remember is "righty/tighty and lefty/loosey."

A rhyme that you might find useful if you are taking chemistry is "*-ate,* I ate; *-ide,* I died." This rhyme helps you remember that cyan*ates* are harmless chemicals, whereas cyan*ides* are extremely poisonous—an important distinction to know. Another rhyme that could help you in your economics course to remember that many jobs are available in a "tight labor market" is "Tell your boss to fly a kite, when the labor market's tight." Some of your instructors may share other rhymes and songs in their subject areas, but with a little imagination, you can also make your own.

Physical Techniques   Using a physical clue can also act as a mnemonic. This can mean physically putting something in a particular place, like putting letters that need to be mailed under your car keys just to jog your memory. Another variation of this technique is to use physical actions or movements to represent steps in a process, lists of items, or cause-and-effect reactions. In other words, in these instances, you are making a physical representation of an abstract idea. For example, instead of the "Thirty Days" poem for remembering the days in the month, perhaps you learned the knuckle method. This method names the months chronologically, counting January on the first knuckle, February in between, March on the second knuckle, April in between, etc. (Don't worry about the fact that you have one in between and one knuckle left over at the end.) Knuckle months have thirty-one days; in-between-knuckle months have thirty. Unfortunately, this method does not give you a clue about how many days are in February; you are on your own to figure that out. Yet another physical technique for learning information is a hands-on process. This includes using a skeleton to learn the bones of the body or using physical representations of molecules to understand molecular structure. The more senses you use to learn something, the more easily you will learn and remember. Using physical techniques can help you to remember everyday errands and tasks. To remember academic information, you can deliberately create your own physical techniques.

Although mnemonic devices made up by others can be very helpful, you should create your own because you will really own them, and they may be even easier to remember than mnemonics that are provided for you.

Exercise 8-E

Directions: Create your own mnemonic device so that you can easily remember the names of the five classic memory techniques (observation, association, clustering, imaging, and mnemonics).

_____

_____

Summary

In this chapter, several aspects of memory are discussed. First, short-term and long-term memory are defined. Short-term memory lasts only about thirty seconds, whereas long-term memory can last a few months, a few years, or forever. However, getting information from short-term to long-term memory takes time, concentrated effort, and an organized method of learning. Committing something to memory is a process that actually includes three stages: input, storage, and output.

Finally, several classic memory techniques are explained. These include observation, association, clustering, imaging, and mnemonics. Mnemonics, an overall term for several memory techniques, include acronyms, which are words made out of the first letters of several words or phrases; silly or sensible made-up sentences; rhymes or songs; and various physical techniques.

List of Terms

short-term memory
long-term memory
input, storage, and output
concentration
environmental distractions
personal distractions
observation
association
clustering

imaging
mnemonics
acronyms
    or abbreviations
made-up sentences or phrases
rhymes and songs
physical techniques

In this box, write your summary question or statement for this chapter.

9 The Power of Making Your Own Visual Organizers

Have you ever heard the saying, "A picture is worth a thousand words"? Although the well-known expression is a little worn out, and the number is surely exaggerated, adding pictures to words can be a powerful means of enhancing your understanding and memory.

In this chapter, you will learn ways to arrange large amounts of information so that the whole picture, a summation of the information, is visible on one or two pages. *Visual organizers,* as the name implies, organize and summarize information by using key words with simple visual connections, such as lines, arrows, or geometric symbols, to show relationships.

The five major visual organizers are:

1. Topic Grids
2. Action-Reaction Arrows
3. Ts
4. Webs
5. Time Lines

Creating visual organizers to summarize various aspects of a topic can help you to learn by stimulating your critical-thinking powers. By creating organizers, you can focus on parts and details and still see the "big picture" all on one page. You may discover new connections you didn't realize existed. You may even find solutions to practical problems by drawing a visual organizer. For example, if you wish to compare two or more cars to decide which make or model to buy, then the drawing of an organizer can help you "see" the details of each likely choice, thus helping you to make an informed decision. Likewise, in college, if you need to see how the various parts of a topic relate to each other, then you can visually make those connections on a page or two by drawing an appropriate visual organizer. By making and studying the organizer, you can learn the details, understand the big picture, and avoid feeling overwhelmed by the amount of information you need to learn.

GETTING A HAND ON IT: MAKING VISUAL ORGANIZERS

The visual picture of a hand should help you to remember the five kinds of personal visual organizers. As you can see from the illustration, each finger and the thumb represents a different visual organizer.

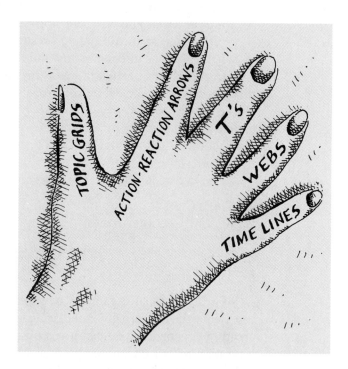

Topic Grids

Because of their concise and logical structure, topic grids provide you with a means of organizing large amounts of information. Just as the thumb allows the hand to hold and grasp many objects, the grid allows you to hold and grasp an infinite number of categories of related information. The thumb of the hand, therefore, with its ability to hold and grasp objects, is a good memory tool to remind you of all the information a topic grid can hold.

The topic grid, as the name implies, consists of a series of boxes, similar to boxes on graph paper, only much larger. If you have a computer with a program that generates tables and graphs, you can use this resource to create grids. Otherwise, with a ruler, you can draw a grid similar to the one illustrated. Be sure to make the boxes big enough to include all the information you need. The following graphic shows the format of a typical grid before any information has been written in the boxes.

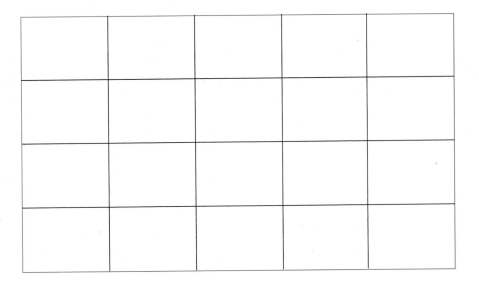

Step 1: Write the name of the general topic above the grid as the title.

Step 2: Leaving the very first box in the upper left corner empty, label each box from left to right along the top row with the name of a subdivision of this general topic. Remember, all items across the top must be parts of the same general topic, classification, or category. The number of items across the top can range from two to as many as you need.

Suppose, for instance, that in your English class you are reading a series of poems related to a certain theme. These poems are being studied as a springboard for writing an essay; in your essay, you are expected to compare and contrast the concepts and poetic devices used in these poems. By creating a topic grid, you can compare and contrast the ideas within each poem, as shown in the following example:

Title: Poems About Animals

	"The Eagle" Tennyson	"Toads" Larkin	"A Bird Came Down the Walk" Dickinson	"The Tyger" Blake

Step 3: Write either questions or key words to generate information about each of the items on the left-hand side of the grid going down.

When you are writing questions and statements down the side of your grid, remember that they must pertain to all the subdivisions listed across the top. In addition, you should avoid writing questions that begin with words like *does, is,* or *can,* because these lowest-level questions (see the Quality Questions Pyramid in Chapter 3) would fill the grid with yeses and noes, making it useless as a visual organizer. The following grid lists some questions you might ask for the poetry assignment.

Title: Poems About Animals

	"The Eagle" Tennyson	"Toads" Larkin	"A Bird Came Down the Walk" Dickinson	"The Tyger" Blake
What is the tone?				
What is the theme?				
Describe the imagery.				

Step 4: Fill in the grid boxes with the answers to your questions for each category.

In the poetry example, look at the first question (What is the tone?) and answer that question in the appropriate box under each of the poems, going across the categories. Or, if you wish, go down the grid, answering each question in the boxes under the first poem ("The Eagle"). Then continue for the other poems, one at a time. Whichever method you choose to fill in the boxes, continue writing brief answers until all the answer boxes of the grid are filled.

When writing answers in the boxes of the grid, use only key words or phrases, not complete sentences. The key words will take up less space than sentences and should jog your memory later when you are writing your essay or studying the information.

Topic grids are useful for many study situations. Whether you are studying for a test, writing an essay, or doing research for a large project, you can organize your information on a grid. Sometimes, when you are dealing with a very complex topic or have lots of sources, you may have to refer back to your sources later for additional information. If that is the case, to save time, it is a good idea to note where you obtained the information in the appropriate answer boxes by using abbreviations, such as T for textbook (with the page number), N for lecture notes (with the date), LB for library book, I for Internet, etc.

The following completed topic grid serves as a visual organizer for education majors who are studying learning disabilities.

Learning Disabilities and ADD

	Developmental Speech and Language	Academic Skills	Unclassified	Attention Disorders (may accompany LD)
Definition	Difficulty making sounds or using language	Behind classmates in academic areas	Delays *not* easily categorized as *specific* LD	Unable to focus attention (*not* considered an LD)
Types or Examples	1. Articulation (speech) 2. Expressive (words) 3. Receptive (understanding)	1. Developmental reading disorder (dyslexia) 2. Writing 3. Arithmetic	Motor skill, language, and/or academic delays Coordination disorders (penmanship, spelling, memory)	Short attention span, easily distracted, excessive daydreaming Some are hyperactive
How it is diagnosed?	Speech therapist (pronunciations, vocabulary, and grammar) Psychologist (I.Q.) Physician (hearing and vocal chords)	Standardized tests, vision and hearing tests, school attendance record	Long-term history of delays	Long-term history: fidgeting, losing things, interrupting, talking excessively, failure to remain in seat, stay on task, take turns
Treatment	Special Education, IEP tutoring, speech and language therapy, counseling, behavior modification	Special Education, IEP, tutoring, counseling, behavior modification	Special Education, IEP, tutoring, counseling, behavior modification	Special Education, IEP, medication, counseling, behavior modification

Step 5: Study the information. Place a piece of paper over all the grid boxes (the answers), read a statement or question, and try to recite the answer for each subdivision across the top. You can work across or down or in both directions to avoid rote memorization.

Topic grids may be useful in every college course—yes, even in math. Some students may say, "Well, I'm taking a math course, and nothing I'm learning could be put on a grid." Such an assumption is incorrect, as the following student example proves.

Topic Grid for Basic Formulas

	Rectangle	Triangle	Circle	Parallelogram
How do you find area?	$A = lw$	$A = 1/2bh$	$A = \pi r^2$	$A = bh$
What does formula mean?	Area = length times width	Area = 1/2 times base times altitude	Area = pi times radius squared	Area = base times altitude
How do you find perimeter?	$P = 2l + 2w$	$P = a + b + c$	$C = 2\pi r$	$P = 2l + 2w$
What do P formulas mean?	P = two times length plus two times width	P = side a plus side b plus side c	Circumference = 2 times pi times radius	P = two times length plus two times width
What does each variable represent?	A = area l = length w = width P = perimeter	A = area b = base h = altitude P = perimeter a, b, c = sides	A = area r = radius C = circumference	P = perimeter A = area b = base h = altitude l = length w = width
Draw an example of each.				

The beauty of a topic grid is that it consolidates and summarizes what could have been several pages of notes, as much as a whole chapter from a textbook, or a combination of both. Topic grids allow you to see relationships, similarities, and differences in the material you are learning. Studying from the grid is much more efficient than flipping back through pages of notes or texts. In addition, the physical and mental act of *creating* the grid itself is a powerful learning tool and stimulates your critical-thinking ability. Finally, when you take a test after studying from a topic grid, that grid and all it contains will become a pictorial reference in your mind, letting you see both the overview and the details.

Exercise 9-A

Directions: Using the directions for creating a topic grid, make a topic grid for the following information.

Ernest Hemingway, born in 1899, was a journalist and a writer of novels and short stories. When he graduated from high school in Oak Park, Illinois, he became a cub reporter on the *Kansas City Star.* He was noted for his terse prose style, which contained much dialogue. He wrote about war and his own adventures, blending realism and romanticism, and was part of the "lost generation," a group of expatriates living in Paris in the 1920s. His most ambitious novel was *For Whom the Bell Tolls* (1940). In 1953, he won the Pulitzer Prize for *The Old Man and the Sea.* He won the Nobel Prize for literature in 1954. When his physical and mental health began to fail, he shot and killed himself in 1961.

William Faulkner, born in 1897, was a humanist who explored questions of human freedom and was noted for his masterly characterizations. He wrote short stories, the most famous being "The Bear," and novels, often set in his fictitious Yoknapatawpha County, describing the regional traditions and culture of Oxford, Mississippi, Faulkner's hometown. Long, complex sentences were trademarks of his style, although he also used stream of consciousness. In the 1920s he lived in the New Orleans French Quarter with other writers and artists. He won the Nobel Prize in 1949 and the Pulitzer Prize in 1955 for *A Fable* and posthumously in 1963 for *The Reivers.* He died in 1962.

Virginia Woolf, born in 1882, was an innovator of modern British fiction, using internal dialogue and stream of consciousness. She was educated at home, her scholarly father having an extensive library. Her best-known works are *Mrs. Dalloway* and *To the Lighthouse.* In the early 1900s, she moved to Bloomsbury (a section of London) with her brother and sister, and they attracted a number of avant-garde artists, writers, and philosophers, who were known for years as the Bloomsbury Group. Besides writing novels, Woolf was famous for her critical essays. Fearing that she was going mad, she drowned herself in 1941.

Action-Reaction Arrows

Action-reaction arrows are effective visual organizers when you need to show cause-and-effect relationships. Returning to the image of the hand as a memory device, just as the index finger points, so does the action-reaction diagram employ arrows to point from the direction of an action (cause) to the direction of a reaction (effect). Action-reaction arrows are adaptable to all topics that involve cause and effect because the arrows may point in any direction (up, down, kitty-cornered, etc.), to show cause-and-effect relationships.

Note how the following action-reaction arrow diagram shows the causes and effects of procrastination.

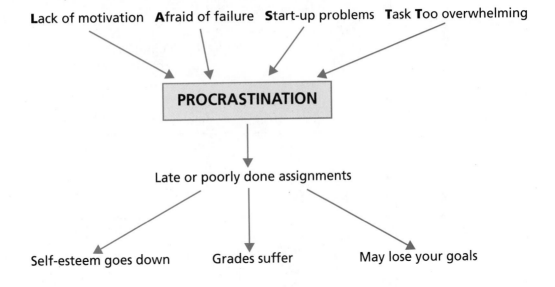

How you design your action-reaction arrows depends entirely upon the complexity of the information you have. You may have one or many causes that lead to one or many effects or results. These results, in turn, might have other ramifications, which themselves become causes leading to further effects. Thus, in many instances you will have a chain reaction of cause and effect: a primary cause or causes that lead to other causes and effects; these, in turn, lead to secondary effects, and so on.

The following student example illustrates the causes and effects of ground-water contamination as discussed in an environmental science class.

Causes and Effects of Ground-Water Contamination

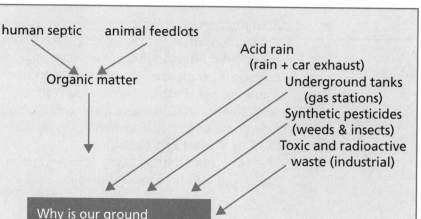

Exercise 9-B

Directions: Create an action-reaction arrow visual organizer by answering the following question (make sure your arrows point from cause to effect).

What has happened to you since you've been in college? Include social, personal (i.e., self-awareness), and educational changes.

Ts

Ts are the appropriate visual organizer to use if you have only two items to compare or contrast, if you are preparing to write an argumentative or persuasive paper (pro/con), or if you are trying to make a decision between two choices. This diagram gets the name T because of its visual shape. To create this visual organizer, you draw a line down the middle of the paper, draw an intersecting line across it at the top, and enter one item on one side of the center line and the other on the opposite side. Thus, the diagram looks like a T, and it is equated with the middle finger of a hand in a *kindly* way, because the middle finger is the midpoint of the fingers and thumb.

You can also think of the T as a balanced equation: Whatever information you put on one side of the T can usually be balanced with comparable information on the other side. If one side has a piece of information but the other side doesn't, leave a blank space on the other side. Notice in the following example how the information on one side is balanced by opposite information on the other side.

Pros and Cons of Returning to College

Pro	Con
Continuing my education	College may have little impact on getting a job
Eventually may end up w/better-paying job	Will have to cut expenses now
Age provides motivation and life experience	Fear of competing w/younger students
Can get student loan	Expensive
Reach my long-term goal	Time-consuming
Meet new people	Takes time out of my social life
Mental challenges	Added stress

In making a decision or thinking through a persuasive argument, no matter which side you favor, pro or con, you should be able to list the information for each side.

You can also use a T as a prewriting technique for a comparison/contrast essay. In addition, a T can act as a study guide to summarize conflicting theories or opinions.

Here is an example of a T created from a student's lecture notes in a world history course. Notice how the student begins with a two-sided question.

Has Marxism hindered or helped Africa's development?	
Viewpoint 1 **Marxism Has Hindered Africa**	**Viewpoint 2** **Marxism Has Helped Africa**
Ndabaningi Sithole	Brenda Powers
Marxist govts. (colonialism) betray Africa's people	Capitalists need colonies to keep economies afloat
Africans are opposed to Marxism—foreign European ideology	Capitalists still use imperialism to make themselves wealthier while making Africa poorer
Africans want to choose social order based on African traditions—pure, simple	Socialism would put needs of people first, offering the only real hope for Afr.
Imperialism = imposition	Social. creates conditions in which nation. div./race discr. are abolished
Marx. soc. destroyed one Afr. econ. after another—mils. die/starve	Marx. teaches that soc. revol. leads to complete elimination of natl. oppression

Exercise 9-C

Directions: Draw a T using the following information about football and soccer.

Among sports in the United States, football is one of the most popular, but soccer has been gaining in popularity. These sports can be compared and contrasted in several ways.

(continued on the next page)

Exercise 9-C *(continued)*

The first set of rules for soccer, which is called football in most countries except the United States, was established in 1863. Currently, a team consists of 11 players, only one of whom, the goaltender, can use his or her hands. Everyone else on the team can use any other part of his or her body—feet, knees, elbows, hips, and head—to get the ball to the goal. The ball, made of leather or rubber, weighs 14 to 16 ounces and is 27 to 28 inches in circumference. The field can be 100 to 130 yards long and 50 to 100 yards wide, but the length must always be greater than the width. Game time varies, but professional games last 90 minutes, broken into two halves. The governing body is the *Federation Internationale de Football Association* (FIFA), and international playoffs between the top teams of each country compete in the World Cup.

Football evolved slowly from the sport rugby in the nineteenth century. The first intercollegiate game was played in 1867 between Rutgers and Princeton. The ball is an oblate spheroid, 11 to 11¼ inches long and 21¼ to 21½ inches around its longest axis. It weighs 14 to 15 ounces and is often called a "pigskin" because that is what it was originally made of, although footballs are now made of leather or plastic, with leather laces on one side, making it easy to grip the ball for carrying or passing. There are 11 players. The ball is kicked to start the game or to make field goals or extra points; otherwise, it is thrown from one player to another or carried to the goal line. The field is 100 yards long (with two additional 10-yard areas called end zones) and is 53⅓ yards wide. Professional games are 60 minutes, divided into 4 quarters, but the actual game time is much longer because the clock is stopped for various reasons. The first professional organization, the National Football League (NFL), was established in 1919. In 1946 the American Football League (AFL) was formed, and the Super Bowl, first played in 1969, is the yearly highlight of professional football.

In addition, many differences exist in the rules, scoring, and manner of play of soccer and football.

Critically Thinking in Writing

Some school boards across the country are considering mandating uniforms for public schools at the grade school, middle school, and high school levels. In a journal entry, critically examine this idea. Begin by writing the question "What are the advantages and disadvantages of public school children wearing uniforms?" at the top of your journal page. Then, draw a T and label one side of the T "Advantages" and the other side "Disadvantages." Brainstorm as many advantages (pros) and disadvantages (cons) as you can for making uniforms mandatory, and put each reason on the appropriate sides of your T. Try to balance each pro with a con. When you finish brainstorming (try to have at least five reasons for each), determine which side, in your opinion, has the strongest argument. Remember, the strongest argument is not necessarily the side with the longest list of reasons. Then, under your T, write a letter to your local public school board explaining why you think students should be required to wear or not wear uniforms according to your conclusion.

Webs

Webs can take many shapes, and continuing the memory device of the hand, the fourth finger, the ring finger, represents this type of visual organizer. Typically, a web begins with a central idea on the paper, which can be likened to a ring on the ring finger. This type of diagram lends itself well to creative thinking and is often best used when brainstorming for an essay or a project. Webs are easy to make and are very flexible. However, because of their open-ended structure, you may be tempted to overuse them. When a more specific visual organizer is appropriate for learning or summarizing the information, you should make the more specific one.

To create a web, begin with a topic, a question, or a key word and branch out from there. This weblike diagram can take the shape of a tree, turkey tracks, or wheel spokes—you name it. Therefore, the resulting diagram is not as predictable in its form as some other visual organizers. It does, however, allow you to generate a great number of ideas. In the following example, using information from a psychology textbook chapter, a student created a web of the five senses in terms of stimuli (S) and receptors (R).

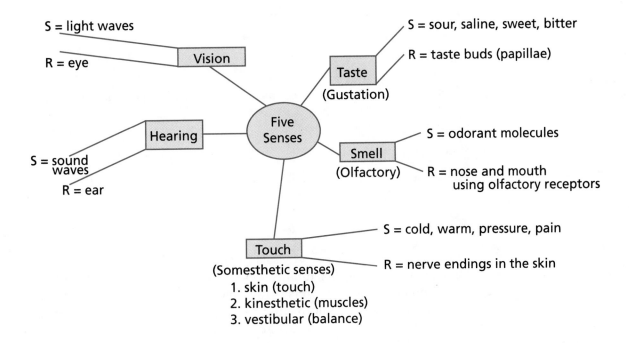

Some webs begin with a general category and move to more specific subdivisions. This pattern resembles a traditional flowchart, which is informally referred to as turkey tracks. This is a good way to narrow down a subject or to show relationships. Following is an example of such a web, using birds as the general category.

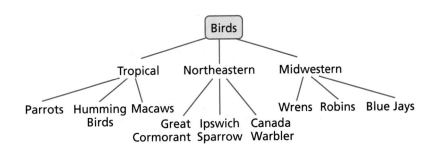

A web can take any shape that is meaningful and useful for your purposes. In such a drawing, you may use lines, as in the examples in this text, or you might make blocks, circles, or a combination of lines and geometric shapes. Whatever is meaningful to you is acceptable.

Exercise 9-D

Directions: Make a web in the shape of your choice using *one* of the following words as the main topic. Then, by brainstorming, branch out with other related words or phrases.

1. Transportation
2. Clothing
3. Sports
4. Electronic games

Time Lines

Time lines may be the easiest visual organizers to make, but like the little finger in the hand mnemonic, they probably will not be used as often as the other visual organizers. Time lines are limited in their use and flexibility because the information they illustrate involves time elapsed, whether it is seconds, minutes, days, years, centuries, or eras.

The structure of time lines is straightforward and fairly simple. They represent chronological events along a straight line, which can be drawn horizontally or vertically. Time lines are good visual organizers if you need to know when various events or steps in a process occur. For example, they could be used in a biology course when you are studying a process that changes fairly rapidly over a period of minutes, hours, or days. Following is an illustration of the development of an embryo during the first week after conception.

Time Line of Week 1 of Embryo Development

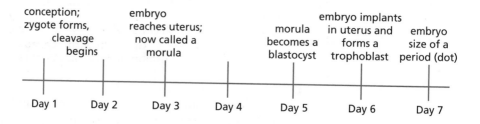

Using time lines is vital in history courses, where much of the content involves dates and events. If you were studying the British monarchy from 1820 to the turn of the century, your time line might look like this.

A Time Line of Monarchs of Great Britain

1820-----------George IV

1830--------William IV

* 1832---------Reform Bill
    (right to vote)

1837-----------Victoria

* Called the Victorian Age

1901-------------Edward VII

This time line is drawn vertically, but it could just as easily have been drawn horizontally.

The larger or smaller line lengths separating each monarch's reign visually reinforce the length of time they ruled.

The time line could also include key words noting other important information about what happened during that period (note examples).

This time line could be extended as you study events which occurred in the 1900s.

In conclusion, time lines can be used as a visual organizer whenever you need to know chronological information or steps in a process.

Exercise 9-E

Directions: Make a time line for the following information.

The length of gestation for various mammals and marsupials varies greatly. Old World monkeys give birth in six months (between 170 and 190 days). Gorillas, orangutans, and humans give birth in nine months. It takes the woolly monkey 225 days, but the marmoset reproduces in 140 days. Marsupials give birth in 12 to 37 days, but the baby stays in a pouch for much longer. Mouse lemurs, small members of the monkey family, give birth in two months.

Exercise 9-F

Directions: Read the following selections and then create the most appropriate visual organizers.

1. The two major economies in the world are the market or capitalist economy and the centrally planned or command economy. Although variations exist in the role government and individuals play in both economies, the broadest differences involve ownership of physical capital and resource allocation. In a market economy, individuals have property rights. In other words, they have the ability to buy and sell goods, and this right provides incentives. In a command economy, the government owns everything, and so individuals do not have a personal incentive to invent new products, for example. In addition, in a market economy, most prices for goods are "freely determined by individuals and firms." In a command economy, the government establishes most of the prices. Many individuals or companies compete in buying and selling in a market economy. The command economy is run by a central government that often allows only one producer of an item or product, which eliminates competition. Another difference is that market economies freely trade in other countries, which can improve their own economy. Command economies are limited in their ability to buy foreign goods. The greater freedom allowed in a market economy makes it (capitalism) more appealing to many countries than a command economy (centrally planned by the government).

(Taylor 57–63)

2. In the late 1950s, two physicians began what is now called the New York Longitudinal Study, interviewing parents and observing children from birth to adolescence. They defined "easy" and "difficult" one-year-old children and "easy" and "difficult" ten-year-old children by their individual differences and temperaments.

For example, easy one-year-olds have a regular rhythm to their lives: They nap after lunch each day and always take a bottle when they go to bed at night. Difficult one-year-olds tend to lie awake after they are put to bed; sometimes they will not fall asleep for more than an hour. Easy ten-year-olds tend to eat only at mealtimes and regularly sleep the same amount of time every night. Difficult ten-year-olds have an irregular rhythm to their lives. Their food intake varies; they may be snackers or refuse to eat at mealtime. They also vary when they will go to bed, falling asleep at different times

(continued on the next page)

Exercise 9-F (continued)

on different nights. Easy one-year-olds have a positive attitude about new situations. They are not afraid of strangers and will readily approach them. If they have to sleep in different surroundings (at grandma's or at a friend's house), they fall asleep and sleep well. Difficult one-year-olds cry or refuse to fall asleep in a new place. Easy ten-year-olds love to go to camp, and the first time they go skiing or do other new activities they enjoy doing them. Difficult ten-year-olds get very homesick if they go to camp, and they are unwilling to try new activities. In terms of adaptability, easy one-year-olds might be frightened of toy animals at first, but learn to enjoy playing with them fairly quickly. Difficult one-year-olds refuse to try new foods every time they are offered. Ten-year-olds who are adaptable might be homesick when they first get to camp but quickly learn to enjoy it. They are enthusiastic about learning everything. Nonadaptive ten-year-olds do not adjust well to new situations, whether it is camp, a new school, or even a new teacher.

(Dworetzky 115)

3. All people, at least once in a while, feel fatigued because they have stayed up to watch the late, late show. However, it is helpful to look at four other reasons why fatigue occurs. One reason is emotional and stress-related: You are overworked or upset over a problem, and you worry about the problem instead of getting a good night's sleep. Your physical state may also be a source of fatigue. Maybe you do not get enough physical exercise, or maybe you are suffering from an illness such as diabetes, kidney or liver disease, or anemia. You need to see your doctor if you suspect you have such an illness. Another source of fatigue might be your diet. If you do not eat well enough, consider taking a multivitamin. Even if you do eat a balanced meal, some nutrients are robbed from your body when you undergo serious, long-lasting bouts of stress. Sleep habits are another source of fatigue. You need to set up a rhythm: Go to bed and arise at approximately the same times each day, avoid caffeine or alcohol in the evening, and know how many hours of sleep you need so that you do not get too many or too few hours per night. It is also helpful not to work on difficult mental tasks right before bedtime.

Critically Thinking Together

In a group of two to three people, come to an agreement about which visual organizer would be most appropriate for each of the three selections in Exercise 9-F. Be sure to provide reasons for the kinds of visual organizers you chose. Then appoint a recorder and make the visual organizers.

Summary

This chapter describes five visual organizers that combine and summarize large amounts of information on a page or two by using key words with simple visual drawings that can be related to the fingers on a hand.

The five visual organizers are the topic grid (the thumb), action-reaction arrows (the index finger), Ts (the middle finger), webs (the ring finger), and time lines (the little finger). Grids are appropriate when you are trying to organize information that is naturally broken into two or more categories. Action-reaction arrows work well to illustrate cause-and-effect relationships. Ts serve as an excellent device to analyze two opposing views or contrasting ideas. Webs, because they are very open-ended and creative, are most useful as a prewriting activity and as a way to see relationships among concepts. Time lines help you to see when events in time or a process occurred and how they relate to one another.

List of Terms

visual organizers
topic grids
action/reaction arrows

Ts
webs
time lines

In this box, write your summary question or statement for this chapter.

10 The Power of Taking Tests

"Testing, testing, testing. One, two, three, testing." When you hear these words, you often anticipate that something exciting and interesting is about to happen. On the other hand, when you hear a teacher use a four-letter word like *test, quiz,* or *exam,* you often dread what is to come.

Testing is an integral part of education because it provides both you and the instructor with a good indication of how much you have learned. Thus, it is to your advantage to develop the necessary skills to become an effective test taker. This chapter will review methods that should enable you to achieve better scores on tests. It will also discuss how to prepare for tests, how to take various kinds of tests, how to minimize test anxiety, and how to analyze your test results.

TYPES OF TESTS

Tests can be divided into three categories: objective, short-answer, and essay. *Objective tests* are recognition tests, which means that the possible answers are provided for you. They include true-false, multiple-choice, and matching tests. The second type of test, *short-answer,* requires you to supply a brief answer, from a phrase to a few sentences. These include completions and definitions. Finally, the *essay test* requires single-paragraph or multi-paragraph answers.

Different types of tests require you as a college student to demonstrate different skills and different levels of comprehension. You need to be aware that literal, factual questions are only one type of question that instructors ask. They may also ask more complicated questions, such as application questions. Application questions require you to reexamine information that you have studied in a class and apply it to a new situa-

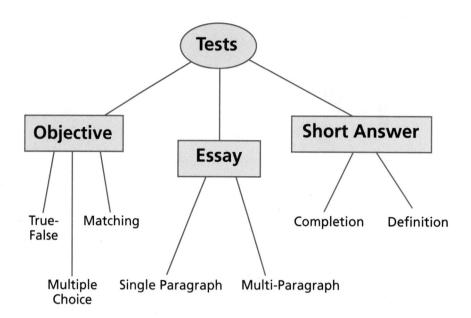

tion. For example, on a test in a nursing course, you might be given a list of a patient's symptoms. Your task on this test would be to consider the patient's history and the list of symptoms in order to identify the patient's problem and to write a nursing care plan. In an English class, after reading Maya Angelou's autobiography *I Know Why the Caged Bird Sings,* you might be asked to write an essay that discusses how the events of the author's early life influenced her writing.

ON YOUR MARK: CONDITIONING YOURSELF FOR TESTS

Starting on the first day of class, you will naturally begin by taking lots of clear, well-organized notes, carefully reading and highlighting your textbooks, and learning new terms by using 3 x 5 cards or some other vocabulary-learning method. By keeping up with your reading assignments and reviewing your notes and terms, you will be conditioning yourself to take quizzes and tests. By repeating information aloud until you have mastered the material, you will be able to store it in your long-term memory, where it will be readily retrievable when needed. This type of recitation is considered the most efficient means of putting information into your long-term memory.

As midterm or final exams approach, your priority—weekly, daily, and hourly—is to get the most out of your time in order to stay on target and avoid undue stress. Just as a runner in training has a daily regimen, you also must have a daily training plan for learning. As a test, midterm, or final exam approaches, you, again like the runner, will move into a more intensified program of study and time management. Beginning one to two weeks before a major exam, it is a good idea to include extra, concentrated study time for preparation in your regular study schedule. By adhering to a carefully planned study schedule, you can avoid cramming and test anxiety.

The week or two before an exam can be stressful because, not only do you need to continue daily study, but you also need to add extra study hours as well as prepare for the upcoming exam. Assuming you have kept up with your notes, textbook reading, and vocabulary words from the beginning of the term, you can benefit from using these tips to prepare for an exam.

- Find out or understand what material is included. Will it include everything from the beginning of the term, several chapters, everything after the midterm, etc.?
- Find out how many exams you will be taking during the week.
- Prepare a study schedule that allows you to attend classes, do your daily assignments, and set aside extra study hours to recite and review for each exam. It may be necessary to cut back on your work or social life during this time.
- Review and recite notes, textbook highlighting, vocabulary terms, handouts, returned quizzes and tests.

GET SET: ACQUIRING A WINNER'S EDGE

When you are facing a major test or exam, like the experienced athlete, you want to gain all the honest advantages you can. You want to be test-smart, well versed enough to know what to expect.

As the exam draws closer, ask your instructor what the test format will be—true-false, multiple-choice, matching, completion, definitions, and/or essay. Often tests, especially midterms and finals, have several formats. The more you know about the construction of the test, the more comfortable you will be as you prepare for and take the test. If, for example, the test is going to include true-false, multiple-choice, matching, and completion (fill-in-the-blank), then you need to study facts, details, and specific information. If the test includes writing definitions of terms, then you will need to recite them to the point of mastery and also know how to spell the terms. If the test is an essay exam, you should concentrate on learning main ideas and supporting details.

As you study and recite information, work in your regular study place, free from noise and distractions. Reciting answers aloud will confirm to you that you really do know the information, which should help reduce your anxiety and boost your test-taking confidence.

You may also find that studying with a partner or a small group is helpful because it gives each of you an opportunity to share notes, information, and ideas. Also, you can weigh and compare what each of you determines is important. Together you can make up study questions and share techniques to help you remember concepts and bodies of information. If you do work in a group, make sure that each member is willing to attend regularly, is prepared, and will contribute to the group discussions.

Sufficient preparation for tests means that you will not have to cram at the last minute. Cramming is usually an exercise in futility. It's like overloading an electrical system. If you try to put too much information into your brain at once, it will overload the short-term circuitry, and you may experience the equivalent of a loss of power or a blackout. In other words, you may not be able to recall the information when you most need it.

One final step in preparing for exams is to have a positive attitude. Some students actually flunk themselves by thinking they are going to fail. One method of preparation you can use is to visualize your success. Imagine yourself taking the test and doing well. As you visualize, focus on the many, many right answers you are able to write down. Just as quarterbacks visualize the perfect pass, basketball players visualize perfect dunk shots, golfers visualize accurate putts, and pitchers visualize the perfect curve ball, so should you visualize your victory before you even begin the test.

GO: TAKING THE TEST

Even when athletes know that they are in good condition and well prepared, they naturally feel tension at the starting signal. Likewise, when you are faced with actually taking a test, you may experience exam nerves. Being somewhat nervous can be positive stress, which is good because it pumps up your adrenaline and makes you more alert.

On the test day, be sure to arrive on time or a little early so that you will not feel rushed. Have an extra pen or pencil and any other equipment you might need, such as extra blue books. While you are waiting for the exam to begin, take several deep breaths and relax your muscles. This will help calm any jitters you might have and get more oxygen—thinking power—to your brain.

When your instructor distributes the exam, jot down "slippery" facts in the margin or on the back of the test. *Slippery facts* are those words, formulas, dates, or other information you are *sure* you will forget. (Of course, check with your instructor in advance to find out if you are allowed to write on the test itself.) Writing down this information will keep you from worrying about forgetting it because it will be there if you need it.

Despite your eagerness to begin the test, listen carefully to any last-minute instructions the teacher gives. Next, look over the whole test to get an overview of its parts and length and how many points each section is worth; then plan your time accordingly. For example, if the test consists of 30 true-false questions worth 30 points and two essays worth 70 points, obviously, you should spend considerably more time on the essay section than on the true-false questions. Also, if your classroom does not have a clock, wear a watch so that you can check the time when necessary. As you take the test, follow your time allotments as best you can rather than getting bogged down trying to remember an answer.

As you start each section of the test, read the directions very carefully. You may even want to read them twice. If you are allowed to write on the test, circle or underline important words. Too often students waste valuable time or lose points on a test because they do not follow directions. For example, if the directions read, "Answer only three of the five essay questions," and you answer all five questions, you will be wasting time. Or if the directions say, "Write out the words 'true' and 'false' when answering the following questions," and you simply write the letters T and F, you may lose points. The few minutes it takes to read the directions may result in a higher score.

If one particular part of the test seems easier than another part, start with the easier part and answer the questions that you are sure you know.

Mark any questions you have omitted so that you can go back and answer them later. Giving correct answers early in the test will build your confidence and help you to keep a positive attitude. In addition, as you go through the whole test and complete answers you know, "forgotten" answers may pop into your mind. Also, some other questions on the exam may provide clues to the answers you were unable to think of earlier. When you have answered all the questions you know, go back to the ones you omitted. When all else fails, you should use logic and educated guesswork to answer any remaining questions. These techniques will be explained later in this chapter.

If you are using a scantron form to record your answers, skipping around may not be a good idea because that could lead you to mark an answer in the wrong place. Whether or not you omit answers on a scantron, be very careful to record your answers in the correct answer box.

If you finish an exam early, do not turn in your test and leave until you have checked your answers carefully. In fact, try to allow yourself a few minutes to reread the directions and proofread—to clarify, add information, correct spelling, or fix other errors. Do not change your answers, though, unless you have a valid reason for doing so. When you are unsure of an answer, your first response is usually right. If other students leave early, you should not be influenced by them. After all, they may be leaving because they have given up.

TAKING OBJECTIVE TESTS

Objective tests, where the possible answers appear on the test itself, include true-false, multiple-choice, and matching tests. For obvious reasons, most students are more comfortable with these test questions than with other types. However, in order to be test-smart, you can still benefit from some helpful tips on taking these types of tests.

True-False Tests

True-false tests can be the least threatening type of test to take because you have a fifty-fifty chance of answering the questions correctly—excellent odds, even in Las Vegas. Even when you know the material thoroughly, you can increase your chances of answering the questions correctly by knowing certain reading and test-taking techniques. These techniques include:

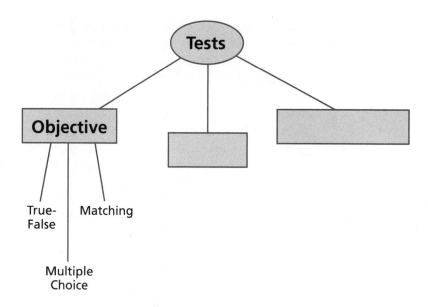

- All-or-nothing words and in-between words
- Negative words
- Partial truths
- Fifty-fifty chance

All-or-Nothing Words and In-Between Words   At first glance, true-false tests may seem easy; however, students often complain that some teachers purposely write "tricky" true-false items. So-called tricky items may simply include qualifying words that have a dramatic impact on the trueness or falseness of the statement. If you are aware of these words and read the items carefully, you should have no problem answering true-false items correctly, assuming that you know the information. These dramatic qualifying words can be divided into two types: all-or-nothing words and in-between words. Examples of all-or-nothing words include words like:

all   always   none   never   nothing   every
exactly   invariably

What these words have in common is that they are so powerful that they allow no exceptions. Therefore, when you come across these words, or others like them, it should be a wake-up call because the lack of exceptions will generally mean the statement is false. Here is a simple example to illustrate this point. Examine the following statement and determine if it is true or false:

T   F   All cars and trucks must have license plates.

At first glance this statement may seem true, but exceptions do exist.

Although *most* all-or-nothing words do indicate false statements, you still must apply logic and critical thinking as you read. For example, think about this statement:

T   F   In the twentieth century, all presidents and vice presidents of the U.S. have been men.

In this case, the answer is true, as you all know. Although most all-or-nothing statements will be false, a few may be true.

When other qualifying words, called in-between words, are placed in a sentence, they modify or alter the meaning of the true-false statement to indicate possible exceptions. Some examples of in-between words include:

few   frequently   generally   many   most   often
sometimes   seldom   usually   probably

When taking a true-false test, be aware of in-between words because statements containing in-between words are almost always true. Look at the following example:

T   F   Usually cars and trucks must have license plates.

If you are aware of the all-or-nothing and in-between words as you take a test, you can significantly increase your ability to read and answer these questions. If you are allowed to write on the test, it is a good idea to circle or underline qualifying words as an additional aid to remembering their significance.

Negative Words   Another important reading technique to help you correctly answer true-false items involves an awareness of negative words. If you read a true-false item too quickly, you may overlook negative words and reach a wrong conclusion. As with qualifying words, if you are allowed to write on the test, circle or underline the negative words to make them stand out.

Negative words include simple ones, such as:

cannot   does not   is not   will not

Other negatives are found in prefixes, such as:

il- (illogical) *un-* (unreasonable) *ir-* (irregular)
im- (impossible) *non-* (nonstandard) *in-* (incorrect)

Be especially careful if two negative words appear in a true-false statement. They will cancel each other out and make the double negative statement positive. Using your awareness of negative words, read the following three statements and determine whether each is true or false.

T   F   1. In a typical year, more than 800 deaths can be attributed to the flu in the United States.
T   F   2. During a nontypical year, more than 800 deaths can be attributed to the flu in the United States.
T   F   3. It is not uncommon for 800 Americans to die from the flu each year in the United States.

The first statement is true according to the Jefferson Health System web site that bases its research on the National Center for Health Statistics (1999). Since the first statement is true, the second statement is false because of the prefix *non-*. The third statement is also true. This sentence has two negatives *(not* and the prefix *un-)* that cancel each other out and make the statement true.

Partial Truths   If any part of a true-false statement is incorrect, then the whole statement is false. Test-taking traps involving such partial truths generally occur in two situations: (1) items in a series and (2) a faulty relationship of words in a sentence. Read the following examples:

T   F   1. The Atlantic coastal states, sometimes subject to devastating hurricanes, are Florida, Georgia, North Carolina, South Carolina, and Washington.

T   F   2.   When John F. Kennedy was forty, he won the Pulitzer Prize for his book *Profiles in Courage;* consequently, at age forty-three he became the youngest President of the United States.

In the first example, a series of items (the states), is listed; however, the state of Washington is not on the Atlantic Coast; it is on the Pacific. Thus, the whole statement is false. In the second example, both facts are accurate, but the connector, the word *consequently*, makes the whole statement false. The first fact did not cause the second one to happen.

Fifty-fifty Chance   One last strategy to remember when taking a true-false test is that there is a fifty-fifty chance that you will answer a question correctly. Therefore, be sure that you answer *all* the questions rather than leaving any blanks.

Multiple-Choice Tests

Multiple-choice test items are made up of two elements:

- the *stem,* an incomplete statement or a question
- the *options,* the choices that complete the statement or answer the question

For example, here is a possible multiple-choice question:

Stem: Which one of the following is not an in-between word?

Options: a. usually
b. often
c. because
d. sometimes

In order to do well on a multiple-choice test, first, it is important to read the stem slowly and carefully. The stem contains the basic information that helps you to understand what is being asked. Thus, you need to look for key words, all-or-nothing or in-between words, and negative words. You may want to underline or circle them if you are allowed to write on the test. This active method of reading helps you to focus your attention and to read accurately and critically.

Second, as you read the options, be sure to read *all* of them with an open mind before you begin eliminating possible choices. Consider all the possibilities and do not cross out one or more of them too hastily.

Sometimes you may know the correct answer immediately, but if you are not sure, you may find the following approach useful. To begin, read the stem with each option as if the stem and option together make a true or false statement. As you read each option, mark it T or F or ?, assuming you can write on the test. (If you cannot mark on the test, do this mentally.) This process of reading and eliminating should produce the correct answer, or at least increase your odds of being correct.

Here is an illustration of the T or F or ? method.

Stem: Which one of the following is an all-or-nothing word?

Options: F   a. usually
               T   b. completely
               ?   c. because
               F   d. sometimes
               ?   e. partially

Two options typically used in multiple-choice tests are "all of the above" and "none of the above." Using the T or F or ? method described above, you should be able to determine if more than one option is correct. If you have found more than one correct answer among the other choices, then "all of the above" is probably the correct choice. On the other hand, "none of the above" is seldom the correct choice. Most teachers would not want to make up a question with all wrong answers. They may simply be including "none of the above" to create the required number of options.

On some tests, the choices may include combined options, such as "both A and B are correct" or "both B and D are correct." In such cases, you will again benefit by using the stem and option T or F or ? method to make your choices.

Matching Tests

In format, a matching test usually consists of two columns of items: the base column on the left, often designated by numbers, and the choices column on the right, often designated by letters.

When taking a matching test, follow these guidelines:

- Scan both columns to determine if the two contain the same number of items. That way you will know whether extra choices exist that you won't be using.

- If extra choices do exist, you would do well to begin with the left-hand column (base) and find their matches in the right-hand column (choices).
- If the number of choices is equal, then you may begin with either column.
- Always match the items you absolutely know first, marking off each choice as you select it. This narrows the remaining possibilities and will save you time.
- Rather than leaving any answers blank, use your critical thinking skills and knowledge of the course to complete any answers you temporarily skipped.
- Sometimes the wording or grammatical clues in the left-hand column will give you a hint as to what type of match from the right-hand column is expected. For example, a left-hand column item might indicate that its match is the name of a person, a date, a definition, a function, a theory, and so on.

TAKING SHORT-ANSWER TESTS

Short-answer tests can be a bit more challenging and unsettling than objective tests because the answers do not appear on the exam. It is up to you to provide the answers—a word, a phrase, or one or more sentences. Short-answer questions include completions and definitions.

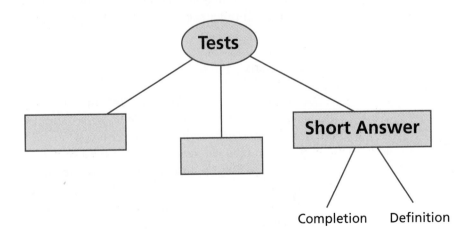

Completions

Completion or fill-in-the-blank tests require you to know facts, details, and specific information extremely well. The statement itself may give you possible clues to what kind of answer is expected—a name, a place, an action, a date, a term, a list, etc. Sometimes other clues—the length of the blank or the number of spaces—will indicate the length of the answer or the number of words required. For example, here is a question from a biology test.

The main water-conducting cells of xylem are called _____

and _____.

In this example, the words "cells of xylem" are word clues that indicate that names of cells are expected in your answer. The two blanks indicate that your answer requires two terms, and the word "the" in "the main" shows that only two correct answers are possible (in this case, the answers are *trachieds* and *vessel members*).

The following example shows other useful clues:

The scientific method used when gathering information includes

_____, _____, and _____.

You should be able to determine from the clue words "method used" (meaning what action needs to be taken) that action words are needed, and the three blanks indicate that three kinds of actions are needed (in this case *hypothesizing, predicting,* and *testing*).

If you are unable to complete a fill-in-the-blank item, you may also find clues to the answer in some other part of the test.

Definitions

In the category of short-answer tests, another type is definitions of terms. A fail-safe way to be able to write definitions is to learn the terms thoroughly by reviewing them frequently.

When you are defining words on a test, the best method is to write complete sentences, unless you are instructed otherwise. In order to do this, combine the term with a verb and give the meaning of the term as clearly as possible. Write the sentence(s) without using the term itself in the definition. Think of this formula:

Term + Verb + Meaning without Using Term

For example, instead of writing, "Recitation means to recite," write, "Recitation means saying the information aloud, in your own words, often enough to store it in your long-term memory." Instead of writing, "Sensory learning refers to using your senses," you could write, "Sensory learning refers to the use of sound, sight, and/or touch to improve your memory, such as by writing your notes (touch), reading your notes (sight), and reciting them aloud (sound)." Notice that in this last definition, the meaning is clarified by the use of an example. Including an example in your definition strengthens your answer by proving that you truly understand the term.

TAKING ESSAY TESTS

Sometimes students panic at the thought of taking essay tests. However, an essay exam need not be intimidating as long as you know the information thoroughly and know how to organize the material.

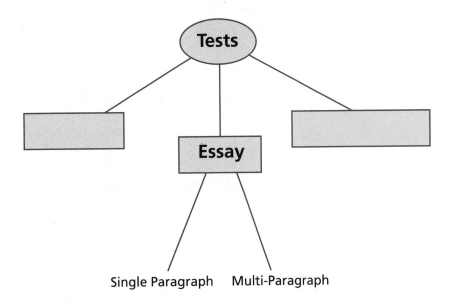

When you hear the words "essay test," you need to know what your instructor means, so you may need to ask. Some instructors may expect answers of a single paragraph; others may be expecting multi-paragraph essays. Some may expect a factual answer; others may expect an application answer.

Regardless of what kind of essay question is asked or how long the answer is expected to be, you must be able to budget your time in order to answer all the questions thoroughly. If you have more than one essay question to answer, start with the one that seems easiest to you because you will gain self-confidence, you will be able to respond quickly, and you will be ready to focus on more challenging questions later.

Understanding Directional Words

Writing an essay of any length requires that you read the question carefully, looking for *directional words.* Directional words are verbs that indicate what kind of information should be included in your answer and how your answer should be organized. For example, each of the following directional words indicates how you should organize your answer and what the focus of your answer should be.

> *analyze:* Break the topic into its logical parts and write about each one.
> *compare:* Show likenesses (although some instructors use the word to mean compare and contrast—check to make sure).
> *contrast:* Show differences.
> *criticize, discuss,* and *evaluate:* Give both positive and negative aspects of the subject and then draw your conclusion(s).
> *describe* and *explain:* Make the topic clear by giving the major details and supporting facts.
> *illustrate:* Explain by giving examples.
> *interpret:* Clarify the meaning or paraphrase the information.
> *justify:* Explain the purpose behind or reasons for a statement.
> *prove:* Provide evidence in the form of facts and details to confirm an assertion.
> *relate:* Reveal connections between or among subjects.
> *summarize:* Give the main points.
> *trace:* Show the development or history of the subject chronologically.

Reducing an Essay to Mini-Questions

In addition to focusing on the directional words as you read the essay question carefully and critically, you must recognize whether the question has more than one part, that is, has *mini-questions.* For example, in an American history course, a question might read:

"Explain the significance of the Civil War one year after it ended in terms of the economy and the social repercussions in both the North and the South and give examples of each."

Stop for a minute and reread that question. How many questions are contained in this large question? If you underline the directional words and key words and number the mini-questions, your essay question would look something like this:

"Explain the significance of the Civil War one year after it ended in terms of the economy in the North (1st question) and South (2nd question) and the social repercussions in the North (3rd question) and South (4th question) and give examples of each" (questions 5 through 8 because you need four examples).

The words *explain* and *give examples* are directional words because they are verbs which tell you what kinds of information should be included. The words *significance of the Civil War* indicate the topic of the essay, and the phrase *one year after it ended* gives the time frame. The words *economy* and *social repercussions* indicate what aspects to focus on in your cause-and-effect explanation. The word *each* reminds you to include the economy in both the North and the South and the social repercussions in both the North and the South. As you can see from the parentheses in the example, this question actually has eight parts, all of which need to be addressed in your answer. By numbering each mini-question, you can make sure you answer all of them.

Once you have determined and numbered the mini parts of the question, you may want to make an informal diagram or outline in the margin of your test or blue book. As an example, for the question above, your diagram might look something like this:

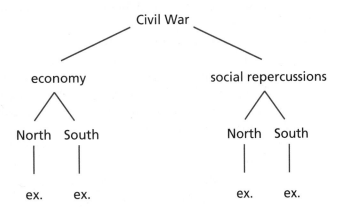

This type of diagram would give you a guide for writing your essay. By listing and grouping ideas, you can determine how many paragraphs you will need and how they will be organized in your essay. A visual outline such as this will also help you to stay on track and include all the required details in your answer.

Exercise 10-A

Directions: Read the following essay question and underline the directional words and circle the key words. Number the mini-questions.

When taking a true-false test, name the reading and test-taking techniques you should use and, when possible, define and give an example of each.

Now, on a piece of paper, draw an informal diagram or outline as a guide for answering this essay question (you do not have to write the essay).

Writing the Essay Answer

Once you have an organizational plan, you are ready to write your opening statement or opening paragraph. That statement is called a topic sentence for a one-paragraph answer or a thesis statement for a multi-paragraph essay. In essence, what you will do is turn the essay question into a general statement. In the Civil War example, your statement might be:

"In 1866, the Civil War had a great impact on the economy and created social repercussions in both the North and the South."

Then, following the organization you established in your thesis statement (or topic sentence) and informal outline, begin writing the body paragraphs of your essay. Write your answer as if you were explaining the subject to a person who knows nothing about it so that you will be as clear, complete, and precise as possible in your answer. Include as many facts, definitions, examples, details, and other information as needed. Write a concluding sentence or paragraph at the end of the essay to wrap up your answer.

When you have more than one essay question to answer, be sure to budget your time accordingly. If, for example, you have three questions to answer and you spend all your time answering only one, even if your answer is very complete, that answer is only one-third of the test. If you do not answer the other two questions, you will fail the test.

If you have miscalculated and you run out of time before you have completed all of your essay answers, rather than leaving a question unanswered or only partly finished, outline the answer as best you can. That way your instructor will understand that you know the major points even though you were not able to write or complete the essay. By outlining, you might get partial credit for an answer.

Finally, if you finish early, do not turn in your test immediately. Use that extra time wisely to proofread your answers by cleaning up any spelling errors, checking your punctuation, and neatly inserting omitted words or added information.

Making Your Essay Presentable

Although your grade is based upon the content of your essay, your instructor may be unconsciously influenced by the appearance of your composition. A neat, legible, well-organized essay is much easier to read and understand than one that is messy and difficult to read. Here are some suggestions for putting your best foot forward by improving the appearance of your essays.

- Consider writing on every other line in case you have time to go back and add more information.
- Leave space between each essay answer in case you think of something that you want to add.
- Write only on the right-hand page of the blue book and number your pages.
- Write legibly.
- Use a high-quality erasable ball-point pen rather than a pencil.
- Indent your paragraphs and leave one-inch margins on each side of the paper.

WEB SITE INFORMATION

For more information on strategies for taking tests, visit our web site:

<http://college.hmco.com/success>

TEST ANXIETY

Many students suffer from test anxiety. Basically, any anxiety is extreme fear of a danger or fear of the unknown. *Test anxiety* is extreme fear of not performing well on a test even though you have prepared adequately. One very difficult psychological reason for test anxiety is fear of not measuring up to expectations, either your own or another's. Some students blame their poor grades on test anxiety when in fact these students simply were not prepared. This anxiety from lack of preparation is not true test anxiety. There is no substitute for preparation for a test. This means regular recitation and review over a period of time, not cramming the night before.

Many students are familiar with the classic symptoms of test anxiety: your mind goes blank, your stomach aches, your hands are icy cold, your skin feels clammy, your concentration wanders, and your mind is scheming about ways to escape taking the test. If you have test anxiety, you may experience one or more of these symptoms or others not mentioned here. Far more important than recognizing symptoms of test anxiety is the ability to relieve it. Here are some suggestions for relieving test anxiety.

- Avoid doom-and-gloom talk about the test with fellow students.
- Find out as much about the test as you can to lessen your surprise.
- Arrive a few minutes early so that you won't feel rushed and so that you will hear any directions the instructor gives.
- Relax—take deep breaths before you start the test.
- Use positive self-talk.
- Focus on the test itself, not on your feelings of stress.
- After you receive the test, jot down slippery facts so you won't forget them.
- Read all the directions carefully before you begin the test.
- Make a time plan, budgeting time for each section in accordance with how many points the section is worth.
- Answer easy questions first.
- Ignore students who leave early.
- Realize that comparing yourself negatively with others can undermine your self-confidence.
- If your test anxiety is not relieved by these suggestions, you may need to visit your counseling center.

Even if you are thoroughly prepared, don't be surprised if you feel a little nervous when you take tests. Some nervousness is natural. Positive stress can give you that needed surge of adrenaline and a winner's edge.

Critically Thinking Together

In a group of three or four people think about specific techniques that you personally use to reduce test anxiety. These techniques should be different from, or at least more detailed than, the ones listed in this textbook. For example, a student might say, "I always get up early enough to eat a good breakfast before I take a big test."

Each student should give at least one technique he or she uses to control test anxiety. One student should act as recorder and write down all ideas from students. Then the group should select the best suggestions (minimum of one, maximum of three) and report them to the whole class.

WEB SITE INFORMATION

For more information on test anxiety, visit our web site:

<http://college.hmco.com/success>

EVALUATING TEST RESULTS

Taking tests in college may not be fun, but you can't escape them because testing is the most used method to evaluate students' learning. If you do well on a test, you feel proud because the good grade boosts your self-confidence, confirms that your good study habits worked, and makes you feel in control of your learning. On the other hand, if you do not do well on a test, you might feel defeated and angry.

For example, how many times have you seen students who get back a test that they failed or did poorly on, moan and groan, wad up the offending test, and throw it in the nearest wastebasket? It's a natural reaction, but not a very helpful one. Instead of reacting negatively, students should analyze their mistakes in order to improve future test scores.

Whether you did well or not so well on a test, you can profit by analyzing your mistakes. To begin your analysis, look at the test items you missed. Try to find patterns. What kinds of questions did you miss? For example, did you miss true-false items, multiple-choice items, definitions, completions, essays? What caused you to miss those questions? Did you misread the question? Did you study the wrong material? Or could other factors have caused you to score poorly on the test? For example, did you not plan and/or use your time realistically?

Each time you get a test back, you can use the following chart to analyze your test results.

Test Analysis Chart

Directions: Look at the test that has been returned to you in order to determine which questions you missed.

Part A Directions: Check all the statements that apply to the type(s) of test you are analyzing.

Objective Test Items
- ☐ I ignored all-or-nothing words.
- ☐ I ignored in-between words.
- ☐ I ignored negative prefixes or words.
- ☐ I did not consider all parts of the statement.
- ☐ I left test items blank.
- ☐ I ignored key words when reading.
- ☐ I jumped to a conclusion before reading the entire question.
- ☐ I did not eliminate options using the T-F-? in multiple-choice questions.
- ☐ I did not use logic in eliminating options.

Short-Answer Questions
- ☐ I did not take advantage of clues on completion questions.
- ☐ I wrote in fragments when complete sentences were required.
- ☐ I used the term itself to define a term.
- ☐ My answer was not specific enough.

(continued on the next page)

Test Analysis Chart (continued)

Essay Tests
- ☐ I did not make a diagram or outline to plan my essay.
- ☐ My essay was poorly organized.
- ☐ I did not develop my essay with enough facts and details.
- ☐ I used opinions instead of facts.
- ☐ I wrote general statements without facts to back them up.
- ☐ I ignored directional words.
- ☐ I did not answer all the mini-questions within the essay question.
- ☐ My writing skills (grammar, punctuation, spelling, sentence structure) were weak.
- ☐ My essay was not neat and legible.

Part B Directions: Check all the statements that apply to your overall test preparation.

Test Preparation Factors
- ☐ I took inadequate notes.
- ☐ I should have read and marked my text more carefully.
- ☐ I did not recite my notes and text material to the point of mastery.
- ☐ I did not use appropriate memory techniques when studying.
- ☐ I did not start early enough or allow enough extra time to study for the test.
- ☐ I crammed.

Test-Taking Factors
- ☐ I misread or did not follow directions.
- ☐ I made poor use of the time allotted for taking the test.
- ☐ I did not underline or circle words on the test to focus my attention.
- ☐ My general reading comprehension was inadequate.
- ☐ I used negative self-talk.
- ☐ I allowed test anxiety to overwhelm me.
- ☐ I was distracted by a physical or emotional crisis.
- ☐ I did not know the information.

Look at what you have checked on the test analysis chart. These are the skills, behaviors, or attitudes that you need to improve before taking your next test.

Critically Thinking in Writing

Fill out a test analysis chart on a recent test you have taken. In a journal entry, write three or more positive statements about what you did successfully. List three or more areas that need improvement. Then describe ways to improve whatever skills, behaviors, or attitudes that caused you to be unsuccessful in your answers. Make specific suggestions for ways to improve so that you will do better on the next test.

Summary

Tests can be divided into three major categories: objective, short-answer, and essay. Regardless of the type of test, you need to begin preparing for it as soon as the quarter or semester starts. Find out as much as you can about the format of the test and prepare for it wisely, using your knowledge of study techniques and maintaining a positive attitude. On the day of the test, by arriving on time, reading directions carefully, and using other test-smart techniques, you can help to ensure that you will do your best.

Objective tests, which can be true-false, multiple-choice, or matching, provide you with possible answers. As you take objective tests, be aware of all-or-nothing words and in-between words, negative words, and partial truths. Be sure to answer all questions.

Short-answer tests—completions and definitions—do not provide answer choices; you have to supply them. Clues about what to write in completion (also called fill-in-the-blank) questions include how the sentence is worded and the length and number of blank spaces. Definitions of terms are clearest when you write them in complete sentences (Term + Verb + Meaning without Using Term).

Essay tests call for answers of one or more paragraphs. Writing an essay of any length requires that you follow the directional words, use an informal outline or diagram to organize your answer, and answer all the mini-questions embedded in the essay question.

Test anxiety can negatively affect your performance on a test. True test anxiety is different from lack of preparation. You can use several mental and physical strategies to control your test anxiety.

Finally, you need to analyze your test results in order to make a strategic plan for improving your future test-taking skills and, therefore, your grades.

List of Terms

objective tests
short-answer tests
essay tests
slippery facts
all-or-nothing words
in-between words
partial truths

stem
options
T or F or ? method
directional words
mini-questions
test anxiety

In this box, write your summary question or statement for this chapter.

Reference Section:
The 16 MBTI Types

In the following "Reference Section," you will find a brief description of the characteristics of your type as well as descriptions of career choices that may be interesting and satisfying to your type. Any personality type can go into any career and be effective and happy, but certain types seem to be drawn toward certain careers. Remember, this section should be used only as a reference; that is, you can consult it for some understanding of your type and others' types, but you need not learn the information. You might want to read only your own type, but you might find it interesting to explore the characteristics of the other fifteen types to help you understand why people behave and react differently. As you read the type descriptions, you may find yourself saying: "Boy, does that ever sound like me," or "This type describes my best friend to a T!" or "Parts of this type were obviously written about my mother!" Certainly you will recognize your own and other people's descriptions.

You may have had no difficulty in determining your preferences in one or more categories. However, you may have had trouble choosing a preference in a given pair of opposites. For instance, you may be relatively certain about three letters of your type: E_FJ, for example. However, when you take in information, you are not sure whether you are a Sensor (S) or an iNtuitive (N). In this case, read both the ESFJ and the ENFJ type descriptions. You will probably find that you identify with one type as a whole more than you do with the other. Whatever personality type describes you most closely, keep in mind that *each type is good* and contributes essential diversity to society. In other words, whoever you are, you're okay.

ISTJ types have a strong sense of responsibility. Although they are generally quiet, private, and reserved, many have excellent interpersonal skills, but they expect a bottom-line, no-nonsense response from others.

They are organized, practical, and self-reliant, having the ability to get things done without being distracted.

In their career choices, ISTJ types generally enjoy working alone or with a small group. They like to use their organizational skills and work with facts and details, rather than theories. They prefer jobs involving responsibility and control and do not mind repetition.

ISTP types are very similar to ISTJ types except they are more versatile and spontaneous. They are objective and tend to wait and see what is going to happen. They are interested in cause and effect, may be mechanically inclined, and often enjoy participating in sports. They are keenly observant and analytical and like to organize facts logically. Their quiet sense of humor is an endearing quality. ISTPs like to work alone or in small groups. In their career choices, they like to have hands-on work and enjoy working with facts, figures, and data, rather than with theories and ideas. They enjoy some action and freedom in their work.

ISFJ types are usually very concerned about the feelings of others, and they do everything in their power to help others. They are good with details, facts, and figures and have a strong sense of duty. They have perseverance and are very responsible, meticulous, and conscientious. They are loyal friends. ISFJs like careers that involve quiet, independent work, and desire jobs that will have an impact on people. They want to work with facts, details, and data, rather than theories, but are always seeking the good of others. Health and education fields are very attractive to ISFJs. They approach their jobs in a quiet, responsible, nurturing way.

ISFP types are tolerant unless one of their inner values is compromised. They thrive on harmony. They care about others deeply, but usually show their feelings by their actions, not their words. They tend to avoid being leaders, but they are loyal followers, usually rather modest about their achievements. They enjoy starting many projects. They are quiet but friendly. They get what needs to be done accomplished but do not like to be rushed. ISFPs do not want to rush their decisions about career choices and may change their majors and career choices often because they want to keep an open mind. They like to work alone or with small groups of like-minded people, often working behind the scenes, and may dislike being in charge. A major goal is to better other people's lives. Their careers often involve hands-on, practical work that allows them to respond to the needs of others with some amount of freedom to do their job.

INFJ types are quietly efficient and are great problem solvers. They enjoy being creative and tend to generate many new ideas. They value harmony and seek the approval of others. They have very strong convictions based on their personal values. They put effort into what they do and feel a need to serve humanity in a useful, orderly way. The future and future plans are more important than the present. INFJs like to work alone or with small groups. They like jobs where they can use their creativity, and they enjoy challenges. They use theories to solve problems, trouble-shoot, and brainstorm new ideas. They communicate well with people both in speaking and writing. Their sense of values is so important that they wish to use this tendency to benefit the development of all human beings.

INFP types are idealistic and true to their personal convictions. They enjoy learning, especially manipulating oral or written language. They like new ideas. Although they are friendly, being sociable is not very important to them. They have a tendency to take on more than they can reasonably accomplish. They are more concerned with helping others than with collecting possessions or controlling their surroundings. Once they accept you as a friend, you are a friend for life. They are flexible, open-minded, tolerant, and enjoy doing things on the spur of the moment. They prefer working alone or in small groups. INFPs like to use their interest in theory and ideas for the good of others. They enjoy freedom and independence in their work and are adaptable people. Careers developing relationships with others and careers that are in harmony with the person's value system are important to INFPs.

INTJ types are self-reliant and often act independently of authority. They value knowledge and competence. They are analytical and often skeptical. They are self-motivated and have good organizational skills. They are always looking for ways to improve practically everything and can be very determined. They are quiet, forceful leaders. Their daring intuition and insights make them see the big picture. INTJs love theory and ideas as they relate to research and pure science. They are creative and innovative and desire freedom in order to investigate cutting-edge discoveries. They want to work independently, constantly striving to create a better product. Some attractive careers may include areas involving research, such as science, engineering, and higher education.

INTP types are more interested in ideas than in people. They have a thirst for knowledge for its own sake rather than for practical uses or human concerns. They tend to be quiet people who dislike large parties and small talk. They are introspective and like using logic and analysis to solve problems. They are flexible and open-minded concerning new ideas and possibilities. Sometimes other types have difficulty following INTPs' complex, abstract reasoning. INTPs are interested in research and intellectual pursuits for the sake of knowledge. They want to have careers that give them freedom to pursue their creative ideas. They often do well in theoretical or scientific areas.

ESTP types are realistic and live for the moment. They are action-oriented people who want to be moving and doing instead of pondering and planning. When faced with problems, they work quickly to solve them. They tend not to be worriers. Socially, they have many friends and are openly accepting of others and themselves. ESTPs do well in careers where they can work and communicate with people. They enjoy jobs where they use their high-level energy and are physically active. They like practical, hands-on tasks and would rather assemble a project on their own than read the directions or listen to explanations. They want to have careers where they have the freedom to bend rules and take risks if necessary.

ESTJ types are realistic as well as practical. They have a high regard for organization, efficiency, scheduling, projects, data, and decision-making. They are determined and tough-minded. Their interest lies more with the task than with the people around them. They make good administrators as long as they can remember to think about the views and feelings of others. They are good leaders and have excellent organizational skills. The qualities and skills of an ESTJ are assets in a variety of managerial and administrative positions.

ESFP types are flamboyant, fun-loving people who savor the present, often to the exclusion of the past or future. They have many, many friends and will go out of their way to help them. Because they like people and physical movement, they love attending parties and participating in sports and/or exercising. They would rather work with facts than theories and provide strength and support in practical situations because of their common-sense approach. ESFPs seem to know what to do in a crisis situation because they think and act quickly for the sake of others. Freedom is a key factor in career choices. ESFPs are good at helping to solve people-problems and try to nurture others toward happiness. Any careers that are people-oriented would fulfill the needs of an ESFP.

ESFJ types bring harmony to almost any situation or occasion and become upset by conflict. Because of their warmheartedness, sympathy, talkativeness, and caring ways, they make everyone feel at home and comfortable. They place others' needs before their own. They are popular people, and they work well with others and make good group members because of their dedication, attention to detail, patience, and their ability to organize and structure situations. They like to help others in a practical, nurturing, compassionate way, and would choose careers that would allow them to give of themselves to others.

ENFP types have the same warm, outgoing personalities as the ESFJs, but they also are vivacious and imaginative. They are very good at dealing with people or situations because of their enthusiasm, their persuasiveness, their good communication skills, and their ability to find on-the-spot solutions. They are open to new ideas, and are capable of doing almost anything they are interested in doing. Sometimes, however, because of their varied interests, they may get bored in the middle of a project. They prefer careers where they can be creative, innovative, and have freedom of choice. These careers are usually people-oriented.

ENFJ types are often leaders. Their tact and fluent speaking ability make them very persuasive. They are comfortable at leading group discussions and are acutely aware of others' feelings, needs, and contributions. They are innovative and future-oriented with strong organizational skills, but they seldom lose sight of how their plans and decisions will affect other people. They encourage camaraderie among others, are tolerant of others' mistakes, and are usually popular and sociable. ENFJs find satisfaction in careers that allow them to use their organizational skills, imagination, creativity, and talent in working with people. They dislike too much detail and repetition in a job.

ENTP types tend to have many interests and abilities and to process information quickly. Because they speak knowledgeably about many subjects and are challenged by the logic of controversy, they will argue either side of an issue—just for the sake of argument. On the job, they are excellent problem solvers, but dislike doing routine tasks. Their fascination with fresh ideas may constantly lead them in new directions, but they are adept at logically explaining these changes of focus. They are noticeable because they are energetic, enthusiastic, and animated.

ENTJ types prefer to be leaders because they like to be in control of themselves, others, and all situations. With great confidence, persuasiveness, and enthusiasm, they want their opinions known on any topic being discussed. Their vision of the future usually results in long-range plans that include concrete organizational plans or products. They have powerful personalities and direct their energies to the outside world and its endless possibilities. ENTJs are likely to seek careers where they can take leadership roles; they are often on the cutting-edge of possibilities and delight in challenges. They are decisive and tough-minded. The ENTJs approach to people tends to be impersonal, but they are good at making policies and future plans.

COLLEGE RESOURCES FOR CAREERS

Almost all campuses have resources that can help you discover more about your interests and abilities and allow you to explore your choices in a major and/or a career. Counseling centers, career centers, student services, and other campus resources have highly trained personnel, testing facilities, technology, and other materials that can provide you with information. Discover what services are provided at your college or university by looking in the student handbook or by consulting your institution's home page on the Internet.

Works Cited and Consulted

Chaffee, John. *Thinking Critically*. 3rd ed. Boston: Houghton Mifflin, 1991.

Dickinson, Emily. *The Complete Poems of Emily Dickinson*. Ed. Thomas H. Johnson. Boston: Little Brown, 1960.

Dworetzky, John P. *Introduction to Child Development*. 4th ed. St. Paul: West Publishing, 1990.

Faelten, Sharon and David Diamond. *Take Control of Your Life*, Emmaus, PA: Rodale Press, 1988.

Levine, Joseph S., and Kenneth R. Miller. *Biology: Discovering Life*. 2nd ed. Lexington, MA: D. C. Heath, 1994.

Loftus, Elizabeth. *Memory: surprising new insights into how we remember and why we forget*. Reading, MA: Addison-Wesley, 1980.

Mader, Sylvia S. *Inquiry into Life*. 7th ed. Dubuque, IA: Wm. C. Brown, 1994.

Malcolm X as told to Alex Haley. *The Autobiography of Malcolm X*. NY: Ballantine Books, 1964.

Myers, Isabel Briggs, and Mary H. McCaulley. *Manual: A Guide to the Development and Use of the Myers-Briggs Type Indicator*. Palo Alto, CA: Consulting Psychologists Press, 1988.

Patterson, Becky. *Concentration: Strategies for Attaining Focus*. Dubuque, IA: Kendal-Hunt, 1993.

Pauk, Walter. *How to Study in College*. 3rd ed. Boston: Houghton Mifflin, 1984.

Piper, Watty (retold by). *The Little Engine That Could*. From *The Pony Engine* by Mabel Bragg. NY: Platt and Munk, 1976.

Rowh, Mark. *Coping with Stress in College*. NY: College Entrance Examination Board, 1989.

Taylor, John B. *Economics*. Boston: Houghton Mifflin, 1995.

Usova, George M. *Efficient Study Strategies: Skills for Successful Learning*. Pacific Grove, CA: Brooks/Cole, 1989.

Index